Information Horizons

In memory of Tom

Information Horizons

The Long-Term Social Implications of New Information Technologies

Ian Miles
Howard Rush
Kevin Turner
John Bessant

EDWARD ELGAR

Published by
Edward Elgar Publishing Limited
Gower House
Croft Road
Aldershot
Hants GU11 3HR
England

and distributed by
Gower Publishing Company
Old Post Road
Brookfield
Vermont 05036
USA

British Library Cataloguing in Publication Data

Information horizons: the long-term
    social implications of new information
    technology.
    1. Society. Effects of technological
    development in information systems
    I. Miles, Ian, 1948–
    303.4'83
ISBN 1 85278 041 X
        1 85278 143 2(PbK)

Contents

Figures

Tables

Preface

Why write another book about information technology? After all in such a rapidly changing field, won't it be out of date as soon as it is produced – just like personal computers seem to be? Needless to say we have high hopes that this book will not be remaindered too soon, or only be used to prop up that short table leg which you have been meaning to do something about. Nor have we written it for our health or to get rich. As generous as our publishers may have been, any money gained is likely to go to restoring our psychological health – strains on which have been the consequence of four independently-minded researchers attempting (successfully we hope) to work collaboratively. Our reasons, as we argue throughout the book, are to help expand the debate over the future social implications of IT in a more systematic way than we perceive has been accomplished thus far in the diverse literature on the subject.

This book arises directly out of a set of studies undertaken by the authors for the Information Technology Economic Development Committee (ITEDC) of the National Economic Development Office (NEDO). The Long-Term Perspectives Subcommittee of the ITEDC asked us to prepare: first, a review of the long-term forecasting literature; secondly a survey of expert opinion; and thirdly our own forecasts. In all cases the time horizon we considered was twenty-five years. The first two studies were published directly by NEDO as its reports, *IT Futures* (1985) and *IT Futures Surveyed* (1986). The third study was drawn upon – along with several other external studies and sources of in-house information – for the ITEDC's own report, *IT Futures – IT can work*

(1987), and is available in mimeo form from the EDC as 'New IT products and services'. We would like to express our gratitude to the Long-Term Perspectives Subcommittee for its encouragement, and for providing the stimulus that brought us together to prepare this joint work. It was with considerable regret that just as we completed this book we learned that the NEDO Information Technology EDC – one of the few bodies in the world which recognised the importance of incorporating forecasting with policy-making – is threatened with closure by painfully myopic government decree.

Initially, it was our intention for this book to be simply a more polished version of the third study we prepared for NEDO. But as we began to rework the material we concluded that it would be important to include considerable amounts of material not addressed in the NEDO study, to bring the role of social theories much more to the fore, and to use a new framework within which to situate the topics discussed. The outcome is a study that bears little resemblance to the original essay, although we continue to express many of the same guiding ideas.

In any case the NEDO study itself is but one of a continuing stream of publications and talks with which the various authors have been addressing the development of information technology. During the course of this book we cite several examples of this stream, reflecting the range of projects we have undertaken in recent years in bringing this book to completion.

This means that we each have several acknowledgements to make. Ian Miles carried out the initial work while funded by the Joseph Rowntree Memorial Trust to study 'The future of work'. His contribution to this book is an input to this project, and he would like to thank JRMT for their goodwill as well as their financial assistance; and his colleague on the project, J. I. Gershuny, for continuing friendship and intellectual stimulation. Much of the reworking of material was carried out while he was funded by the Programme on Information and Communication Technologies of the Economic and Social

Research Council, of which this book may also be considered an early output. Howard Rush and John Bessant are indebted to the Brighton Business School for the time and encouragement to undertake this research; and to Carlota Perez and the Venezuelan Unido/Fomento PAI team, with whom they have been working, for helping educate them on technology issues of relevance to the Third World.

We want to thank our working institutions for providing a vital environment in which this work could be carried out. This book would have been immeasurably weaker without the fertile ideas with which we are surrounded, and the personal and intellectual support that is available, at the Science Policy Research Unit, University of Sussex, and the Innovation Research Group, Brighton Polytechnic. Among our colleagues we would particularly like to thank for advice are Ken Guy, Marian Whitaker, Lesley Turner, Dave Paskins and Dirk Crossfield. We are grateful to Judy Herbert for help with the graphics.

Finally we would like to thank those we have interviewed in the course of our studies (too numerous to list) for the time they have spared us; and our families and friends without whose emotional support and tolerance none of this would have been – worthwhile!

I.M., H.R., K.T., J.B.

Brighton, 1987

1. Images of the Future

Throughout the 1980s the media have been full of pronouncements about the long-term consequences of the 'information revolution'. Images of dramatic and sometimes cataclysmic change are bandied about, and a host of commentators offer themselves as instant authorities. Unfortunately little basis is provided in most of this material whereby readers can judge the relative merits of the divergent forecasts. Assumptions are rarely specified, forecasting methods are described in very broad terms (if at all), and considerable faith seems to be a prerequisite to taking any analysis seriously. It is as if we are expected to take our pick of the experts we prefer – often apparently on the basis of little more than their charismatic qualities – or of the futures that are on offer on the grounds that one or other caters best to our prejudices or accords with our propensity of optimism or pessimism. Given that these forecasts concern a topic of prime importance, the clamour that they create is doubly unfortunate.

How can we find our way through this morass? If the prophets were talking about the distant future or about events beyond our control, we might not need to. But the developments around IT that are portrayed are often happening – or starting to happen – right now. And choices that are made now may be of decisive influence over the course of events. This chapter proposes that we can apply a simple classification to the recent forecasting literature; it outlines three approaches to thinking about the future – specifically, the role of IT in future society

– that we can broadly identify in this literature. Throughout the book we attempt to flesh out the different
viewpoints associated with each approach and consider
what their broad social implications are.

Although there is considerable redundancy and rep-
etition in this literature, many of the leading commentators have added their own slants to the debate about
IT. As well as diversity in content, in matters big and
small, there is also diversity in style and aim. While
some authors write as if in splendid isolation, others
provide oblique criticisms of previous analysts, and yet
others present a smorgasbord of the speculations gleaned
from the literature. A few have explicitly drawn on their
own experience in practice with, or on their own more
or less systematic research into, uses of IT. Some issue
warnings in order to stimulate what they believe to be
the most appropriate policy responses; others portray
utopian futures for precisely the same reason. Some
provide armwaving impressions of the deep underlying
characteristics of social change, in stark contrast to those
who provide detailed quantitative estimates of very
specific features of future trends.

Given the diverse backgrounds and interests of the
authors writing about IT, any attempt to classify the
literature will inevitably yield categories which are rather
rough and ready. Certainly the more subtle, and the
more prolific, authors are not always easy to place. It is
not our purpose in this book to provide an elaborate
literature review or bibliographic study: we have presented this elsewhere.[1] This book sets out to develop our
own view of the future – or rather of key issues and
choices that are liable to determine what sort of future
is created – partly by elaborating the implications of our
perspectives through a dialogue with other viewpoints.
In the manner of classical philosophers, if not with their
perspicacity, we will orchestrate and conduct an argument
with three ways of thinking about IT.

In this chapter then we shall present a first approach
to outlining some major differences in assumptions that
are present in the IT debate; and thereby locate our own

assumptions. By comparing and contrasting the three distinct perspectives or viewpoints on the nature and the social implications of IT, we hope to be able to illuminate issues of relevance to today's policy-makers, official and non-official. We have labelled the three viewpoints the continuist, transformist, and structuralist schools. Their main features are outlined in Table 1.1.

Of course in the manner of a classical philosophical dialogue the three viewpoints are essentially our own construction. We believe they reflect distinctive themes and positions present in the literature: we have not dreamt them up, but rather found them to provide a useful framework for thinking about the strands of the material we were reading – and indeed for understanding our own reactions to some of the developments we were witnessing. But they are our own construction in the sense that we have sought out underlying themes and positions in the work of different authors, and drawn parallels where these may not have been explicitly present in the texts themselves. We have imposed a coherence in perspectives which is imperfectly present in the debates around IT. Thus hopefully we have been able to clarify these debates somewhat. But this does mean that there are probably few people who would accept that any one of our three perspectives completely accords with their own views. All we can say is that we have found this framework a useful one ourselves,[2] and we invite readers to determine whether the dialogue below contributes to their own understanding.

THE THREE SCHOOLS

It will be readily apparent that there is considerable disagreement concerning the scale and pace of change that is liable to be associated with IT. Our discussions and reading of the literature suggest that it is misleading to think of this as simply an argument about more or less 'impact' of IT, or faster or slower diffusion of the technologies and their applications. The distinctions we

Table 1.1 **Three perspectives on the nature of information technology**

Continuists	Transformists	Structuralists
IT is merely the current stage in a long-term process of developing technological capacities. 'Revolutionary' claims overstated.	IT is revolutionary technology based on synergistic and unprecedented rapid progress in computers and telecommunications.	IT has revolutionary implications for economic structure and may lead to reshaping many areas of social life
Rate of diffusion of IT is and will be much slower than claimed by interested parties. Likely to be many mistakes, failures and discouraging experiences.	Positive demonstration effects, and proven success of IT in meeting new social and economic needs, will promote rapid diffusion and organisational adaptation.	Diffusion of IT will be uneven, with some countries and sectors proving far more able to capitalise on potential.
Main features of society liable to remain unchanged by use of IT: change will come from social and political initiatives.	As major a shift in society anticipated as that between agricultural and industrial societies. IT will change bases of political power and social classes.	Social change like that experienced in earlier 'long waves'; need for new organisational structures, styles and skills; changes in issue and leadership.
Forecasting can be largely based on extrapolation of past experience. In practice forecasts	Forecasting requires identification of 'seeds of future' in exemplary	Forecasting requires cautious use of both preceding methods, together

Continuists	Transformists	Structuralists
are usually short- or medium-term, relate to narrow fields i.e. individual industries or services, and are based on trend analysis or conventional modelling approaches.	organisations and experiments. In practice forecasts are typically long-term, scenarios derived from mixture of intuition and generalisation of 'leading edge' experiences.	with such approaches as historical analogy. In practice forecasts are often restricted to such topics as change in industrial organisation and employment.

draw between the first two perspectives seek to identify rather more fundamental differences in approach.

The two extreme views that are so evident in the IT debate concern the nature both of the technological change that is currently taking place and of the social processes which this technological change facilitates and with which it is inextricably intertwined. One viewpoint, which for reasons that will become obvious we call the transformist perspective, stresses the fundamental nature of this change. For this perspective, the emergence of IT represents a major metamorphosis of civilisation. It is provoking a shift to what they describe as the 'information society'; a shift that is as significant as the historic transitions between hunter-gatherer and agricultural societies, and subsequently between agricultural and industrial societies. IT is a revolutionary technology in that nothing will be the same again once the IT revolution has run its course.

For the transformist perspective there is a synergy (a favourite transformist word) between emerging 'post-industrial' values and the properties of IT. Experience with IT is likely to speed up value change as it exposes people to new information and, more important, new ways of dealing with information – but particular social values also facilitate the application of IT in ways that make best possible use of its potential and which are bound to accelerate its diffusion. Cultural differences, a subject we shall return to when addressing the question of national differences in our conclusions, are thus seen as playing some role in the process of design and adoption of technology, so that groups and countries that are further down the 'post-industrial' route will be the vanguard of the information society, and provide valuable guides to the future with IT.

At the other extreme, there is the continuist perspective, which is highly sceptical about the magnitude of these changes. This perspective stresses the emergence of IT from earlier generations of computer and communications technologies and thus is less inclined to see it as a revolutionary technology, whatever that may mean; continuism and talk of 'revolution' go together badly, almost to the same extent as transformism goes well with talk of 'synergy'. Certainly to some extent there is disagreement about the pace of change: the continuist perspective is particularly cautious about the rate of diffusion of the more advanced forms of IT, whereas it sometimes seems as if the transformist literature skips blithely from the problems of current technology to an imagined future where all these problems are resolved by technological advance.

For the continuist view the issues around IT are similar to those posed by other innovations; they tend to focus on specific information technologies – computers, information services, new media, and so on – one at a time, to describe them as incremental and isolated incremental changes. New information technologies are adopted for familiar reasons, to increase competitiveness, efficiency, productivity, to satisfy consumer aspirations and increase convenience. In spite of the fact that many new skills and organisational frameworks are required, these are not considered to involve radically new learning processes in the ways hinted at by the transformist view. However, learning processes always take time, and this means that adoption and diffusion of IT is bound to be much slower than technological enthusiasts imagine: social institutions channel technological choices and often resist rapid change. This approach, then, shares the transformist identification of cultural differences as a significant factor in technological change, but tends to view them as inhibiting rather than facilitating factors. Thus IT is not seen as something which should lead to countries departing from their established trends of inventiveness and innovativeness. Rather, what changes do occur will be more a matter of political and managerial astuteness.

In the 1970s continuism was the most common approach, and in many ways the most acceptable viewpoint in most quarters. Since then it has taken rather a battering, but some commentators continue to advocate it as a corrective to the hyperbole of the transformist approach. It even appears to be staging something of a comeback, as despite the rapid diffusion of IT, evidence of major changes in working practices and ways of life is less apparent. Furthermore many small businesses and proud parents have discovered that purchasing microcomputers has not resulted in the much-touted improvements in their business's performance or their children's educational achievements, that they were led to expect.

As might be expected, a third viewpoint can be located which in many respects falls between these two. However we are less interested in the 'middle ground' than in mapping out a distinctive position, which we label structuralist. This perspective shares with the transformist view the perception that IT represents a revolutionary technology. However this is not seen as something new within industrial society that will lead to a transition to a completely new social order, but as being more likely to facilitate a further development of industrialism –

perhaps to 'superindustrialism' – than to lead to its being superseded. Previous technological revolutions such as electrification have succeeded in reshaping many of the institutions of industrial society (work patterns, training, the leading industrial sectors, the relationship between sectors, and so on) without bringing about a new form of civilisation: IT has its own specific characteristics but should be viewed in terms of the propensity of industrial societies to shift direction in response to technological development.

Thus elements of continuity and transformation are wedded together in this viewpoint, not just averaged-out. The structuralist perspective would agree that the changes of the next few decades cannot be extrapolated from those of the last few. But it would also propose that it is possible to descry much of the likely form of the new technology system from analysis of the problems that have beset industrial society in recent years, and which innovation around IT is largely designed to overcome. Ideas of 'long waves' are congenial to many structuralists, who view our current problems and uncertainties as reflecting at least in part the trough of such a wave.[3]

PLANTING OUR FLAG

We should remark that while we seek to draw on the better analyses of each school our own sympathies are more inclined towards the structuralist perspective. Why is this?

We agree with the idea that IT is a revolutionary technology. A leading writer of recent years, whom we would place in the structuralist school, has described the conditions for what she terms a shift in 'technological style' or 'technoeconomic paradigm' a structural change around a technological revolution. In this analysis a major source of change is a shift in what is perceived to be the expected structure of costs, and the 'commonsense' way of organising production. Both are related to the emergence of a new key factor which has:

- low and descending relative cost
- no serious constraints on supply
- the potential to be used across sectors in a wide range of applications
- the ability to lower the costs of capital, labour and products as well as to change them qualitatively.[4]

In terms of this analysis earlier 'industrial revolutions' are seen as largely based on such new factors. Revolutionary new technologies, such as steam-based energy for machines and transport, low-cost steel, and abundant oil-based energy, enabled these changes in critical features of major production processes and products.

We agree that IT possesses the characteristics of a revolutionary technology as set out above. It radically increases the speed of operations, the amount of information processing (at reduced cost) that can be handled by a device of a given size, and so on. Improvements in these core features are continuing, as Chapter 2 illustrates. And information processing is a feature of all production processes (even if it is not recognised in the classical economist's three factors of labour, land and capital), so IT can be applied widely across the formal economy, and beyond, as the following chapters will show.

But to accept the revolutionary nature of IT does not mean siding with the transformist approach: this divergence is implicit in the structuralist argument that there have been several technological revolutions since the Industrial Revolution of the early nineteenth century. These revolutions have been associated with major social change, shifts in the balance of power between nations, new ways of life, and so on. But the association between technological revolution and social change is a complex one, which cannot be adequately described in terms of the impacts of technology. And while the social change

can be considerable – we do not rule out the possibility
that opportunities for even more profound change which
might have been seized in the past may yet be seized
in the future – it is not necessarily as momentous as the
transformation of civilisation we are sometimes led to
believe IT is instigating.

This does not say we reject the view that in the long
term IT is bound to raise issues of a civilisational nature.
Indeed it raises issues more profound than those posed
by the agricultural and industrial revolutions, whose
main challenges to human existence, in the form of
ecological crises, are in many ways only just beginning
to confront us. These earlier revolutions challenge humanity's relation to nature; in the long run we believe that
'artificial intelligence' and similar developments will not
only challenge our relationships to our artifacts but also
raise questions about what it is to be human; or what
it is about human beings that we should value. The
emerging potentials of biotechnology – genetic engineering, the scope for creating 'artificial species', life extension
and advanced psychopharmacology – will present challenges of a similar magnitude too; the future is bound
to present much scope for philosophical dialogues. While
it is certainly not too soon to debate such issues, and
we should note that they are actually raised infrequently
in the literature we are considering, they are beyond our
immediate horizon, being challenges whose full force
will not be appreciated until well into the next century.
Our concerns in this book are with the set of structural
changes that are currently under way, and with what
might be their results over the next few decades.

In considering these more immediate prospects we are
struck by the cogency of the structuralist approach.
While transformism is correct to stress the revolutionary
potential of IT, it seems rather loath to concede that this
potential has to be seized, and shaped, by human
beings for their projections to be realised. Technological
determinism – the view that technological change follows
an inevitable path, and that social institutions have to

adjust to cope with this (or can at best hinder the process) – is an inadequate guide to the real processes of technological development. The continuist perspective is justified in emphasising the resistance to change that is often experienced. But beyond this there is a very substantial process of social shaping of technologies that needs to be seen as more than just a faster or slower acceptance of predetermined technological hardware.

This point is made repeatedly in the serious literature on industrial innovation and is based on a great many case studies as well as elaborated within the context of formal economic modelling.[5] The course of technological development, or what are termed 'technological trajectories' within evolutionary approaches to technical change, is determined by social factors on both the supply and the demand sides, often called 'technology push' and 'demand pull' (Figure 1.1). On the supply side the scope for possible innovations is based on the scientific and technical information available and how far particular innovating organisations are able to monitor this ever-accumulating information. The way in which scientific and technical (and market) information accumulates and is organised is itself a product of the socially determined priorities for pure and applied research of different kinds, as set by governments, higher education and industrial establishments.

At any one time there are liable to be many innovations waiting in the wings: often there will be many innovations that are more or less appropriate to carry out a particular task.[6] Motor cars, for example, could be powered by electric or steam motors as well as petroleum engines: the design characteristics of the different propulsion mechanisms are not identical of course, and petrol engines have to date been dominant because of their advances in terms of price, size and performance. But in the future fuel cells or hydrogen engines may achieve design superiority. Extant and potential alternative technological solutions for any problem will be 'selected out' by innovators and users on the basis of the perceived

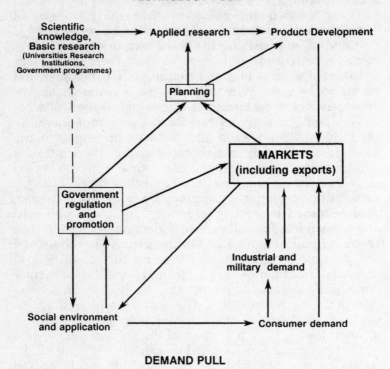

Figure 1.1 **Technology push and demand pull**

superiority of the various options in the circumstances of use.[7]

The supply-side is only half of the picture. The market is an important source of selection itself, as our mention of 'users' implies. The market for an innovation is not just the product of sovereign consumer decisions as elementary economic texts would have it. Markets are structured by regulations, and public agencies may themselves be major sources of demand. Consider the role of state purchasing decisions in the Strategic Defence Initiative (Star Wars) at present: this is hardly a matter of multitudes of individual consumer decisions. But whatever the source, powerful new demands, which may reflect major state purchasing decisions or the results of other policies, can trigger off a set of innovations, as the following quote suggests:

The strength of the German demand for ersatz materials to substitute for natural materials in two world wars spurred on the intense R & D efforts of I. G. Farben and other chemical firms. The strength of the military/space demand in the American post-war economy stimulated the flow of innovations based on Bell's scientific break-through in semiconductors and the early generations of computers. . . Conversely, the absence of a strong market demand for some time retarded the development of synthetic rubber in the US, the growth of the European semiconductor industry. . . or of colour television in Europe after the war.[8]

In the examples mentioned the author is talking of a whole class of innovations applied to a particular end. Market forces also select among technologies designed for a particular purpose. This is illustrated in the competition between electronic typewriters and word processors (or between electronic mail and telex). The transformist perspective tends to paint a picture in which the more advanced forms of IT will quickly triumph in such a situation, on account of their technical superiority. But there is still a substantial market for electronic and even mechanical typewriters, and this cannot be viewed as entirely a matter of inertia or conservative attitudes.

It is far from the case that the most technically sophisticated devices come to be selected in the market. Nowhere is this more true than with personal computers, where IBM machines and their clones occupy a dominant position in most western markets, even though they are regarded by specialists as lagging well behind machines from other suppliers. Another example may be emerging in the case of High Definition Television, where a

Japanese system, which is widely proclaimed as technically superior to European alternatives, is being resisted by Europeans in favour of their own more incremental system, an argument which appears to be based on more than just jealousy of the quantum step represented by the Japanese system (see Chapter 5).

How can such apparently perverse market and regulatory decisions be accounted for? Sometimes they are due to national self-interest predominating. The conflict over appropriate systems for High Definition TV can certainly be interpreted in this way, as can the earlier dispute about colour TV standards, which effectively gave a number of European national manufacturers protected markets. Sometimes specialist or protected markets play a role: their particular needs may determine the course of development of technologies in ways that affect users more generally. But often it is because of the simple fact that technological frontiers are only one of the criteria that are important to users.

Equally influential, if not more so, can be factors such as: having the guarantee of good maintenance and technical support; knowing that your purchase will be compatible with that of clients and partners; being able to use new technologies alongside your installed stock with minimal retraining needs, and even with your old software; and having reason to believe that a good supply of software will continue to be available. As the saying goes, 'no one ever gets fired for buying IBM'. Such factors can be important determinants of technological development: the preponderance of IBM-type systems has meant enormously more effort going into developing software and peripherals for them than for alternative systems (some of which may have been intrinsically better suited to the applications in question). The European argument for an incremental High Definition TV system has some similarities: it is suggested that this will allow users of conventional TV sets to receive the new broadcasts, and vice versa, whereas the Japanese technology proposes completely new chains of equipment from the studio to the viewing public.

To return to our main argument, the point is that market selection – and the establishment of standards by regulatory bodies or by a *de facto* process – has an important feedback effect on the R & D process itself. A differential flow of profits concentrates R & D efforts remarkably (though rarely entirely). As already noted, more software has become available for IBM machines, just as more video programmes have become available on the dominant VHS standard than on its competitors such as V2000 and Betamax. The concentration of effort does not necessarily mean that all leading-edge innovations will happen here; it is notable that certain user-friendly software innovations were pioneered by Xerox and Apple (for example windows, icons, the mouse, desktop publishing), although they have since been emulated for IBM machines and clones.

It is commonplace to hear of technology-push and demand-pull theories of innovation as if these were exclusive alternatives. The reality is more like a coupling between the push and pull processes, which may develop over many years, and in which one or other factor may be dominant at different phases. Structural features of organisations and markets are crucial to the development of new products and processes – something which is often ignored by the transformist and the continuist perspectives.[9]

THE STRUCTURE OF THE BOOK

Having made our own prejudices clear, in favour of the structuralist viewpoint, we should again emphasise that all three perspectives are to some extent portrayed in caricature here and throughout the book. Of necessity we have simplified and unified what are in reality elaborate (and evolving) viewpoints. Each exists in more or less critical versions, in more or less deterministic versions, with more or less emphasis on the role of strategic choices and social influences on the development and use of IT. Despite this diversity, we believe that efforts at systematisation (even as caricatures) can prove a helpful guide to a dauntingly large and seemingly amorphous literature. In the process of piecing together the viewpoints of the three schools it was only natural to find within this growing mass of literature a number of continuities and discontinuities. Their coverage of issues tends to be rather selective. We have therefore found it necessary to construct 'ideal-type' arguments in areas where they are silent. This systematisation also helps us locate our own viewpoints with more clarity.

We have also outlined the reasons why IT is a revolutionary technology: it substantially changes the cost and quality of information processing. As information processing is a component of all human activities, IT can potentially be used to transform many aspects of our lives. This does not mean that IT will suddenly materialise in all these activities. Indeed, as the profiles in Table 1.1 suggest, the different approaches vary in their understanding of how IT relates to ongoing processes and underlying mechanisms of social change, and their appreciation of the rate of change in, and speed of diffusion of, IT. Even within each school applications are seen as developing and diffusing unevenly through the economy and society.

One way of thinking about this corresponds to the structure of this book, and it is helpful to set out a very simple model of the structure of economic life (Figure 1.2). Some sectors of the economy largely produce materials, goods and services for other industries to use. They produce energy, minerals, agricultural products, tools, equipment and knowledge that are embodied in the production process, and hence into the final products, of other industries. They produce intermediate goods and services. The consumer goods and service industries consume these intermediate products, and themselves create final goods and services supplied to consumers. Here we term this latter group the 'household sector', since it is seriously misleading to view households' only economic role as that of passive consumers of final

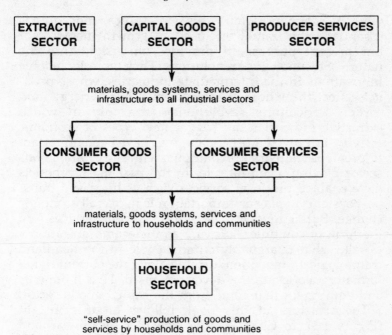

Figure 1.2 **Model of economic life**

products (and of course providers of labour inputs to the formal economy). There is considerable, if unqualified, actual production of goods and services by 'consumers' themselves, consuming 'final' goods and services to make their own 'self-services'.

Figure 1.2 naturally presents a simplified view of affairs. It omits the feedbacks that are essential parts of the system – the flow of labour and money from the household sector into industries, in particular. And in reality things are not so neat as we have indicated: for example agricultural produce and energy supplies are often sold direct to consumers without being 'packaged' by food industries or utilities. Nevertheless as a rough

view of economic affairs this will suffice, indeed it is
essentially the framework used in growth models. For
our present purpose, it provides an insight into the
nature of technological revolutions. They typically involve
innovations in the intermediate industries, whose products affect the whole of the system. Cheap energy (and
earlier, agricultural revolutions) is a way in which
extractive industries can trigger new types of economic
activity. Improved tools and engines have been important
to previous industrial revolutions, with the capital goods
sector playing a central role. In the past these products
have enabled producer services such as improved transport systems to play an important role in overall economic
change. But IT involves contributions from services – in
the form of computer software and telecommunication –
to take what is arguably an equal role in the heartland
technological innovation, driving along the current transformation alongside the developments of IT components
and equipment that come from the capital goods sector.

The structure of this book follows on this insight
(Figure 1.3). In Chapter 2 we consider these heartland
technologies – the component technologies that are the
basis of the 'IT revolution'. Although our schools of
thought disagree as to rates of change, all three appear
to share similar notions of the key types of development
of IT over the coming trends, and this chapter provides
a menu of the principal devices which will form the
foundations of the chapters on application. In Chapter 3
we consider the integration of technologies – the IT
systems that are of general social and economic significance and that are formed by the combination of IT
components and software. Whereas the core technologies
are widely agreed upon, there is significant disagreement
as to the degree of enthusiasm displayed for their
application by households, formal social institutions, the
workforce and other groups of social actors. Chapter 4
considers these applications (and the different perspectives) in the various sectors of the formal economy to
which the heartland technologies diffuse, and where IT
innovation shapes the given applications to specific

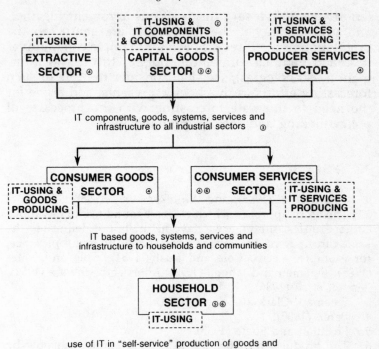

Chapters

② Technology Trends
③ Using IT
④ Putting IT to Work
⑤ Living With IT
⑥ Acting on IT

Figure 1.3 **Structure of the book**

purposes. Chapter 5 goes on to consider the 'household sector' – applications of the final products of IT in everyday life. In Chapter 6 we expand this discussion in order to consider activities such as education, social participation and some rather important 'final' applications of IT in public services and in communities. Finally, in Chapter 7 we shall attempt to tie the (enormously diverse) threads of our argument together, and probe some of the issues that are central to the orientation of the three schools (for example competitiveness and national differences, public attitudes to information technologies); we shall consider the role of such forecasting efforts as this book represents, and argue for the need to integrate forecasting with the processes of policy-making and social experimentation.

NOTES

1. Bessant *et al.* (1985); and Whitaker *et al.* (1988).
2. This is an approach which we have found useful in various earlier studies, although we have naturally not delineated the same three perspectives when addressing different topics. See, for example, Acero, Cole and Rush (1981); Cole and Miles (1985); Freeman and Jahoda (1978); Miles and Schwarz (1984); Bessant *et al.* (1986).
3. Freeman, Clark and Soete (1981).
4. Perez (1985).
5. Freeman and Soete (1985).
6. The production of printed text, for example, can now be carried out by various sorts of mechanical and electronic typewriter. While some might consider these to be obsolete technologies, new models are still being introduced in new materials or more portable versions. Alternatively one can use dedicated word processors or multipurpose machines of various types (laptop, desktop, terminals to mainframes) which run any number of text-handling programmes and can operate dot-matrix, daisy wheel, inkjet or laser printers. Long distance communications can be carried out by telephony or radio communications, morse code, and so on.
7. Noble (1984).
8. Freeman (1981).
9. Metcalfe (1986).

2. Technology Trends

Thirty years ago the public perception of computers was of mysterious machines, often referred to as 'electronic brains'. Somehow, through a combination of flashing lights and spinning tapes, they were able to solve the complex mathematical problems posed by their white-coated operators. Data were fed into these mammoth calculators, which then applied inscrutable processes to provide objective answers. At that time any prediction that in the 1980s computers would be commonplace in homes would have been greeted with bewilderment: where would people find room for them; how could they afford them; what could they be used for?

In contrast the telephone was already familiar to all. It was found in an increasing proportion of homes, and considered relatively mundane in comparison to the new wonders of television. The prospect of a marriage between telephone and television – which would now be called a videophone – was considered a natural development.

Looking back to this period gives a salutary reminder of the dangers of technological forecasting. No one could predict the microprocessor because the crucial first step – the integrated circuit – had not been taken. This is not to deny that there were visionaries who were able to conceive of computing equipment with the sort of capabilities that have only become available with micro-electronics. There were indeed such visionaries, although even they tended to think of future computers as massive centralised machines, without hitting upon the idea of small and portable microcomputers – except, presumably, inside the robots of popular literature. And when AT & T introduced their Picturephone in the 1960s there was insufficient consumer demand to make the new service commercially viable.[1]

Despite the dangers, forecasts of information technology developments for the remainder of this century and well into the next are plentiful. These range from papers in scientific journals examining the likely progress in a single technology, to extravagant descriptions of the technological infrastructure of the next century. In this chapter we draw on many of those sources to present our own forecast from a structuralist perspective. This gives us the freedom to mix the extrapolative approach of the continuists with the more speculative identification of seeds of the future, which we associate with the transformist view.

Our mixture of methods will vary with the technology considered: some technical developments are so recent that long-term forecasts cannot be extrapolated from the data available, while other trajectories are well established. It will also vary according to timescale, as the further we look into the future the more likely it is that some of today's seeds will have grown and blossomed, while others will prove to have fallen on stony ground.

IT covers a remarkable range of technologies, and there are numerous dictionaries of IT with thousands of entries, which suggests our task is enormous if not impossible. Fortunately this is not a dictionary: the selection of technologies is in itself part of the forecast, indicating those we consider likely to be of prime importance in the closing years of this century, and the opening decade of the next.

Not only is the range of technologies broad, but they are becoming increasingly interconnected in a process that is often represented by the convergence of two lines, as, for example, in Figure 2.1. This illustrates the chronological development of IT from its separate origins in computing and communications, but fails to show the extent of the interconnections between technologies. A more detailed representation might bear more resemblance to a street map of Mexico City – extremely complex,

23

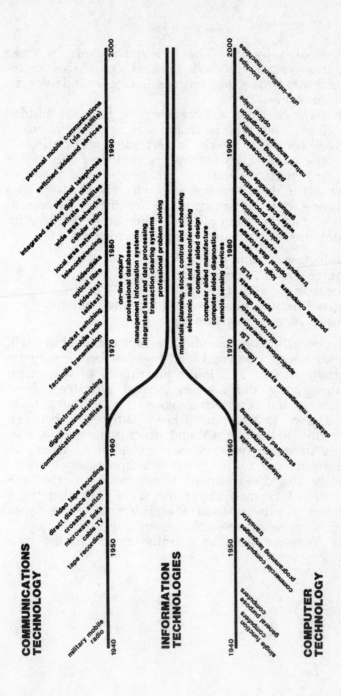

Figure 2.1 Some key events in the convergence of information technology
Source: Bessant et al. (1985).

and outdated by the time it is published. To make
navigation easier we have divided our discussion of
forecasts into two sections: core technologies and integrating technologies.

What we call core technologies are generally hidden
from view – silicon chips inside plain grey metal boxes,
optical fibres under the city streets, satellites orbiting far
above the earth. Each technology performs one of five
basic information-handling functions: production or
collection of data, storage and retrieval of data, data
processing, data transmission, or the display or presentation of data. For example the technologies required for
broadcasting a television programme include:

- production – camera
- storage – videotape recorder
- processing – videotape editor
- transmission – broadcast and reception antennae
- presentation – television set.

Each core technology may be a technical marvel in itself,
but they need to be combined together before they are
practically useful.[2] This is the function of what we term
the integrating technologies, which effectively bind
together several core technologies, thus enabling them
to be applied to a myriad of tasks. Differences between
the continuist, transformist and structuralist perspectives
become in many respects more pronounced when we
move from core to integrating technologies: there is
relatively less disagreement about trends in the core
potentials of IT than about the ways in which these
potentials may be realised. We shall discuss the issues
around integrating technologies in more detail in due
course; first we need to examine trends in the core
technologies.

CORE TECHNOLOGIES

Microelectronics

The first integrated circuits, with transistors and their interconnections formed directly on tiny pieces of silicon (hence the term silicon chip), became commercially available in the early 1960s. Ever since their introduction developments in the manufacturing process have enabled the number of components and the complexity of the circuit on a chip to increase rapidly.

In 1964 it was predicted that the number of features in a state-of-the-art integrated circuit would double every year.[3] This prediction has been sufficiently accurate to be named after its author, 'Moore's Law', although this suggests an inevitability which does scant justice to the sustained efforts of scientists and engineers, and the commitment of vast sums of research and development money in laboratories and factories around the world. In the early 1970s chips with tens of thousands of components become available, and the term Large Scale Integration (LSI) was coined to describe these. A few years later a new description, Very Large Scale Integration (VLSI), was considered necessary as the level of integration rushed past 100 000. Chips with over a million components are now commercially available, and these are likely to be termed Ultra Large Scale Integration (ULSI, naturally).

It may seem that having achieved the million mark there can be little more to be gained, yet each increase in integration brings numerous benefits:

- lower costs per component, since the number of components on each chip rises faster than the production costs
- lower assembly costs for electronic equipment as each chip replaces many discrete components (or, nowadays, many smaller chips)
- faster switching speeds, leading to faster and more powerful computers

- more reliable equipment, with fewer interconnections which are likely to be the source of faults
- smaller and lighter equipment, requiring less power, which multiplies the range of potential applications.

Increasing integration has therefore been crucial to improvements in performance and reductions in cost of all kinds of electronic equipment. These in turn have stimulated demand for better versions of existing products and enabled new markets to be created.

The explosive growth in chip complexity has been achieved primarily by reducing the size of the components on the chip and the distance between them. This minimum feature length has been reduced from about 10 microns (0.01mm) for the most advanced commercially-available chips of the mid-1970s to around 1.2 microns today (and less for experimental chips).

The optical lithography techniques traditionally used in chip manufacture can be improved to reduce the minimum feature length to around 0.5 microns.[4] Major reductions beyond this are possible with alternative techniques using X-rays or electron beams in place of light. However it is generally predicted that at around 0.1 to 0.2 microns the devices and connections on a chip will become so small that fundamental problems will affect the operation of the microelectronic circuits.[5,6]

The rate of reduction in minimum feature length is therefore likely to become less rapid as technological limits are approached, and each incremental reduction requires increasingly expensive manufacturing plant. Figure 2.2 shows the historical and expected trends in best-practice minimum feature length. The initial pace of development in chip technology was set by American manufacturers such as Intel and Texas Instruments. However the late 1970s saw substantial coordinated investment by several major Japanese electronics manufacturers, and by the mid-eighties these companies had become technological leaders in chip production and the dominant world suppliers.

With the physical limits to development of silicon chips now in sight, although still many years away,

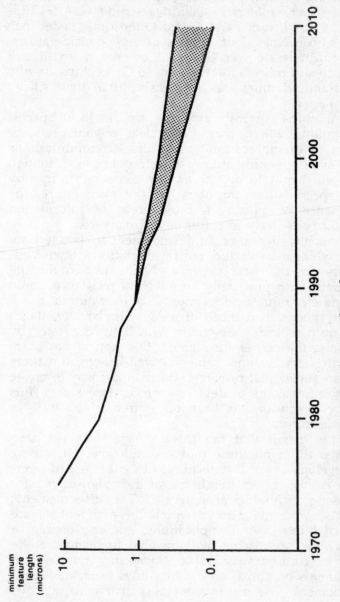

Figure 2.2 **Trends in minimum feature length**

27

increasing attention is being given to an alternative semiconductor material – gallium arsenide (GaAs). Chips manufactured from GaAs are up to ten times faster than their silicon equivalent, operate at higher temperatures, and require less power. GaAs is, however, more difficult to refine and process than silicon, so GaAs chips are fifty to a hundred times more expensive than their silicon equivalent.[7]

GaAs chips currently available are aimed at specific applications where they have clear advantages over silicon, for example as components of telecommunications equipment operating at very high frequencies. Although they will begin to appear as key components in very high speed 'supercomputers' in the near future, the dominance of silicon in most areas of information technology is likely to continue for many years.

At much earlier stages of development are two technologies which may produce radical alternatives to semiconductors in the next century. New superconducting materials, with practically no electrical resistance, could provide electronic devices capable of operating at much higher speeds than those of today. Similar advantages arise from replacing electricity with light (generated by lasers) as the carrier for signals; that optical fibres are replacing conventional cables is well-known, but there are also substantial research efforts under way to create optical equivalents of devices such as transistors. Thus we are beginning to hear of 'optronics' as well as microelectronics.

To the extent that the three perspectives we have sketched differ on these topics – and others involving the development of core technologies – it is not in terms of the reality of past trends nor of their significance for increasing technological potential. The disagreements will be about the rate at which these potentials are converted into useful applications, and the degree to which new approaches will be able to overcome the limits to continuing advance (increasing numbers of components on chips) on existing lines of technological development. The continuist perspective will put considerably more stress on the obstacles to innovation faced in these two respects, while transformism tends to portray these obstacles as transitory problems at best. A structuralist view would lead us to expect that develop-· ment will most probably be very uneven, with some aspects of core potential being developed, and some aspects being seized upon for applications, much more rapidly than others: the pattern of development will be determined by constellations of powerful interests (such as military research programmes, or efforts to maintain national leads in specific core technologies) as much as by the intrinsic nature of microelectronic technology.

Microprocessors By the early 1970s semiconductor technology allowed the essential circuits for the central processor unit of a simple computer to be squeezed on to a single chip – a microprocessor. With additional chips and peripheral devices such as a keyboard and display, small general-purpose computers – capable of being programmed to perform an endless variety of tasks – could be assembled.

One measure of the 'power' of a computer is the word length of the processor, which is measured in bits. The significance of this is that the sort of operations processors carry out, for example the multiplication of two numbers, can be performed in much fewer steps, and hence faster, by, say, a 32-bit processor than an 8-bit processor. Increasing integration has led to a range of 4-bit, 8-bit, 16-bit and, more recently, 32-bit microprocessors being introduced. The latter has become the most common word length for mainframe computers and minicomputers, offering a balance between complexity and performance, and therefore there is unlikely to be any move towards microprocessors with a word length over 32 bits. Developments in the short term will concentrate on increasing the speed of existing designs, reducing their cost and adding the functions performed by ancillary chips (which act as the 'glue' between the microprocessor and the devices which surround it) on to the microprocessor chip itself.

Looking further ahead towards the last decade of the century, three separate aproaches that are currently being pursued seem likely to be of considerable importance:

• The addition of a number of co-processors to operate in conjunction with the main processor, each dealing with specific tasks such as graphics or network communications. By maintaining compatibility with current designs, these microprocessors would form the basis of future business microcomputers.
• Microprocessors such as the INMOS Transputer with processing, memory and communications functions on a single chip. Computers containing several Transputers could break tasks down into operations capable of being performed simultaneously by the processors working in parallel. These would find applications in areas such as computer-aided design and engineering, and providing robots with the ability to interpret pictures of their surroundings provided by video cameras, for example.
• Reduced instruction set (RISC) microprocessors, which are much simpler than most existing designs but operate at higher speeds. These may form the basis for specialised microcomputers intended for applications requiring, for example, understanding of speech. By the early 1990s RISC microprocessors manufactured using gallium arsenide are likely to be commercially available, but the high costs of GaAs chips will limit the range of applications.[8]

Memory Memory chips, with a simpler design than logic chips such as microprocessors, have traditionally had the highest density of components. Figure 2.3 shows the increasing storage capacity of the most common form of memory chip from the 1Kbit chips of the early 1970s. Further reductions in minimum feature length will lead to 16Mbit chips by the middle of the next decade, and eventually to 64Mbit chips. Advances beyond this will require major design and production changes, for example the further development of three-dimensional chip technologies.[9,10]

Semiconductor manufacturers have generally tried to keep the physical size of chips as small as possible. The

31

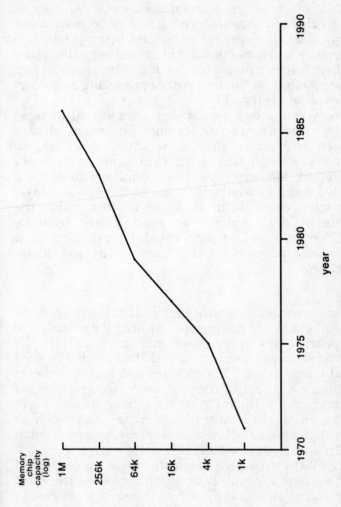

Figure 2.3 **Memory chip storage capacity**
Source: Prince and Due-Gundersen (1983).

costs of production are closely related to the cost of processing each silicon wafer – a thin circular disc cut from an ultra-pure silicon crystal from which tens or hundreds of chips are manufactured by a sequence of photographic and chemical processes. Smaller chips mean not only more chips per wafer but also better production yields, since occasional unwanted impurities in the wafer will affect a lower proportion of the chips. Both have a significant effect on the unit cost of producing each chip, and hence on profitability.

Memory is the one area where a significant increase in chip size may occur. Memory chips are already produced with spare circuits, which can be used to replace those in an area of the chip found to be faulty when tested. Memory capacities a hundred times those predicted could be available in the early 1990s on single 'wafer-scale' chips. With batteries to ensure that the contents of the memory are continuously retained, 60 million bytes of storage could be provided in a transportable package about 100mm square and 10mm in thickness.

Application-specific integrated circuits   For many years the design of electronic equipment required the selection of appropriate chips from those mass-produced by the semiconductor manufacturers, and their assembly on a printed circuit board. The complex and lengthy process of designing a chip, coupled with the expense of producing chips in anything less than quantities of millions, meant that only high-volume users (such as the computer manufacturers and motor industry) could consider using custom-built chips.

Since 1980 increasingly sophisticated computer-aided design and the availability of libraries of standard 'cells' have reduced significantly the time required to design complex chips for particular applications. During the same period new production processes have been introduced, allowing small batches of chips to be produced quickly and at reasonable cost.

These developments enable application-specific integrated circuits (ASICs) to be designed and produced for many more applications. The ASIC market is thus considered by many as a major growth area for the future.[11] As the design systems required become both cheaper and more powerful (aided in part by ASICs themselves), chip design will become a feasible proposition even for very small companies. The design can then be forwarded to a chip manufacturing company acting as a 'silicon foundry', producing chips for a range of customers.

Data storage

The dominant technology for storage of large volumes of data is currently the magnetic disc. These range in capacity from the now familiar floppy discs (typically holding a few hundred thousand bytes of data) up to multi-surface disc packs used by mainframe computers and capable of storing several billion bytes. Magnetic tapes are still widely used for archival of data and for storage of security copies. However, the future competition for magnetic discs will come from semiconductor memory (including the wafer-scale chips described above) and optical discs.

As can be seen from Figure 2.4, semiconductor memory gives access to data around a thousand times faster than magnetic discs, but is at least ten times more expensive. There is relatively little room for improvement in disc access times, which are governed primarily by the electromechanical parts of the disc drive.

Magnetic disc storage capacities may increase by a factor of ten in the near future with the introduction of techniques such as vertical magnetic recording, in which magnetic particles are perpendicular to the disc surface rather than flat. However the technical advantages of semiconductor memory, including reliability and power consumption as well as speed, will inevitably lead to it displacing magnetic disc technology for data storage in

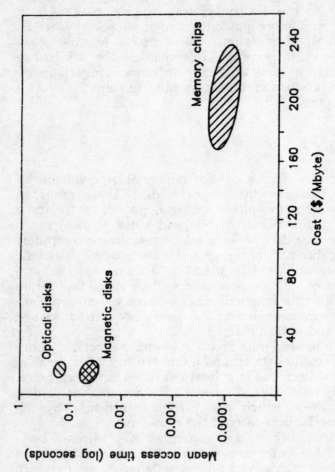

Figure 2.4 Data storage costs and performance

many application areas, particularly in portable equipment.

At the other extreme the development of optical discs provides very low cost data storage, although with relatively slow access times. The inability to erase data from an optical disc will limit initial applications to the replacement of magnetic tape by 'write-once read-many' discs, and the creation of a new method of information distribution on read-only discs.

There is considerable research into optical discs on which data can be erased and overwritten, as on a magnetic disc, with various alternative materials being investigated. The requirement is for a material a small area of which will switch between two states (colour, transparency or even shape) whenever a laser beam of a specific type is concentrated on its surface. With reduced access times through improvements to the laser which reads and writes to the disc, optical discs are likely to become the standard for high-volume data storage by the turn of the century.

Telecommunications

The conversion of telecommunications networks to carry signals in digital rather than analogue form has been taking place at an increasing pace over the last two decades.[12] This enables telecommunications to take advantage of developments in digital microelectronics, giving higher reliability, improved performance and reduced operating costs.

The general approach that has been pursued to date has been to introduce digital transmission on major trunk routes, and more recently to replace electromechanical switching equipment by more reliable digital exchanges (which are essentially highly specialised computers). Programs along these lines are well advanced in most countries, so that the USA, Japan and most of Europe expect to have completely digital trunk networks by 1990. However small rural exchanges are unlikely to be replaced by digital versions until they have become completely obsolete (or too costly to maintain), which may not be until well into the next century.

The major technologies for high-capacity transmission have traditionally been coaxial cable and microwave radio relay systems. Although both can be used to carry digital signals, the newer technologies of optical fibres and satellites are generally considered to offer both technical and economic advantages.

Optical fibres   Optical fibres are thin strands of very pure glass, which carry digital signals as pulses of light generated by lasers or light-emitting diodes. The combination of strength, flexibility, light weight and small diameter enables them to be installed easily, and the use of light pulses avoids problems of electromagnetic interference.

The performance of optical fibre systems can be measured by two factors – the speed with which signals are transmitted, and the distance a signal travels before it begins to fade and blur, requiring a repeater to boost the strength. The first commercial installations in the early 1980s carried signals at up to 34 million bits per second (around 500 simultaneous telephone calls) with distances of 8–10 km between repeaters. Within five years the problems of producing and installing fibres with a thinner central core had been overcome, enabling a more 'concentrated' beam of light to be carried. Together with improvements to the electronics used to send and receive signals, this led to the introduction of systems carrying 565 million bits per second – sufficient to carry almost 9000 simultaneous telephone calls – with a repeater spacing of up to 45 km.[13]

The economic advantages of higher speeds and fewer repeaters are stimulating considerable research, which may be expected to continue to produce new performance records for some years to come. For example, several channels could be transmitted simultaneously over the same fibre, at different wavelengths. Since this only requires changes to the electronics and not to the fibre itself, installed optical fibre systems could be upgraded in the 1990s to carry several billion bits per second. New systems with capacities similar to those at present would only require repeaters at intervals of around 250 km.

Early next century fibres made from fluoride glass rather than silica glass will enable the installation of transoceanic systems carrying signals at billions of bits per second, and with repeaters at 2000 km intervals.[14] By reducing or eliminating the number of repeaters these systems would have a longer lifetime and lower mainten-ance costs.

Satellites Satellite communications technology has improved rapidly since the first commercial satellites were launched in the mid-sixties, as shown in Table 2.1. This has been achieved through a combination of increasing launch capability, which has allowed larger, more powerful satellites to be deployed, and advances in microelectronics. The main applications to date have been in international television distribution and in voice/ data communications. Only the United States makes extensive use of satellites for domestic services, although countries such as Canada have used satellites for improv-ing communications to scattered communities.

Table 2.1 **Development of satellite capabilities**

Generation	Year introduced	Design lifetime (years)	Voice circuits	Television channels
I	1965	1.5	240	–
II	1967	3.0	240	–
III	1968	5.0	1 500	–
IV	1971	7.0	4 000	2
V	1980	7.0	12 000	2
VI	1987	· 10.0	30 000	3

Source: Intelsat (1985).

The increasing number of satellites has already caused problems with saturation of the transmission frequencies allocated for satellite telecommunications, particularly in North America. These problems have been alleviated by the allocation of an additional band of higher frequencies, and by using tighter transmission beams, allowing satellites to be more closely spaced in orbit without interference between signals. Earth stations required for reception of these higher-frequency transmissions are smaller and cheaper than their predecessors, enabling satellites to be used for transmission of television signals either for distribution via cable networks or direct to consumers.

Experiments with an even higher band of frequencies are now taking place, with commercial use anticipated from the late 1990s allowing expansion of existing services. Furthermore the relatively small size of earth station required (less than 1 metre in diameter) is expected to lead to increasing application in the area of mobile communications.[15]

Satellites deployed in the 1990s will be capable of transmitting and receiving signals in all three frequency bands, with sophisticated microelectronics for on-board switching and signal processing, enabling them to carry a wide range of services with very efficient use of frequencies.[16] In the longer term the assembly in space of large 'platforms' has been proposed by many as a means of providing significant increases in capacity. The feasibility of this approach will be tested by the space stations planned by the USA and USSR for the next decade.

Although there appears to be a clear technological path forward, a fundamental change in the applications of communications satellites is commencing. The reason for this is that optical fibres are overtaking satellites as the most cost-effective method of introducing new capacity on most of the high-density long-distance routes, for example between North America and Europe. A gradual changeover to optical fibres on such routes seems inevitable, and may well lead to substantial capacity increases which will initially be only partly utilised. The result would be a change in the role of satellites to the provision of complementary services,[17] including:

● on low-density routes, particularly those to countries in the Third World
● to ships, aircraft and vehicles in remote areas
● over geographically difficult areas, such as mountainous regions and groups of islands
● high-capacity links required at short notice or for short periods, for example at major televised sporting events
● as a means of providing internal and independent telecommunications networks for multinational companies.

Core forecasts

The last thirty years have seen the first communications satellite, the first silicon chip, the first optical fibre. The momentum of development is such that long-term forecasts of the capabilities of established core technologies do not differ radically, with practically all commentators anticipating continued rapid growth. This is why we have not attempted to elaborate distinctions between continuist, transformist and structuralist perspectives in respect of the various core technologies, at least not in any detail.

Divergences between forecasts are far more prevalent when there are expectations of discontinuities in technological development, as we have already briefly noted. One example of such a potential discontinuity is the recent discovery of ceramic materials which function as superconductors at temperatures much higher than those previously considered achievable (although still well below room temperature). From our structuralist viewpoint we acknowledge the potential of this breakthrough, but we do not anticipate it having a major impact on our core technology of microelectronics until after the turn of the century. A transformist forecast is likely to seize upon the discovery as yet more evidence of the accelerating rate of change: research funds will be diverted into this area, so that understanding of how to use the new technological potential will be established rapidly. The continuist perspective will be sceptical of the current interest in this area, as reflecting in part at least hyperbole from funds-starved researchers; as a topic on which we need to wait for further evidence before attempting any extrapolation; and as one that is bound to involve many major technological challenges before a wide range of commercial applications is possible.

In part our own caution is a result of historical analogy with the time taken from the discovery of the transistor to the widespread replacement of valves and magnetic storage by the new technology. The reasons for such caution will become more apparent as we examine integrating technologies and the ways in which these affect the rate and direction of diffusion of innovations.

INTEGRATING TECHNOLOGIES

Computers

Trends in computers (and integrating technologies in general) are less open to quantitative representation than those in their component technologies. Performance measurements certainly do exist but these are not universally accepted. Thus, for example, 'mips' (millions of instructions per second) are occasionally referred to as 'meaningless indicators of performance'. The problem is that there are many dimensions of performance to be taken into account, including those relevant to all the different classes of components that make up the computer system, and specific performance issues are posed by the particular applications for which it is used. For example users of microcomputers may well gain more benefit by replacing a floppy disc drive with a hard disc drive – increasing their data storage capacity and reducing the time needed to retrieve data – than by changing to a faster microprocessor and being able to manipulate the data more rapidly. Similarly the speed at which a computer can perform multiplications is irrelevant to users of word processing and database software.

Since the late 1940s computers have been designed on principles established by von Neumann. This 'von Neumann architecture' is based upon a central control unit performing a program of instructions in sequence (although high processing speeds enable computers to appear to carry out several tasks simultaneously). Development has for the most part been due to improvements in the size, cost, speed and reliability of the components. In the 1960s IBM consolidated its early dominance of the mainframe market, which continues to this day, with the introduction of the System/360 range. However a much smaller company, DEC, was able to create a new market for their minicomputers such as the PDP-8, which was sufficiently compact and low-priced to be used by departments within companies, in laboratories and on the factory floor.

This story was repeated in the 1970s with the success of microcomputers such as the Apple II, the first of which were produced in a garage. On this occasion IBM responded with a range of microcomputers which have been extremely successful in the 1980s, although Apple remains a major competitor with their innovative Macintosh range. The entry of IBM into the microcomputer market prompted a host of established and new manufacturers to produce 'clones', which were generally better and cheaper, the two most notable being the portable computers produced by Compaq and Toshiba.

When they are installed computer systems are typically expected to have a life up to seven years, during which time enhancements such as increased memory and disc storage may be made. By the time that replacement is considered, the major investment will generally have been not in hardware but in packaged and custom-developed software, and in staff training. Computer manufacturers therefore attempt to provide 'backwards compatibility' in their products, which enables the existing software to be used on new hardware, but in doing so imposes considerable constraints on the design.

The continuist viewpoint would take factors such as this inertia, effectively generated by the vast amount of existing software, as evidence that we will still see for many years the further development of computer systems based around architectures introduced in the 1970s, such as those of the IBM S/370 and DEC VAX machines. Advances in semiconductor technology will enable smaller and cheaper versions of such systems to be designed and manufactured, for example as single-user workstations intended for computer-aided design. At the opposite end of the range, large computer systems now support hundreds or thousands of users in activities crucial to the day to day operations of organisations. The reliability and performance demanded for such applications will increasingly be met by systems incorporating several processors working closely together, sharing access to discs and in some cases to memory. In addition to giving high levels of performance, these systems have the ability to continue operating when faults occur.

The transformist perspective looks beyond the entrenched position of existing architectures to alternatives which can provide major improvements in speed – considered necessary to provide computers of the 1990s with human-like capabilities in areas such as language and reasoning. The most common approach to achieving this is based upon parallel processing of instructions whenever possible, using computers with tens or hundreds of processors. These may be conventional microprocessors communicating with each other via a single shared data highway. Alternatively custom-designed 'nodes' consisting of processor, memory and communications interfaces may be used, each communicating only with its nearest neighbours. In both cases the major technical challenges of constructing the hardware have been overcome, but the development of software to take advantage of parallel processing is still at an early stage.[18]

The structuralist perspective will tend to see these two views as complementary rather than exclusive. The investment in software (and in training and peripherals), combined with the essentially conservative purchasing policies of major corporations, will ensure a continuing dominance of computers based on existing architectures in most of what are currently their strongest areas. These include maintaining corporate databases, processing transactions for organisations such as banks, airlines and government departments, and providing personal computing facilities such as word processing and spread-sheets. We expect parallel processing architectures to become increasingly favoured for highly computational applications in areas such as weather forecasting and image processing, where vast volumes of data are put through diverse sets of operations. These developments will provide the base required for the development of software and skills, which will gradually filter through to existing applications and enable expansion into new areas.

Software developments and artificial intelligence

The pace of development in software has been relatively slow in comparison to the changes in the physical hardware of computer systems. A succession of program-ming languages have been introduced, each enabling hundreds or thousands of the low-level instructions which can be interpreted by the computer processor to be automatically generated from simple statements. Of these thousands of languages only a handful have been widely adopted alongside the ancestors of them all: Cobol for commercial applications and Fortran for technical use, both of which have been much improved from their original 1950s versions. Some of the most successful new languages have been those which can be learnt quickly and easily, without a lengthy training in programming. Simple 'query' languages were first designed to enable users such as managers and librarians to retrieve information from databases. Many of these languages have now been extended to form 'fourth generation' languages capable of being used for creating and updating databases, as well as for data retrieval and reporting. Meanwhile languages such as LOGO have been successfully learnt by children in their earliest years at school, and Basic has become the most popular language for use on home computers.

Despite these advances, software now dominates the cost of computing, largely because of its inherently large labour content (much of which is modifying and maintaining existing programs, rather than new systems development). The supply of trained computer staff has continually lagged behind demand, and this problem is exacerbated by the continual need for retraining as new hardware and software is introduced.

As the reliability of computer hardware components has improved, aided where necessary by the use of duplicate components and systems to provide 'non-stop' processing, software has also become the dominant factor in the reliability of computer systems. Increasingly ambitious projects, such as the Strategic Defence Initiative, require development of software containing millions of lines of instructions. (In this particular case it will never be fully tested, which has prompted questioning of the technical feasibility of the entire project.)

One solution to the problems is seen to lie in increasing formalisation of software production – its long-awaited transformation from a craft to an engineering discipline. The hope is that 'software engineering' will not only make the production of software more systematic and its maintenance more routine, but that it will also prepare the ground for the automation of much software development, thus helping to decrease costs and enhance system reliability.

In recent years increasingly sophisticated products to assist in the creation and testing of computer programs have become available, in the form of Integrated Programming Support Environments. Since these offer the prospect of major improvements in productivity, in maintenance of existing software as well as writing of new programs, they can be expected to spread rapidly into commercial use. Considerable research is taking place into reducing the time required to prepare software specifications through the development of formal specification languages, which may be text-based or diagrammatic. However computer users are generally very slow to adopt new computer languages, as amply illustrated by the continuing widespread use of Cobol and Fortran.

A second approach has been the attempt to provide methods for development of more 'portable' computer programs capable of operating on many different models of computer. This approach is particularly associated with supporters of the non-proprietary Unix operating system, itself a highly portable program, which tries to make different computers appear to be identical. Unfortunately suppliers and academics have been unable to resist the temptation to 'tinker' with Unix, and as a result the original Unix has fragmented into many different versions. A single standard, to be called Posix, is now being defined with the intention that the separate versions should change to meet this by the 1990s. Posix will meet similar problems to those faced by new computer languages, with the added difficulty that computer manufacturers are likely to view it as a threat to the revenues they earn from proprietary operating systems.

The problems of the software development process result in enormous waste of an already scarce resource, namely trained software staff. If they are not fixing mistakes in existing programs they are making minor modifications, or converting software written for one computer to work on another. Even when developing supposedly new systems they are often re-inventing the wheel, producing yet another stock control system or word processor to add to the thousands previously written. While this does result in improvements to software (few users of the Lotus 1-2-3 spreadsheet would choose to revert to the original VisiCalc), it also acts as a restraint on the development and diffusion of innovative applications.

One of the longest and most vociferous debates regarding the future of IT concerns the development of software incorporating artificial intelligence (AI) techniques, collectively known as Intelligent Knowledge-Based Systems (IKBS). Research into AI began in the United States in the 1950s, with the twin goals of using computers to help to understand human thought processes, and improving the capabilities of computers in areas such as language and learning. Early researchers began ambitious projects, such as automatic translation from one language to another, and quickly discovered that such tasks required not only faster and better computers but also fundamental research in areas such as linguistics and neurophysiology. So for many years AI was seen as an area of outstanding potential application, yet as one with such a low probability of success that the funding of academic research was restricted.[19]

By the late 1970s the first commercial applications of AI research were just beginning to appear. Perhaps the best known example is XCON, a computer program which embodies the expert knowledge required to configure VAX computer systems.[20] The success of XCON has been a major factor behind widespread interest in development of similar 'expert systems' for solving problems and providing advice in areas ranging from employment legislation to geological prospecting.

Every expert system developed has been confined to a narrow domain of knowledge, which is stored in the form of facts and heuristics (or 'rules of thumb') in the knowledge base of the expert system. For example MYCIN is a medical expert system which can diagnose blood infections and recommend treatment, using its knowledge base and information about a given patient provided by a doctor (in a dialogue with the computer which may last up to two hours). The performance of MYCIN is impressive within this domain but it knows nothing of other branches of medicine, even closely related areas such as other infectious diseases.

The 1970s also saw the development of INTELLECT, which enables information to be retrieved from databases using enquiries phrased in natural language, rather than the highly-structured query languages generally employed. INTELLECT has fulfilled a similar role to XCON, demonstrating that AI research has reached the stage of commercial exploitation, in this case in the area of AI known as natural language processing. However like XCON its performance is limited – it can translate enquiries into the form required to search the database but does not understand the subject matter.

Increasingly powerful computers, together with new approaches to language processing, have prompted renewed efforts in machine translation between languages. The European Community is funding a major project in this area, and a system capable of providing a rough translation of scientific and technical papers in several fields is available.[21] These are often sufficiently accurate for a scientist to understand the contents, although the output will generally be polished by a professional translator.

Software to enable computers to convert speech into text has also appeared commercially during the 1980s. Generally this includes a vocabulary of only a few hundred words, and requires the user to speak slowly and distinctly. This is sufficient for many applications, such as recording of faults found by a quality control inspector while walking round a piece of equipment (for example an aeroplane or automobile), or for providing routine banking services over the telephone. The main current objective is recognition of continuous speech,[22] enabling the development of products such as a voice-driven word processor or 'talkwriter'. Primitive talkwriters are already on trial and are expected to be commercially available by the early 1990s, but the cost alone will deter most computer users from throwing away their keyboards for some time.

The final major area where commercial applications of AI are now appearing concerns vision, in particular the provision of robots with the capability to see their surroundings and, more important, to interpret them. Existing vision systems, such as General Motors CON-

SIGHT, can only interpret images in two dimensions.
This enables them to be used for tasks where the outline
is enough to identify the object, for example picking
components off a conveyor belt. By using carefully
controlled lighting vision systems can gain information
about surfaces, but true three-dimensional vision requires
separate images from two cameras. While simple 2-D
vision systems are likely to become a commonplace
feature of factory automation in the 1990s, 3-D systems
will be limited to those dealing with well-defined tasks,
such as guiding a vehicle through a familiar factory.

The transformist perspective sees artificial intelligence
as the key to the 'second computer revolution', producing,
for example, machines which can translate speech from
one language to another, resulting in enormous changes to
human communications and society. Some commentators
anticipate the eventual evolution of computers into an
ultra-intelligent species, or even the creation of human-
computer hybrids.[23]

Of course there is a more cautious continuist view.
This looks back on thirty years of research, concluding
that it has produced only a handful of commercial
applications in highly-specialised areas. Although
additional problem-solving techniques are slowly being
provided by artificial intelligence, human capabilities
such as understanding language and applying commonsense reasoning are considered to be beyond reach of
any machine in the medium-term future.[24]

A structuralist view would be that the recent progress
in expert systems and language processing is bound to
provide valuable tools to improve productivity in many
tasks, for example fault diagnosis in machinery, and
document translation; and will make computer systems
easier and 'friendlier' to use. While systems incorporating
these tools will become more widespread in the 1990s
there are still many years of research ahead into the
representation of 'deep knowledge' for systems approaching human levels of capability in reasoning, language
and vision. In particular implicit knowledge of the
'rules' of social interaction – in which there may be a

considerable variation in the interpretation of the same
act or the same spoken sentence in different circumstances
– requires extensive explication.

There remains a long way to go with AI research. But
the development of research programmes centred around
AI, such as major parts of Alvey in the UK, Esprit in the
EEC, and MCC in the USA, are of significance. They may
be seen as strengthening (and perhaps permanently
transforming) academic-industry links and as providing
models for similar programmes in other areas of technological research.[25]

Integrated Services Digital Network

The next few years will see the completion of the change
to digital operation – the digitalisation of the major
elements of telecommunications networks in Europe,
Japan and North America. This has been justified on the
basis of reduction of the costs of installation, operation
and maintenance of the equipment which provides the
telephone service, rather than on the provision of new
services. In addition to the public telephone network,
telecommunications authorities operate networks for
special applications such as telex and data communications, some of which already use digital signals.

Attention is now switching to the next stage, the
integration of these separate networks, so that multiple
services can be carried on a single digital network; and
the extension of digital operation beyond trunk lines
and major business users to customer premises more
generally. In planning for this all telecommunications
authorities have faced the same problem: the existence
of millions of miles of twisted-pair cables in local
networks, and the installed base of telephones and other
equipment. The approach being adopted worldwide is
to utilise the existing cabling to carry digital signals,
to which computer-based equipment can easily be
connected. However existing analogue equipment (such
as conventional telephones) will need to be either

completely replaced or have a 'black box' added to translate signals between analogue and digital forms. (This would be rather like a mirror-image of the current 'modems' that translate computer data into a form which the analogue telephone network can handle.)

International standards have been agreed which propose that existing cables be used to carry signals digitally at a speed of 144 000 bits per second, although only 64 000 are required for a single voice channel. The spare capacity would be available for transmission of data, enabling a variety of additional services to be used without affecting incoming and outgoing calls. Some services will be improved versions of those currently available, for example high-speed facsimile and viewdata, while others may be new services, such as slow-scan videophones. It is this capability for voice and data services to be provided over the same cable which makes the proposed systems more than just a technological updating of the telephone network, and this is reflected in the term which has been adopted – the Integrated Services Digital Network or ISDN (Figure 2.5).

Pilot versions of ISDN are already operational in several countries, and few technical problems are expected in introducing the network on a wider scale. Nationwide access will be available in most industrialised countries by the mid-1990s, although the more complex structure of the telecommunications industry in the USA may result in slower implementation (and now seems to be giving rise to some criticisms of the whole ISDN approach). The growth rate of ISDN usage will be determined by customer demand for the new services (examples of which are listed in Table 2.2), for which they will have to purchase new equipment as well as paying operating costs. Business users of existing services such as telex, viewdata, electronic mail and facsimile seem likely to form the majority of initial ISDN users.

The experience with the French viewdata system, Teletel, suggests that rapid diffusion of new telecommunications services into the domestic market will require bold decisions on equipment costs, tariffs, and services

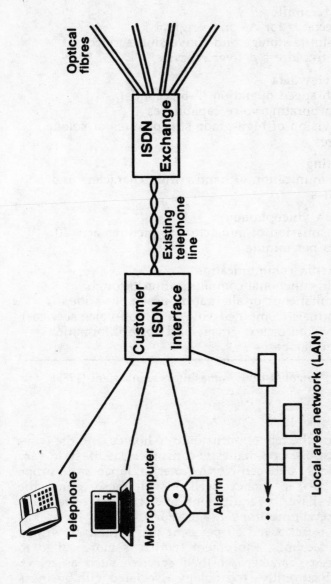

Figure 2.5 ISDN

Table 2.2 **Examples of future ISDN services**

Digital facsimile
  − 4 seconds for A4 size original
  − facsimile storage and conversion service
  − multi-address delivery service

Digital viewdata
  − high-speed operation (2–6 seconds)
  − incorporating voice capabilities
  − provision of high-grade still pictures or colour
  pictures

Telewriting
  − communication of handwritten characters and
  graphics

Slow-scan videophone
  − transmission of monochrome pictures at 8–10
  frames per minute

Multi-media communication
  − multi-functional communication through
  simultaneous or alternating usage of various
  terminals (combined voice and non-voice services)
  − provision of text, image and voice information
  from databases

Source: Adapted from Yamashita and Asastani (1985).

provided. The rate of diffusion into homes, and the types
of service used by domestic consumers, is likely to vary
considerably between North America, Japan and Europe
on the basis of policy decisions on these topics, the
installed base of equipment and cultural differences
in telecommunications usage. For example, Japan has
recently experienced 50 per cent per annum growth in
sales of facsimile equipment (which is more suited to
their large character set than services such as telex).
Although currently a technology associated with business

use, facsimile transmission may be a major factor in spreading domestic use of ISDN in Japan.

Broadband communications network

Planning for introduction of the ISDN began as early as 1972, the first stages being primarily concerned with the establishment of international standards. Work is now in progress on defining the next stage, which will require the installation of optical fibres in the local network.

From a continuist perspective current ISDN developments are expected to be sufficient to keep telecommunications engineers, service providers and the users of telecommunications equipment busy for the foreseeable future. But the transformist viewpoint looks beyond this; indeed sees this as merely a transitional stage to a much upgraded communications network. Such an improved network will enable the introduction of further new telecommunications services, especially those seen as requiring the very high capacity (broadband) channel that can be provided by optical fibres. Examples of such new services are given in Table 2.3.; they share in common the need for large quantities of data (such as those required to make up a video frame) to be delivered rapidly through the communication channel.

Although many of the standards developed for the current generation of ISDN will be applicable to the optical fibre network, there are still problems to be overcome, particularly in the provision of switching systems. (The continuist perspective will stress the existence of such problems, and point to efforts being made to reduce the need for broadband networks – for example, by developing data compression techniques that allow much more material to be crammed into existing or ISDN lines.) Optical fibres are already being installed in some local networks, but apart from a few experimental networks[26] they are initially being used primarily as cable television networks, with additional

Table 2.3 **Examples of future broadband network services**

Very high-speed facsimile
- high-resolution facsimile
- 2–3 seconds delivery time for A4 size original

Colour facsimile
- 30 seconds for A4 size original

Video circuit service
- transmission service for video signals
- supply of television programmes

Videoconferencing
- conferencing with colour television standard pictures
- direct connection, reserved connection, multi-point connection

Videophone
- visual communication using colour pictures and high-quality voice
- small-group videoconferencing

Video response system
- provision of diversified information (including still pictures, video, voice and music) from central libraries
- remote access to interactive video

Source: Adapted from Yamashita and Asastani (1985).

telephone and viewdata services in some cases. These networks could be the first to carry broadband ISDN services as they become available around the turn of the century.

The evolution to a complete optical fibre network will require enormous investment in installation of the fibres and new switching equipment: the costs for Europe have been estimated at $400 billion for a planned programme over the period 1990–2005.[27] Given the expenditure in the 1980s and 1990s on the introduction of digital transmission, new exchanges and the ISDN, we feel that continuist caution is not altogether misplaced in this instance. In most cases it is likely that the programme will commence later and take much longer, although for reasons of national prestige or industrial policy some countries may well seek to accelerate broadband programmes that are now only in preliminary stages. Priority is likely to be placed on connection of business premises, where there will be much higher demand for the interactive services which can only be provided by a broadband network, such as videoconferencing. The availability to households of ISDN services over the existing (still largely telephone-based) network, coupled with terrestrial or satellite television broadcasting, will limit the extent to which private consumers are prepared to invest in connection to the broadband network and purchase of new equipment. Unless there are massive governmental subsidies, we anticipate that the result will generally be a transitional period of several decades before optical fibre networks are widely available in industrial countries – some time well into the next century.

Computer networks

The use of telecommunications networks to allow remote access to computer systems began in the 1960s, enabling the development of applications such as airline reservation systems. Initially simple terminals were connected over the public telephone network to a mainframe computer located elsewhere, using either a permanent leased line or a dial-up connection. These were primarily used for collecting and distributing data within organisations. For example, a customer order could be entered directly from a terminal in the showroom, with the delivery details immediately printed at the warehouse.

As companies introduced computers into several sites methods of direct computer-to-computer communication were developed, allowing exchange of data. Different 'network architectures' were introduced by each of the major computer manufacturers, enabling their own computers to be linked together. Incompatibilities in the methods adopted made connection to computers from other manufacturers difficult, although with 70 per cent of the world's mainframe market traditionally held by IBM most companies provided some form of 'gateway' to IBM's System Network Architecture (SNA).

By the 1980s large organisations were installing thousands of computers each year. So long as there were just mainframes and minicomputers there had been some chance of purchasing from one or two suppliers. The microprocessor opened the floodgates. In offices the Apple on one desk could not talk to the IBM on the next; and executives struggled manually to enter the latest sales data (as printed by the mainframe) into their Lotus 1–2–3 forecasting model. On the factory floor engineers wondered how to connect the GEC programmable-controller to the Unimation paint-spraying robot (perhaps through the Hewlett-Packard production control computer), so as to ensure that the robot stopped painting imaginary car doors every time production was halted.

Two technologies emerged over the last decade claiming to solve the problems of interconnecting large numbers of computers from different manufacturers: packet switching and local area networks. Packet switching networks have been established in most major industrial countries since the early 1980s. Operated either by the public telephone authority or by private companies, they use a nationwide grid of communications lines dedicated to data transmission, to which anyone may attach a computer. To send a message over the network it is first divided into standard-sized 'packets', to each of which the address of the destination is added. In the network packets may be mixed with those travelling between different computers, or they may be sent via different routes to avoid congestion. The network carries each packet to the correct destination, where they are reassembled in the correct order to reconstruct the original message.

Naturally the network itself depends upon sophisticated computer systems to control the flow of traffic. Fortunately international standards have been agreed in areas such as the size of packets and addresses of computers, so packet switching offers a means of transferring data between computers from different manufacturers in different countries and belonging to different organisations.

Local area networks (LANs) are concerned with the interconnection of computers within a small geographical area, for example an office, factory or hospital. When first considered in the 1970s there were many high expectations, and as many rash promises. The concepts of packets of data and uniquely-addressed computers were to be combined with high-speed transmission through coaxial cables. Each computer could be reached by installing a single cable around the building, with the ends of the cable joined to form a ring in some cases.

Many LANs have been successfully installed based on these principles, but few live up to the initial expectations or promises. Connection of microcomputers from a range of suppliers, or even different models of computer from the same manufacturer, is far from common. (Some LAN suppliers have adopted the Henry Ford approach – you can connect any computers you want, so long as they are all IBM PCs.)

Over the years manufacturers have attempted to impose order by proposing their LAN technology as a standard. In a cooperative move rarely seen before in the computer industry, DEC and Intel backed the Xerox-developed Ethernet. Announced in 1980, Ethernet is still the nearest thing to a LAN standard for office use. More recently IBM introduced their own Token-Ring technology, different from Ethernet in almost every respect.

Standards are universally recognised as the key to the success of communications networks, and recent years have seen the emergence of a new standard-bearer. The International Standards Organisation (ISO) has received widespread support for its 'reference model' of Open Systems Interconnection (OSI). The OSI model (Figure 2.6) is structured as seven layers, each providing a specific service and with a clearly-defined relationship to the layers above and below. The lowest three layers are

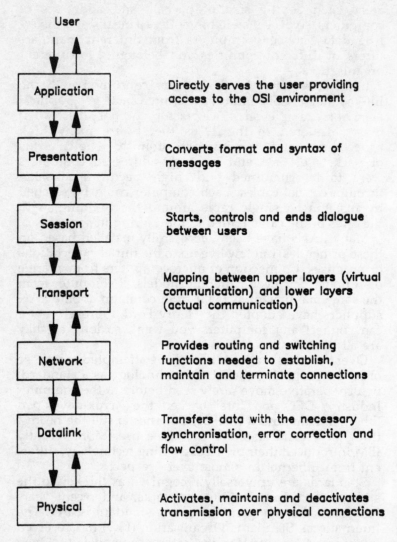

Figure 2.6 **ISO open systems interconnection reference model**

concerned with the networks themselves – the processes by which links are made, data are transferred, and links are then disconnected. The upper three layers define a 'virtual' network, which always appears the same regardless of the type of network actually used to transmit data. The fourth layer acts as an intermediary between this virtual network and the different types of network below, 'mapping' the messages from their virtual network format into that required by whichever network is to be used to transmit the messages. The intention is that users and software on different computer systems should be able to communicate effectively regardless of the type of computers and ISO seven-layer model network used.

In practice the ISO began not by developing new standards from first principles but by adopting and adapting existing standards: for example the X.25 packet switching, Ethernet and Token-Ring standards have all been incorporated within the lowest three layers of the OSI model. As attention is now switching to the higher levels this approach is continuing, but with the ISO taking a stronger, more pro-active, role. For example, in 1986 they insisted on modifications to a proposed standard from IBM before it was adopted as part of the model.[28]

From the transformist perspective the chaotic history of computer networks is easily overlooked; thus it is assumed that by the 1990s OSI will be developed to the point where all computers can communicate easily, opening the way to the opportunities and problems of a new information age. But a typical continuist in this area – say a weary computer programmer poring over the latest SNA specification from IBM – knows from bitter experience that getting the message through to its destination is the easy part, compared to getting the recipient to understand it. (As an analogy, consider your reaction to receiving through the mail an income declaration form sent by the Inland Revenue, printed in Swahili.) These people see OSI being discussed in committees and at conferences, but have yet to see the products behind the promises.

From a structuralist perspective we respect the advances made towards OSI, in particular the unprecedented levels of cooperation between computer manufacturers, telecommunications companies, governments, standards authorities and users. The OSI model is however facing danger on two fronts. The first is the attitude of IBM, with their apparent intention to preserve their own SNA in parallel to OSI, which will inevitably weaken the impact of OSI. The second is the tendency of standards to quickly become obsolete under the pressure of rapid technological change.

Integrating forecasts

Standards have long been central to the development of national and global telecommunications, and are becoming increasingly important in computer technology. Continuist, structuralist and transformist perspectives all tend to agree on their desirability – their differences primarily concern matters of the feasibility and implementation of standards. Thus transformist views of integrating technologies are liable to take the existence of OSI and ISDN on paper as sufficient indication that they will become established in reality (and, what is more, that they will function as intended technically, and be made to work by the major actors involved).

The continuist perspective, particularly as expressed by sceptics within the usually gung-ho computer industry, is much more cautious. Such sceptics point to incompatibilities within many existing so-called standards,[29] and to the difficulties of producing workable and effective standards (reflecting best practice rather than lowest common denominators) in international committees containing representatives from many organisations.

Our (structuralist) forecast has veered towards what might be seen as a continuist conclusion in this area. The comparative torpor of development in what we have called integrating technologies, when viewed next to the dynamic changes in the core technologies, is likely to be a bottleneck to the successful commercial exploitation of new products and services. Slow movement towards standardisation will restrict the size of markets in areas such as viewdata terminals and software packages. Yet progress is being made, with OSI a particularly welcome example of cooperation between suppliers and users.

NOTES

1. Martin (1978).
2. The necessity for this is illustrated by the well-known conundrum: who bought the world's first telephone – and what did they do with it?
3. Noyce (1977).
4. Gregory (1986).
5. Pfeister *et al.* (1985).
6. Barker (1986).
7. Robinson (1984).
8. Robinson (1987).
9. Fischetti (1986).
10. Lewyn and Meindl (1985).
11. Fischetti (1986).
12. The replacement of analogue equipment by digital equivalents – a process commonly termed 'digitalisation' – has been under way for about twenty years, with the most familiar examples in consumer products being the digital watch and the audio compact disc player. In analogue equipment quantities are represented by 'analogy', for example electrical signals which fluctuate according to sound received by a microphone. Digital equipment operates with all measurements converted to numerical values, which allows greater use to be made of microelectronics. As a result, digital equipment is generally both more reliable and more accurate than analogue equipment. Digitalisation of the telephone network will result in higher quality speech transmission, faster connections, and fewer mis-routed calls.
13. *British Telecommunications Engineer* (1986).
14. Ranner *et al.* (1986).
15. Norbury (1986).

16. Kay and Powell (1984).
17. Rowland (1985).
18. Wallich and Zorpette (1986).
19. For example the cuts made as a result of the report to the UK Science Research Council by Sir James Lighthill in 1973.
20. For more information on commercial applications of AI see Winston and Prendergast (1984).
21. The Computerised Online Translation for European Languages service, provided by the European Centre for Automatic Translation.
22. Say 150 words per minute and an initial vocabulary of 30 000 words, with the ability to add to the vocabulary.
23. Feigenbaum and McCorduck (1983).
24. Weisenbaum (1983).
25. Office of Technology Assessment (1985).
26. For example in Mitaka, Japan and Biarritz, France.
27. Mackintosh (1986).
28. Hayes (1987).
29. For example the existence of a book attempting to explain the differences within the RS232 standard used for interconnecting computer equipment.

3. Using IT

We have discussed in Chapter 2 the remarkable developments in IT and outlined trends that are liable to continue into the foreseeable future. This raises an important question; what is it that drives such technological development forward at such a rapid rate? Although basic scientific curiosity plays a part, the main motive can be seen in the potentially vast range of applications for IT, which make it, in the view of some commentators, likely to become the biggest industry in the world with sales approaching $1000 billion by 1990. Furthermore, although the trends in cost and performance of the various constituent elements of IT are of considerable interest in themselves, the major impact of information technology on society will not be widely felt until the technology is used in the industrial, commercial and domestic contexts. In this chapter and the next we are concerned with how the technology is applied within industry and commerce; and in Chapters 5 and 6 we consider questions of final demand and the consumer use of IT.

We have already argued, and it is implicit in the distinction between the three perspectives, that there is a range of choice in respect of the speed and extent to which the technology is implemented, in what configuration, and so on. This chapter discusses some general issues likely to shape the way in which those choices may be made, looking at the supply and demand side; and Chapter 4 discusses in more detail the applications potential and practice that is emerging in major sectors of the economy.

Table 3.1 **IT applications by economic sector**

System type	Sector						
	1	2	3	4	5	6	7
Integrated text & data processing	+	+	+	++	++	+++	+++
Transaction clearing	+	+	+	+	+++	+++	+
Online enquiry systems	+	+	+	++	+++	++	+++
Management information systems	+	+++	++	+++	+++	++	++
Professional problem solving	++	+++	++	++	+	++	+
Professional databases	+	++	++	++	+	+	++
Electronic mail and teleconferencing	+	++	+	++	++	++	++
Material planning, stock control, scheduling systems	++	++	++	+++	+++	+	+
CAD and draughting	+	++	+++	+++	+	+	+
Computer-aided manufacturing	–	+	++	+++	–	–	–

System type	Sector						
	1	2	3	4	5	6	7
Computer-aided fault diagnostic systems	++	+++	+++	+++	++	+	−
Remote sensing devices	++	+++	+++	+	++	+	−

Key
Plus symbols indicate level of application of IT anticipated in specific sectors over the period to 2010.

1 agriculture etc.
2 extractive
3 construction and utilities
4 manufacturing
5 goods services
6 information services
7 people services.

Source: Miles, Rush, Bessant and Guy (1985).

CONVERGENCE AND INTEGRATION

Many IT applications have been developed in the recent past, and all sectors of the economy have been influenced by these developments. Table 3.1 indicates a range of technological options which are becoming available across the primary, secondary and tertiary sectors of the economy. Figure 3.1 indicates these in diagrammatic form and also identifies ways in which the trajectories of much technological development on the applications side are also 'converging'.

Such lists of technologies may seem impressive but in one very significant respect they fail to convey the really important features of the new technological trajectories.

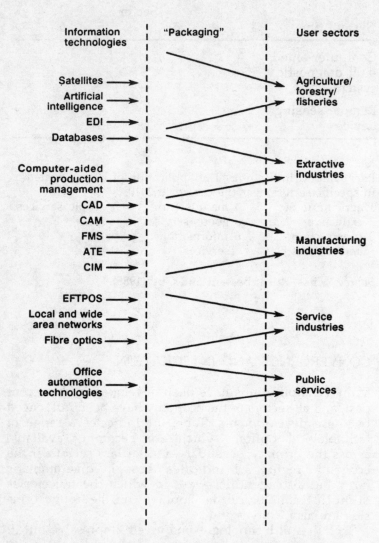

Figure 3.1 **Convergent technologies of production**

When treated in isolation they tend to suggest ways of replacing old technologies and rationalising standard activities; in essence doing what we have always done a little better. Thus robots replace paint sprayers, word processors replace typewriters, and so on. But this is to ignore the real significance in the evolution of IT-based technological trajectories: the re-integration of functions that were long ago separated in the industrial division of labour.

We can see here one of the important dividing lines between the structuralist, transformist and continuist schools of thought. The continuist perspective focuses attention on the application of IT as an incremental process with a gradual evolution of better ways of carrying out traditional processes; as new technologies are essentially applied so as to substitute for existing systems. In contrast the other schools of thought recognise that IT offers the opportunity for completely new ways or working.

An example of this reorganisation might be the way in which the major stock exchanges of the world now function – the original process of market-making and dealing has been radically transformed by IT. A continuist view would have expected technological change to involve the gradual application of IT as an aid to conventional broking activity; for example, as a more sophisticated calculating or display device. By contrast a transformist or structuralist view would have seen the possibilities for radical change, exploiting the communication capabilities for IT to move to 24-hour all-electronic dealing on a worldwide basis.

It is important, however, to note a second point on which the structuralists and the transformists differ, concerning the role of organisational change in support-ing such technological leaps. Whereas the transformist view sees change as discontinuous jumps into totally new ways of doing things, the structuralist view recog-nises that without considerable adaptation and change on the part of the organisational systems into which IT is being introduced such innovation may fail to fulfil its potential. In our stock exchange example the structuralist perspective would stress the importance of training and the development of new skills; reorganisation of the dealing and broking firms to make them responsive to a wider range of customers within shorter timescales; of their adapting procedures to make better use of (rather than simply to fit) the technology; of .the need for changing regulatory codes and institutions to control such new ways of working, and so on. We will return to this theme later.

FACTORY AUTOMATION

Let us first explore integration a little further, and, in particular, examine why putting IT elements together into integrated systems is of such potential benefit. For this we will use the example of manufacturing, although the same pattern is emerging right across the spectrum of the formal economy.

Rather than applying one item of new technology to each of the functions now performed as a distinct stage of production, IT offers the possibility of integrating functions towards a total system of production. Thus the options of Figure 3.1 converge; for example, computer-aided design, flexible manufacturing systems and computer-aided production management come together into computer-integrated manufacturing (CIM).

This integration of functions can extend beyond the integration of what (in earlier phases of industrial evolution) became divided parts of the 'grand areas' of industrial operation – design, production, marketing and distribution. Thus the example of CIM could well involve computer-aided design linked to manufacturing (using FMS and a variety of automated manufacturing, measuring and test equipment, responding to the electronic and/or optronic codification of designs); with overall planning and coordination also using a variety of computer aids and drawing on databases produced, and reacted to, by the various sub-systems. In addition links to customers and suppliers will be 'informatised', and some elements of the tasks of placing orders and accepting commissions will be automatically incorporated into the overall production process.

Such a 'factory of the future' would involve a complete integration of these various sub-systems via some form of high-capacity local area network, with the possibility of supervisory control by a large master computer talking to a variety of smaller sub-system control computers. This can be seen as part of a long-term trend involving integration first *within* spheres of manufacturing activity and then *between* them.[1] Figure 3.2 illustrates this process of integration within and between spheres.

We can see this pattern of integration throughout the production process. For example, in the area of design the traditional activities of concept design, draughting, detailing, modification, production planning, materials planning, and so on, have gradually become integrated as elements in a computer-aided design system. Developments in CAD have enabled it to move outside the design sphere; for example, by generating the control information to drive various forms of computer-numerical control (CNC) machine tools it is possible to operate a CAD/CAM (computer-aided design and manufacturing) system. Similarly links are now available into the coordination system so that material requirements planning or works order scheduling can be generated using the data held in the CAD system. In some models for the fully integrated factory, the main database on which all the constituent elements draw is generated by the CAD system, thus putting design at the centre rather than the periphery of manufacturing activity.

Similar patterns can be found in the other two spheres of manufacturing. For example in production the trend towards integration of machine functions, with handling and transport systems within a manufacturing cell, now features complex linkages between shopfloor computers controlling physical operations and those responsible for the planning and supplying of production. Figure 3.3 illustrates this type of integration in the field of metal-working production.[2]

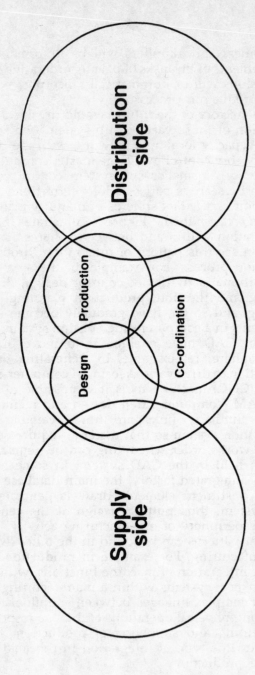

Figure 3.2 **Integration beyond the firm**

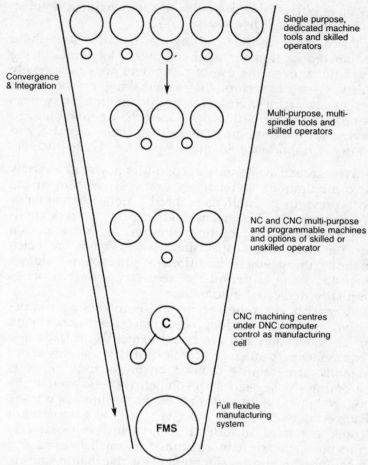

Figure 3.3 **Convergence and integration in metalworking production**

That IT permits the integration of hitherto discrete activities and functions in the manufacturing process does not explain why there should be such enormous current interest in its doing so. For example a recent survey of UK senior manufacturing executives suggested that the majority (over 70 per cent) believed that computer-integrated manufacturing (CIM) was relevant to their business and would be their main investment focus in the next five years.[3]

There is of course nothing particularly new about automated equipment in the context of manufacturing operations; even the use of computers goes back nearly thirty years in sectors like steelmaking or the larger process industries. However the integration of systems is now markedly further developed than heretofore, and several factors combine to make it an issue of central and strategic importance in manufacturing. These include:

● Widespread availability of computer power in a variety of configurations at relatively low cost (in comparison with previous generations of 'hard' – non-programmable – automation). This means that in many sectors/applications automated solutions become a viable option for the first time, especially in areas such as batch manufacturing where traditionally production volumes were too small to permit the necessary scale economies to justify dedicated automation.
● A market environment in which increasing competition, shorter product lifecycles, greater customer demand for customisation and growing fragmentation leads to a requirement for much greater flexibility within the plant. Manufacturing agility rather than productivity alone is becoming the key factor in competitiveness, even at the high volume, commodity end of the business spectrum. Thus economies of scale are giving way to economies of scope: examples include the move in steelmaking to mini-mills, the shift in chemicals to small batches and in engineering the development of flexible manufacturing systems for machining and assembly.
● The role of automation; programmable technology permits more rapid changeover of plant to make different specifications/products and increases flexibility without necessarily incurring the traditional cost penalty in productivity terms due to unproductive set-up times. At the same time the increasing use of computer-based systems in coordination activities facilitates solution of the production management problems involved in planning, scheduling and keeping track of a larger number of smaller batches.

• The possibilities for more efficient use of resources which are opened up by networking and computer-integration. Digital Equipment, for example, in a recent report describing their Clonmel CIM facility in Eire, point out that through the use of the company's world-wide computer/communication network the plant can access up to 15 000 computer systems. For a task like design this means that a vast resource of specialised knowledge – distributed geographically throughout the world – can be brought to bear on the problems of a particular plant through a single computer terminal and appropriate communications software.[4]

Above all, such computer-integrated facilities attract interest because they offer radical improvements in a number of traditional problem areas confronting manu-facturers. These improvements include:[5]

• reduced lead time, both for existing and new products
• reduced inventories, especially of work-in-progress
• more accurate control over production and better quality production management information
• increased utilisation of expensive equipment
• reduced overhead costs
• improved and consistent quality
• more accurate forecasting
• improved delivery performance.

It is also important to recognise that the potential application of such integrated automation extends right across the industrial spectrum – unlike earlier generations of automation, which were confined to larger scale industries; for example in the high volume/low variety mass production businesses, where traditionally the pressure has been to try and produce as much as possible as cheaply as possible while maintaining quality standards. Emphasis was placed on productivity and this was achieved through extensive capital investment and automation; economies of scale were critical to success. However the pattern is changing and the pressures now are for greater flexibility and agility, even in commodity-type businesses. As a result major firms in these industries are exploring and investing extensively in CIM; for example in margarines, oils and fats; in fibres and in a variety of chemicals production.

In the mass batch industries, such as automobile manufacture, the pattern has been one of approximations to flow processes through the use of expensive special-purpose equipment (such as transfer lines) and powerful models of production organisation and management (such as the production line concept, developed from the ideas of Taylor and Ford in the 1920s and still the blueprint for much western factory organisation). Attempts to achieve scale economy have led to the use of expensive automation of the 'hard-wired' variety. However the pattern is moving towards more flexible and integrated approaches; increasing use is being made of programmable controllers, robotics and flexible manufacturing systems, and of CAD/CAM. At the same time organisational changes are leading to smaller workforces and plants producing with greater flexibility and quality through the application of alternative management approaches, such as 'just-in-time' manufacturing and total quality control.[6]

One effect of this is that the pattern of competitive advantage may shift. Some firms, such as General Motors, are attempting large-scale CIM ventures of a highly complex nature (as in the Saturn project in Detroit), which are aimed at high volume production. But others, such as the UK's Rover Group, are trying to use integrated manufacturing as a means whereby they can survive as a small but flexible producer.[7] Once again this supports the view that CIM and related approaches may open up new opportunities based on economies of scope rather than simply of scale.

In the case of small batch manufacturing such as capital goods or aerospace the opportunities opened up by CIM are considerable. Traditionally the problem here was to manage the trade-off between productivity and flexibility. The more different batches a firm produces the more difficult their manufacture is to manage. Sales are harder to forecast: purchasing of raw materials so as not to overstock but also not to hold up production is complex; keeping track of products at various stages of manufacture is complex and as a result guaranteeing deliveries is problematic. Moving through several different production stages often gives rise to unbalanced operations with bottlenecks and under-utilisation of plant; it is often the case that in many metalworking plants products spend only 5–10 per cent of their time within the factory actually being worked upon. The rest is wasted waiting to get on to machinery or being pushed aside to allow higher priority items through; in being 'lost' somewhere in the system, and in finished product stores awaiting orders. Estimates suggest that as much as £23 billion may be tied up in the UK in such stocks, mostly of work-in-progress.

As a result of such complications and uncertainties in the production process, lead times (from receipt of customer orders to delivery) are often over-long and delivery is hard to guarantee. Attempts to resolve the problem by employing progress chasers and other indirect workers to expedite production add further to the high manufacturing cost.

The above problems increase with flexibility; the more variety which is introduced into the product range, the more they are exacerbated. Nor is this a rare experience; estimates suggest that a large proportion (perhaps 75 per cent) of engineering production involves batches of less than 50.[8] Thus the attractions of integrated automation technologies such as FMS and CIM, which offer both productivity and flexibility, are considerable and it is particularly in this sector that much of the current interest in advanced manufacturing technology can be found.[9]

Even at the extreme end of the manufacturing spectrum – very high variety, very low volume production and 'one-off' production (such as in prototype work) – there are still attractions in some aspects of integrated automation. In fields like sub-contracting the possibility of enhancing flexibility and responsiveness through the use of CAD/CAM and CNC in the hands of a small number of highly-skilled craftworkers has considerable attractions. Notably several small firms in Scandinavia have begun to exploit the opportunities opened up by 'flexible specialisation' to enter and defend small market niches in engineering and capital goods.[10]

THE EMERGENCE OF NETWORKING

The trend towards convergence requires, at its heart, the putting together of different technological elements in hardware and software. This process of integration is not just a matter of pushing different bits together; what is required is a complex 'gluing' operation. Indeed if we think about the process of gluing two things together it is in fact a complicated procedure. There are usually two sub-tasks which are crucial; preparing the different surfaces so that they fit each other, and applying the correct glue in the appropriate manner. The analogy works in the IT field where these two can be identified with the issues of standards and networks respectively.

Another feature in common is the fact that we tend only to glue things together ourselves if we are do-it-yourself enthusiasts or accident prone; otherwise we tend to buy pre-assembled items rather than kits. Of course there are some things we buy as components, for example hi-fi systems, power tools and supplies or small word processors and printers. But these are essentially situations where the operations to be performed are relatively standardised – and even in these cases there are many frustrating incompatibilities – and there is a trend towards the sale of complete systems (for example racking hi-fi sets or personal word processor plus printer configurations).

Integration of IT equipment, that is, interrelation of the functions performed by discrete pieces of equipment, requires that there be effective communication between them. For domestic consumers this demands some form of network to link the equipment; local area networks will suffice within single site organisations but communication between organisations and sites requires a highly developed telecommunications infrastructure. The installation of LANs is something that many organisations have displayed some reluctance to undertake and high-volume networking through the telecommunications grid will require the easier access provided by the development of the ISDN (described in Chapter 2) capabilities at national level. Since ISDN is unlikely to be available for a decade at least, the development of IT-based integration is likely to be at best partial, until the end of the century.

The analogy here might be with a national electricity grid; ISDN is an information grid which will be as necessary for the diffusion of IT-based innovation as mains electricity was for innovation around the electric motor. Further, just as some large firms have sufficient resources to provide their own power generation capabilities, so it is likely that in the future more and more will develop internal capacity for information transmission, and thus it is likely to be innovation in smaller firms and the private household which will be most dependent upon infrastructural change. We shall return to this issue later; first, let us consider some of the other dimensions of the 'gluing' problem.

Preparation of the 'surfaces' to be connected in IT-based systems is usually discussed under the heading of 'standards'; and the development and agreement of standards for data communications is a topic of considerable interest at present. The comparison could be drawn with highway infrastructures; until there are clear guidelines about which side of the road to drive on, what speeds are permissible, where parking is allowed and what size of vehicle is to be catered for, even a motorway is useless – a comparison that is more apt with a multi-route city centre than a single motorway. As we have seen, ISDN systems appear to have established a standard transmission rate (as well as a standard for control and switching). But there are problems in data communications associated with the networks and terminals that feed into and out of ISDN. Various standards are currently competing, and considerable attention has recently been focused on the conflict between Open Systems Interconnection (OSI) and IBM's System Network Architecture (SNA).[11]

The OSI approach developed by the International Standards Organisation offers the advantage of being supplier-independent – the concept is essentially one of *open* systems. In outline this is attractive since it means, at least in theory, that any user can plug in different items of IT equipment from different suppliers and there will be network compatibility. In practice the main problem is that only some of the seven levels or layers of interconnection envisaged (Figure 2.6) have actually been implemented. By contrast, proprietary systems such as IBM's SNA have the advantage of being more fully developed and ready for use.

One indicator of the way this trend to standardisation is moving can be seen by returning to the topic of factory automation. With the new generation of computer aids – robotics, flexible manufacturing systems, computer-aided design, computer-aided production management, automated test equipment, and so on – comes an urgent need for effecting interconnection between them. Since it is extremely unlikely that all these items would come from the same supplier, one key requirement would be for tolerance of many different types and sources of IT equipment, that is, an open system, which is also supplier-independent.

Among major users facing this problem was General Motors, which in 1984 had around 200 000 programmable devices from a large number of different suppliers which required some form of integration. Their response was to develop a standard called the Manufacturing Automation Protocol (MAP), which was modelled on OSI principles; this has now been adopted and endorsed by most of the major IT suppliers in the USA, Europe and recently in Japan. Several semiconductor manufacturers are now producing the control chips which will enable networks using MAP to operate; as a result of this MAP is a strong contender for the standard for factory automation applications of IT.

It should be stressed that MAP is not a General Motors proprietary product but a standard available to any interested user (although their strong presence as a user of IT equipment has undoubtedly helped to establish the dominance of this particular standard). Because of this openness, and the urgent need for some resolution of the growing problems of incompatibility, MAP has received support from government and advisory agencies.[12] A similar standard-setting venture covering the design office has recently been announced by Boeing, and this Technical Office Protocol (TOP) was recently demonstrated working in conjunction with MAP at several factory automation exhibitions in the USA and Europe.

Despite such apparent endorsement by suppliers, users and other agencies including government, the MAP standard is still far from universally accepted. Concern has been expressed by suppliers (such as DEC) that the system is too complex and that simpler alternatives would suit many user requirements; and these comments are echoed by users particularly concerned at the slow speed with which MAP-supporting equipment is becoming available and at the changing nature of the standard.

OFFICE AUTOMATION

It should be noted that trajectories of this kind also exist for organisations whose central tasks are more concerned with information or financial flows. Thus the office or bank of the future is liable to base its integration around the particular forms of information processing, storage/ retrieval and communication with which it is concerned. For example, the 'office of the future' is usually depicted as based on a system of workstations linked together (and to more high-powered or specialised equipment) with local area networks, and more broadly making access to high-capacity wide area networks. Figure 3.4 illustrates this general pattern of convergence.

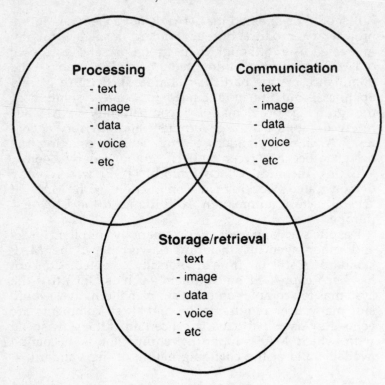

Figure 3.4 **Integration in office activities**

The automation of administrative tasks was the first major commercial application of computers, and telecommunications have long been accepted as a fundamental requirement for effective business communication. Initially used for bulk processing of repetitive transactions, the reduction in size and cost of computers led to their increasing use for word processing, while computer networks enabled the introduction of services such as electronic mail within organisations. As a result the need for integration and interconnection is as great in the office as in the factory, yet standardisation is no further advanced.

As suggested in Chapter 2, this is partly attributable to the fact that adhering to a single supplier with proprietary standards is becoming less feasible than in the past. Only managers with severe myopia, or extreme paranoia about their employment prospects, can justify selection of equipment from a single supplier for every purchase, and even the standards of IBM itself no longer cover their full range of products.[13]

We will continue to discuss the question of standards repeatedly in this study, but at this point the matter of standards in office automation systems arises. OSI is widely seen as the vehicle for international agreement on new standards for office automation, especially by Europeans and IBM's competitors. The lower, most basic, levels of the OSI model are sufficiently well established to be implemented for physical interconnection of computers (and to have been agreed to by IBM). Capability to connect to OSI networks is now becoming a major criterion in equipment purchasing by organisations in both the private and public sector in western Europe, including, for example, government agencies.

It is at the higher application levels of the OSI model that standards are few, and only slowly emerging. The first, known as X.400, specifies a format for electronic mail messages – the text of the message and additional information such as identification of the sender. This is a relatively straightforward application, requiring only limited interaction between the sending and receiving computers.

It might appear that defining similar standards, such as those for word processing documents, would be no more difficult. However the history of word processing development in the 1980s illustrates the problems of attempting to produce standards for a changing technology. Within that period documents have become increasingly complex, first with the inclusion of different styles and sizes of typeface, then with the mixture of text and graphics as desk-top publishing emerged.[14]

More problems arise with applications involving higher levels of interaction, rather than transfer of complete files of data. Standards to allow access to data held in a computer database by a system elsewhere on a network will need to define the format of a host of different types of request and response, including those to preserve the security and integrity of the database.

The speed with which these higher-level OSI standards are defined will be critical to the rate of integration of office systems. Issues such as the complexity and evolution of standards are likely to cause similar concerns to those already being voiced about MAP. In addition the highly-fragmented nature of the software industry, which includes many small independent companies, will inevitably delay the 'migration' of software to conformance with new standards.

AUTOMATED FINANCE AND TRADE

Other service sector actors, such as banks, are likely to use even more advanced network systems, as is already apparent from their current performance (they have made massive investments in terminals and telecommunications networks). Another important consideration behind their use of high technology is the requirements for security that are associated with their particular type of high-value information. Those financial information flows which also involve retailing and other service industries can also be integrated into these systems – for example through the use of electronic funds transfer (EFT) – and such integrated systems also permit improved distribution and materials management. Figure 3.5 provides an illustration of such an integrated network to support EFTPOS systems (electronic funds transfer at point of sale).

Several benefits arise from this kind of operation. While the application of IT to discrete activities like those of cash registers in retailing, or the automation of cheque clearance in banking, offers advantages of speed, accuracy and better information availability, these are once again basically improvements on the traditional way in which

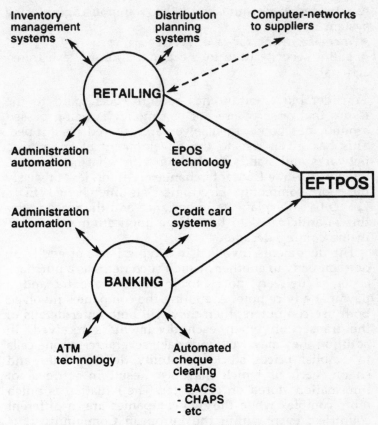

Figure 3.5 **Integration in an EFTPOS system**

these functions have always been discharged. But an integrated EFTPOS system offers several other benefits which are associated with changing the whole concept underlying the retailing operation. These include:

- acceleration of overall transaction process
- optimisation of total system through better information availability; for example the stock management and distribution process can be significantly improved when accurate information about the numbers of goods sold

can be fed back quickly to the warehousing/ordering
system
• increase in the range of services offered
• better security (due to the elimination of cash transactions).

Considerable attention has recently been paid to the
issues that arise where not just money is being passed
around, but goods themselves are ordered or shipped.
This has given rise to the development of specialised
networks and standards dealing with what has become
known as Trade Data Interchange (TDI); or, less precisely
but more commonly, Electronic Data Interchange (EDI).
Let us try to explain its importance and the reason why
this is anticipated to be a large application area for IT
in the coming decades.

The documents involved in a typical sale of goods by
one company to another include such items as a purchase
order, a delivery note, an invoice, a cheque and a
payment advice note. Assuming the companies involved
both use computers, then they will both enter details of
the transaction when each document is received. In
addition they may well undertake several telephone calls
to establish prices, stock availability, delivery dates, and
so on, each of which may also result in retrieval of
information stored on computer. The situation is much
more complex when the two companies are in different
countries: even within the European Community it is
estimated that paperwork accounts for 8% of the cost of
goods crossing national boundaries.[15]

These protracted procedures can be simplified using a
computer-based direct ordering system, allowing the
purchaser access to the supplier's computer to make
enquiries and place orders. In the 1980s viewdata
technology has been successfully used by several UK
companies to provide this service, for example in the
office stationery industry. The advantages to the supplier
are that the purchaser takes over tasks previously carried
out within the company; and that the system can be
used as an additional marketing channel to advertise

new products, special offers, and so on (and even to collect complaints and thus get rapid feedback on problems associated with new product specifications). For the purchaser there is easy access to information and reduced order lead-times, but the details of the order still have to be entered to their own computer. There is also new equipment to be purchased, training to be undertaken, and increased telecommunications charges.

Direct ordering systems have no impact on the financial transactions involved in orders, and the advantages are weighted towards the supplier rather than the purchaser. By building on the availability of packet-switched networks as a means of exchanging data, EDI aims to replace a significant proportion of business documents and telephone calls with equivalent electronic messages.

During the last twenty years forms of EDI have been introduced within two industries which require high levels of information exchange between companies. The first is the SWIFT network for electronic transfer of funds between banks, and the second SITA which carries data between computers operated by airlines. Both have required substantial investment in computer systems and dedicated communications networks, and the 'products' that are traded are largely paper-based ones.

More general EDI systems are now offered by two operators of packet-switched networks in the UK, and by numerous others in the USA and elsewhere. Forecasts from industry sources portray this as an activity with massive growth potential. Industries such as construction, chemicals, pharmaceuticals, shipping and motor manufacturing are carrying out trials with these systems, and cooperating to develop standards for documents specific to their business.[16] Advantages quoted for EDI are often expressed in terms of reductions in the time from order to delivery, or lower stock levels – particularly appropriate for manufacturing industries. However EDI can also be beneficial to service industries, as illustrated by the decision to use EDI to carry data between a thousand insurance companies, brokers and underwriting syndicates on the London insurance market, which is expected to cut the maximum time to complete documentation from nine months to two or three weeks.

The principles behind office automation and EDI also apply in the context of those services which are more people-based, such as hospitals or transportation systems. Here again IT permits not only automation or computer-aided performance of discrete functions but also the possibility of considerable integration of tasks, for example in a hospital management information system. And, as in the examples we have dwelt upon, the benefits associated with integration are likely to be considerably greater than those due to discrete innovation.

It is important however not to underestimate the problems which integration poses. Just as the benefits associated with applying IT to discrete functions or activities are relatively limited, so too is the scale of problems which need to be addressed. As the level of integration increases, so there are new problems to be solved – such as software compatibility, relationships between different functional areas, demand for new kinds of skills and for flexible disposition of those skills, and the evolution of new organisational forms to support the novel ways of performing functions which IT facilitates.

Here again we see the distinction between the transformist and structuralist view, with the latter placing considerable emphasis on this need for simultaneous innovation of both technology and the organisational context into which it will be applied. The transformist view sees the potential pattern of technological integration but does not always consider some of the problems of structural adaptation. For example, in the case of EFTPOS the technologies to facilitate the arrangement have been available for some time; but the actual large-scale innovation has been repeatedly delayed by disagreements between banks and retailers over systems, costs and standards.

COMMON THEMES

The exact form and pace of change is bound to be different across different sectors of the economy, but in general we anticipate a shift towards systems integration to be common to most areas of the formal economy. (We shall see in Chapter 5 that similar developments are also plausible in the informal domestic economy of the household sector.)

These common trends are likely to occur for a number of reasons:

• systems integration will enable greater improvements in productivity than can be gained from stand-alone equipment (for example, by virtually abolishing delays in reprocessing and transmitting information between various stages of production)
• IT will enable more monitoring of process and product performance, and thus more rapid diagnosis of problems and opportunities
• while initially threatening 'information overload' IT will also enable larger quantities of information to be processed, and more complex problems to be handled
• IT will also enable greater variety, flexibility and rapid response to changing demands in the marketplace.

There are differences among our three schools of thought in the perception of the rate and extent of impact of this technological trajectory. For the continuist perspective the pattern is likely to be one of gradual, incremental change based on a slow replacement of existing equipment and facilities with IT. This viewpoint will emphasise the problems that have often been experienced by firms which attempt to move into radically new systems (especially if they are the firstcomers).

In contrast the transformist perspective sees the technological trend as practically inevitable: the advantages it offers are so great that it is bound to be adopted. What problems in implementation there are simply represent stages along the learning curve towards full and widespread diffusion of the technology.

The structuralist viewpoint argues that, like all major technological changes, use of the new technologies will not be trouble-free. There is likely to be a long learning period during which mistakes will be made, components will fail, 'hacks' and frauds will find ways of breaking into supposedly secure systems, tried and tested procedures will be inadvisedly dropped in favour of oversold modernistic methods, and people will persist in circumventing integrated systems in order to preserve craft or professional demarcation barriers. But these are likely to be marginal rather than central issues. Most private and public organisations are responsive to the majority of the benefits identified above and thus there is good reason to anticipate that the technological trajectory will be established, although the rate of change may be slower and less of a leap than predicted by transformism.

The structuralist approach, as we have seen, is also more cautious in terms of organisational questions, pointing out the need for considerable adaptation before such advanced technological systems can be expected to deliver their full potential benefits. Most current organisations operate in largely disintegrated fashion – a consequence, in part, of the Ford/Taylor philosophy of management which has dominated manufacturing and much of the service sector for the past fifty years. This is based on factors like high division of labour, functional specialisation, emphasis on rigid procedures and bureaucratic controls, relatively long hierarchies and a basically 'mechanistic' approach to performance.

IT-based systems, by contrast, offer organisations opportunities to integrate functions, to operate in highly flexible fashion, to respond rapidly and, in short, to emphasise a much more 'organic' form of operation.[17] Viewed in these terms IT, particularly in its more integrated forms, can be seen as a somewhat inappropriate technology for many organisations. The full benefits from successful implementation are only likely to arise if the organisation can adapt along a variety of dimensions. These vary but would typically include the need for closer functional integration, shorter hierarchies, greater delegation of responsibility and autonomy to the operating units – for example the shop floor – and an increasing emphasis on providing the necessary training and staff development to ensure a good match between technology and the skills required to support it. The question of the role of technology in the long-term strategy of the firm becomes increasingly important and this requires a major rethink about the processes whereby major investments are justified, with a move away from purely quantitative techniques such as ROI (return on investment) calculations.[18]

An issue which may become increasingly prominent in the light of the development of what is. variously termed 'convergence' and 'integration' (really two closely related processes) is what we may call 'packaging', that is, the process of assembling discrete items of IT into integrated systems. Without such packaging the major benefits of IT are unlikely to be realised. This is particularly true in the manufacturing sector where the range of data communications that are likely to be involved means that rather more skill will be required here than is taken, say, to put together an amplifier and cassette player in a home hi-fi system.

Returning to the automated factory example, it is clear that putting together a manufacturing system for, say, CAD/CAM would involve major difficulties even if suitable software and network standards were available. Choices of system components – which CAD system; which post-processor to produce the machine tool control programs; which machine tools; which robots; which transport system; and which overall control computers – are followed by the need to consider how best to put these elements together into a suitable system configuration. Even large companies have relatively little experience in buying complete systems, and, with the exception of the large process industries, the concept of a single supplier offering a turnkey package solution is often new to many firms in manufacturing.

Further problems are posed by the fact that at least three aspects of such a system need to be considered:

the hardware indicated above, the software which drives it, and the organisation in which it is to operate. Thus to invest in even a modest CAD/CAM integrated facility poses serious difficulties for the potential user; at the level of full computer-integrated manufacturing these difficulties may seriously limit the achievement of the full benefits on offer from the technology.

In order to deal with the packaging problem various solutions have emerged, ranging from attempts on the part of suppliers to put together their own turnkey packages, to joint ventures between different types of suppliers; the emergence of specialised consultants who offer to act as an overall 'managing agent' for big projects – what we have termed 'systems integration contractors' – and the setting up of totally new businesses by users in which to implement integrated systems.

The packaging operation can be undertaken in various ways, even if end-users themselves shy away from the complexities. Major IT firms seem to be pursuing strategies, involving both in-house R & D and purchase of specialist firms aimed at providing them with complete portfolios, so that they can establish divisions centred on packaged automated systems, office automation systems, and so on. These developments are of some significance to European countries, whose IT firms currently have relatively little presence in the emerging 'packaging' industries. Decisions about standards and infrastructural developments may well play a crucial role in determining the room for manoeuvre of UK firms and authorities in these respects in the next decades, and the monitoring of developments in this area is an important task.

In terms of our different schools of thought, the continuist viewpoint would argue that such problems testify to the difficulty of moving too fast to an integrated configuration of IT. This viewpoint would favour a more incremental approach, perhaps an 'islands of automation' strategy, based upon gradually introducing IT systems and letting them evolve into an integrated network at a pace with which the organisation can cope in terms of its skills in configuration, implementation and operation.

The structuralist perspective, on the other hand, would argue that the need for integration agents in the short term is simply an indication of the need to evolve new industrial structures on both the supplier and user sides. On the supply side it is clear that reorganisation and the formation of new kinds of alliance between suppliers of software, hardware and systems expertise is needed before any kind of total or turnkey package can realistically be offered. For the users the requirement, as we have seen, is for organisational adaptation and particularly greater integration between functions; in skills profile and in company strategy, if the introduction of advanced IT systems is not to lead to computerised chaos.

The transformist approach sees the problem as less serious since it expects considerable technological development towards establishing suitable integration without the technological systems. Thus the problems of configuration and linking together of suitable packages will be obviated with the emergence of 'intelligent' systems based on knowledge engineering.

To conclude, we have argued that realising the full benefits offered by IT will depend on developing applications which integrate into systems. Putting such systems together is not a simple matter and will depend critically on the process of packaging systems together, on standards to facilitate this and on the establishment of a suitable high-capacity network infrastructure in telecommunications – essentially the ISDN/OSI idea. A pivotal factor in the direction in which IT develops – for both intermediate and final demand applications – and the speed with which such technologies become available (and to which groups) will be the pattern of development of this telecommunications infrastructure. For this reason we consider it to be a major strategic issue and it can be argued that it is a major rate limiting step in determining whether or not it is possible to realise a transformation in manufacturing and services, as opposed to an incremental change.

ACCEPTANCE OR REJECTION OF IT APPLICATIONS

Much of the discussion surrounding the possible application of IT is characterised by a strong element of
determinism. That is, there often appears to be little
questioning whether or not the technology could or
should be applied, but instead attention focuses on how
and in what configuration. Even in the Third World the
debate has shifted away from whether or not IT is
'appropriate', to considerations of the relative costs of
failing to adopt the technology and the consequent
implications for participation in international trade.

Why should such an apparently strongly deterministic
picture arise? In large part it is, as we saw in Chapter 1,
because information activities of one kind or another
make up a part of overall activity within an industrial
or commercial sector. Since almost all activities have a
high information intensity, and some (such as banking
or insurance) involve little else, it follows that any
technology offering improvements in how those activities
are performed – which IT does – will have attractions.

The strength of this argument is reinforced by the
implications such improvements in information activity
have for productivity and competitiveness. It encourages
a belief that failure to adopt IT poses threats of competitive
disadvantage and that to keep ahead requires rapid and
widespread use of the technology. This view is promoted
by the supply industry and, increasingly, by national
governments, as illustrated by statements like 'we cannot
afford to let the UK miss the microelectronics boat'; or
'the choice for UK firms is stark – automate or liquidate'.[19]

Its force can perhaps be judged by the response of
groups such as the trade unions. Such groups might be
expected to oppose the introduction of a technology
liable to have considerable implications both on the level
of employment and on the qualitative pattern of skills
distribution and work organisation. While the unions
expressed considerable concern about the potential
impacts of IT, the general view is that it is necessary to
support its introduction since the consequences of a

failure to adopt would be much more serious in terms of competitive weakness.[20]

A third strand in the picture comes from the supply side, where massive investments in R & D are being made, as we saw in Chapter 2. In order to ensure a share in what are generally acknowledged to be massive potential markets the supply industry needs to make heavy and continuing investments in R & D which in turn increase the range of potential application of the technology, and thus the pressures for a future with IT.

Of course the views of our different schools differ on this. For the continuist perspective what is happening is simply a matter of extending the pattern of general industrial development, in which succeeding generations of technology have been adopted and diffused with simultaneous adaptation on the part of organisations and society at large. That there are short-term dislocations and discontinuities, and that the rate of development and the extent of availability of technology outstrip organisational capacity to assimilate it are seen as manifestations of the frequently-observed learning curve effects common to all technological changes.

The transformist perspective, by contrast, anticipates (indeed claims to see) a revolution that will sweep away old structures and bring about an information society. This view places considerable faith in the power of technology to force the pace of such change, by making available such attractive alternatives (in terms of cost, service, performance, and so on) that there is clearly only one way forward. Thus in the case of EFTPOS systems linking banks and retailers, the argument would be that such networks are clearly superior in many dimensions of the present system; they are, for example, faster, more secure, more accurate and offer banks and retailers several ways to improve the efficiency of their operations, such as reducing inventory costs. The benefits to these two groups will eventually filter through to the customer in the form of lower costs, more efficient and higher variety services, and so on. Thus there is a strong case for moving as rapidly as possible towards this type of system; the flaw in the argument is simply that it is too strongly rooted in the technological trajectory and does not consider in detail possible sources of resistance or obstacles to such innovation.

From a structuralist perspective the apparently overwhelming thrust of technology in this context can partly be explained by considering notions such as that of long waves. Current ideas of long waves really began with the Russian economist Kondratiev, were advanced further by Schumpeter, and in the last decade have been used by a number of commentators as a way of thinking about relationships between major technological changes – such as railways, steam power or electricity – and long-term patterns of (and fluctuations in) economic development. Some writers take a rather mechanical view of long waves, seeing them as regular cycles; others see them as more contingent and unpredictable; and the rest abandon the concept and talk instead of successive 'regimes of accumulation' or 'phases of capitalist development'. But in these approaches IT is typically seen as another major revolutionary technology that makes changes possible in the rules of the game. As with previous long waves (or development phases) we can expect to see considerable transformation of structures within society, as a consequence of important social actors developing new strategies while playing within the new rules of the game (or trying to bend these rules), of their seizing on the new opportunities that are available. These include major changes in employment patterns, in skill structures, in location and organisation of production, in the evolution of alternative processes for production, and so on. In each of these cases we can find similar shifts in structure associated with earlier long waves; for example the major shifts in employment due to the first steam-power based Industrial Revolution. Thus the structuralist view could be summarised as one which recognises the long-term inevitably of major social change; which sees such change as having an important technological dimension; but which tries to go beyond seeing change as confined to a technological dimension or driven by the technology as such, so that social change is merely a process of adaptation to technological imperatives. Social change – and technological change – is brought about by the interplay of social actors, using the (technological and other) means at their disposal to advance what they take to be their interests.

INFORMATION MANAGEMENT

It is clear that whatever position on the underlying trend is adopted, IT will be an important technology because of the centrality of information to so many activities. This raises an important question about our overall ability to exploit such a powerful new set of tools to carry out information activities more efficiently: what is termed 'information management'. Information management skills are not those associated with learning to use IT-based systems but rather those concerned with using them to their full potential. In many ways, as we have already seen, this will require new ways of thinking and working – not merely doing essentially the same task a little better. Examples here would be the integrated office or factory mentioned earlier in the chapter. A key dimension of information management is the ability to make sense of increasing amounts of information. One feature of IT is that it facilitates the production of vastly increased quantities of data: but to convert this into useful information is not necessarily a straightforward process. Cheap information processing does not necessarily mean cheap information. Making sure that the right information is available in the right place at the right time is a management skill likely to be much in demand in the future.

Successful information management requires the development of skills in planning, configuring and operating IT-based networks and systems which take into account fundamental changes, such as:

- shifts in industrial structure, with changing relationships between organisations (such as those in the supply and distribution chain, with closer linkages and longer term planning and cooperative activities such as R & D via CAD linkages)
- changing patterns of industrial ownership and control, with the possibility of decentralised operations managed (via networks) from a highly concentrated centre
- changes in the pattern of production economics, with the traditional advantages of economies of scale being replaced or at least paralleled by economies of scope: that is, the ability of plants to produce small batches efficiently with high utilisation of capital equipment so that considerable product flexibility can be offered to meet changing market demand for more variety
- changes in skill structures within firms, with increasing demand for multiple skills at all levels and for flexibility in working practices and disposition of skills to support increasingly integrated operations based on IT
- shifts in the location of physical operations and activities, with the growing possibility of 'distance working', 'telecommuting' and other forms of operation via networks.

In particular information management skills require the ability to make choices about the optimal arrangements for particular situations. Evidence suggests that IT, unlike earlier generations of technology, offers considerable flexibility – at least in the early systems/software design phases – in the way in which a task can be carried out. It appears that there is not necessarily a single 'best' way of organising such a system, which might be suggested by the technology, but rather a set of alternative options which may be more or less appropriate in different organisational contexts. Thus the skill required here is to match the technology and organisation to get as close a fit as possible.

The evolution of such information management skills and the setting up of alternative organisational and societal structures as a consequence forms a key part of the thinking in the structuralist school of thought. Without such a systematic shift in the way in which the design and implementation of IT is approached it is unlikely that its true potential for improving information activities can be tapped.

This issue is given less weight from the transformist and continuist perspectives. The former assumes that technological developments will inevitably lead to greater efficiency and other advantages, and imperfections are taken to reflect short-term problems of availability of suitable technology rather than structural problems on the user side. The continuist view will also fail to recognise information management as a specific requirement: organisational innovation is seen as part and parcel of the continuing requirement for firms to adapt to survive, rather than anything that is particularly associated with or changed by IT.

NOTES

1. For a detailed discussion of this, see Kaplinsky (1984).
2. For a description of this kind of automation within the production sphere, see Bessant and Haywood (1986).
3. This survey and a discussion of some of the problems and benefits of CIM can be found in Mortimer (1985).
4. O'Malley (1987).
5. For discussion of the benefits offered by CIM, see Bessant and Haywood (1985).
6. See, for example, Schonberger (1986).
7. Altschuler *et al.* (1984).
8. Bessant and Haywood (1986).
9. Bessant and Haywood (1985).
10. Christenson (1987).
11. An example of this was the need for government intervention in the UK to stop the telecommunications service supplier, British Telecom, from adopting SNA for a major project.
12. For example, in the UK the Department of Trade and Industry sponsored a major awareness-raising event in 1986

to demonstrate MAP and its ability to link many different types of IT equipment. Since then it has backed several events which have featured MAP strongly and is partially supporting the establishment of a conformance testing centre for MAP and other standards.

13.   For example IBM's System/3X minicomputers will not be included in their new Systems Applications Architecture.

14.   There are several 'page description languages' used in desk-top publishing for describing the image of each page, which may form the foundation of a new document standard.

15.   Basil de Ferranti, MEP, quoted in the *Guardian*, 16 July 1987.

16.   Fortunately the basic standards already exist, thanks to organisations such as the Simplification of International Trade Procedures Organisation (SITPRO).

17.   Burns and Stalker (1961).

18.   For a detailed discussion of such adaptation, see Child (1987).

19.   These statements were made in 1978 by the UK Department of Industry, in publicity surrounding the launch of a government support scheme for investment in microelectronics technology; and in 1982 by Kenneth Baker, Minister for Information Technology.

20.   See, for example, Trade Union Congress (1979).

4. Putting IT to Work

We have explained in Chapter 3 some of the underlying forces shaping the application of IT in the economy, and some of the critical issues that this pattern of innovation raises. Here, and in Chapters 5 and 6 we shall explore how the technology is being, and is likely to be, applied within different economic sectors. This chapter focuses on the sectors of the formal economy, and we subsequently turn to the informal, household and community sector.

IT is becoming almost universally applicable, and since information-processing activities of all kinds are central to our working and domestic lives, in this respect our view is much closer to the transformist than to the continuist perspective. Given this scale of application, it would be an impossible task to present an exhaustive list of applications in the formal or informal economies. Instead we have attempted to identify the leading trends and to illustrate these with exemplary instances.[1]

By the same token we have not attempted to cover the full range of the Standard Industrial Classification on a sector by sector basis but have grouped various sectors together which have activities in common. These groupings are as follows:

- agriculture, forestry and fisheries
- extractive industries (mining, oil, and so on; also the energy producing industries)
- manufacturing industries (batch and process)
- construction
- utilities (water, gas, electricity, and so on; essentially concerned with the distribution of such utilities)

- services
  - goods-based or physical-process based (for example storage, distribution, transport and retailing)
  - information-based or data-processing based (for example telecommunications, financial services, broadcasting)
  - people-centred or biological/psychological-process based (for example health care, education, welfare services).

This is a step on from the conventional 'three sector' model of the economy, which only differentiates between a primary sector (agriculture, mining, and so on), a secondary sector (construction plus manufacturing plus utilities), and a tertiary sector (services). In particular it is worth pointing out that our divisions within the service sector differ from those usually applied; however it can be argued that the 'traditional' breakdown into subsectors like public services, transport and distribution, communications, and so on, is not very helpful when discussing the impact of a pervasive and integrating technology such as IT. (On the other hand we are not following the transformist approach of adding a fourth 'information sector' to the conventional three sectors. While some service activities – such as telecommunications – do centre on information processing, we would argue that there are important information activities in all spheres of the formal economy, and that it makes little sense to classify many diverse activities as constituting an 'information economy' distinct from the rest of economic life.)

Within the discussion of each sector the key trends in application of IT are introduced, followed by a discussion of the following issues:

- the type, range and likely timescale of application
- the geographical distribution and rate of diffusion of applications (for example between developed, newly-industrialising and Third World countries)
- the impact on the productivity and competitiveness of the sector which IT applications may facilitate

- quantitative and qualitative trends in employment which may be associated with IT
- the impact on organisational and industrial structures.

THE IMPACT OF IT ON CORE AND PERIPHERAL ACTIVITIES

Before we begin our review it will be useful to examine the application of information technology at a more general level. Our structuralist approach to this is based on a simple insight. All activities in the formal economy can be roughly classified into 'core' and 'peripheral', where core activities relate to the direct production task and peripheral to those supporting it – such as coordination and communication. For example we can list the core tasks for our sectors (Table 4.1).

This is admittedly a very schematic approach to defining the main tasks of each sector. It obscures some important distinctions within sectors (for example process versus assembly, mass production versus small batch, within manufacturing). But we suggest that it does prove helpful in identifying and understanding the technological trajectories that emerge as IT is applied to the different tasks within the formal economy.

As well as core activities there are what we may term peripheral activities in all these sectors: many of these activities are common to all sectors, although they too, along with the core tasks, vary to some extent. Peripheral tasks include planning, administration, coordination and communication, among others. For example, office support in manufacturing is not directly concerned with making anything but covers the (none the less important) tasks of planning, procuring materials, scheduling the flow of material through the plant, keeping track of inventories and production status, keeping records on quality and maintenance, processing sales orders and invoices, and so on.

Table 4.1 **Core activities**

Sector	Core activities
Agriculture	growing things
Extractive industries	extracting materials and energy
Utilities	delivering material services such as power and water
Construction	designing and erecting buildings, roads, etc.
Manufacturing	processing materials in various ways to produce goods
Physical services	storing, moving, repairing, selling, exchanging, changing the physical state of goods
People-centred services	taking care of, educating, changing the physical or mental state of people
Information services	storing, moving, processing, changing the state of data and information

Until IT as we know it had been developed, there was relatively little scope for the application of new technology to the information-processing components of many of the core tasks identified above. The core activity centrally involves features other than information processing, and the informational components of the work would typically vary tremendously according to the particular materials (or people) being processed and the environments being worked in. Some core activities were susceptible to computerisation, for example in the case of process control systems in the chemicals industry and power stations. And sometimes a division of labour which standardised the core tasks and reduced the scope for decision-making within these tasks would allow for computerisation of these activities removed from the core task. But in the case of many core tasks there was limited applicability of expensive large computer systems; and technologies other than IT have greater impact in these instances – for example, biotechnology in agriculture, mechanisation in extractive industries, materials technology in construction or machinery and process technology in manufacturing. The exception to the generalisation that before IT there was little scope for applying technologies to information-processing tasks (to which we will return later) are the information-based services; in these cases, as the name suggests, the core activity involves the storage/retrieval, processing and communication of information.

By contrast most peripheral activities involve extensive information activity – in storing, processing or communicating information. Consequently we can see or expect to see IT applied extensively to these tasks – indeed, this has already been the case for many years among larger organisations.

The availability of new and powerful technologies means that the process of innovation within both core and peripheral activities is likely to change in the future. IT can increasingly be applied to diverse core activities, where it is quite possible to use new technologies in the course of all sorts of production processes. This is not simply a function of their increasing power but also of falling cost, increasing reliability and availability of standard user-friendly packages and increasing choice of configuration from small systems to large-scale highly integrated options.

Thus, for example, office automation technologies (which in the mid-1970s were the province of large organisations) have begun to be commonplace – to the extent that basic low-cost word processing/database systems (computer, software and printer) are available (and selling well) as consumer products, used by many small businesses and individuals such as writers and journalists.

Similarly the application of network-linking computing and communication is increasingly evident in many developing countries and in sectors (and countries) not traditionally considered at the forefront of technology usage. Examples include online medical support databases in Africa, microcomputers in education or satellite TV in India and banking automation in Argentina.[2]

IT applications are also likely to increase their penetration of core activities, although not to the same extent. Thus manufacturing is likely to become increasingly automated, with individual plant items monitored and controlled by computers or microprocessors, and with the linking up of these discrete elements into manufacturing systems; offering overall supervisory control and opportunities for optimal scheduling, more rapid feedback of production status and increased speed of response. Taken a stage further IT offers the chance to link core and peripheral activities within the same IT system, for example by linking the order processing/customer invoicing systems to the production system via a factory automation network of the sort discussed in Chapter 3. It also opens up the possibility of links back along the supply chain and downstream along the distribution chain. Nor is such a pattern confined to manufacturing; similarly increased use of IT in core activities and subsequent integration between the core and periphery can be seen in areas like mining or agriculture.

A third point which should be borne in mind is the changing role of peripheral activities. Although it is possible to see them as primarily providing support for the productive core activity, in many cases they are assuming considerable strategic importance as the environment within and outside the firm changes. For example, the increasing emphasis on rapid response to specific customer requirements in the marketplace means that information systems (such as for market intelligence,

competitor monitoring, new product developments, legislative changes, and so on) assume a key role. The well-
informed firm is likely to be in a better position to
respond in the right way at the right time, and thus
increase its competitiveness. Or again the growing
pressure on manufacturers to manage high and rising
material costs moves emphasis away from trying to
improve processing of those materials (core activity) and
towards better materials management. There have been
some spectacular improvements in this area, with
reductions of 70 per cent or more in the inventories that
are carried; IT applied in the peripheral activities of
inventory control and production scheduling is of criticial
importance in this process.[3] (Thus we reiterate that our
distinction between core and peripheral activities in no
way corresponds to one between important and less
important functions.)

The extension of such trends can lead to the emergence
of peripheral activities as core activities in their own
right. From providing support to core activities within a
sector the systems may evolve to a point where they
provide, or themselves become, a saleable commodity and
can form the focus of a new business. Diversification of
this kind can best be seen in the information services
sector, where there has been an explosion of growth in
online databases, value-added networks and, to a lesser
extent, producer services of the information management
type. For example, one of the biggest database services
in the world is operated by the Lockheed Corporation –
originally an aircraft manufacturer. (Often it is activities
that were previously regarded as minor burdens for firms
that turn out to be tradeable commodities, sometimes
even among the most profitable parts of the portfolio.)

In the sectoral analysis which follows we shall try to
draw out this distinction between core and peripheral
activity and use it to highlight the focal points of IT
application. But first we will take this opportunity to
further elucidate our view of technological trajectories as
they relate to the application of IT.

Traditional views of innovation, as we saw in Chapter

1, often see the emergence of new technologies as a consequence of two forces – demand (or need) pull; or supply (or knowledge or technology) push. In the former it is the perception of a 'need' (which may not yet be a recognised market or public policy demand) which draws innovation out of the supply side – the underlying concept being that 'necessity is the mother of invention'. In the case of the latter, by contrast, the emergence of a new technology for whose application new opportunities can be created is key – the underlying concept here being that of a 'solution looking for a problem'.[4]

These models, while helpful at a basic level, are somewhat simplistic. But they do correspond quite closely to the guiding tenets of the continuist and transformist perspectives respectively, in so far as the former stresses the organisational requirements for innovation, the latter the attractiveness of the technological potential (although each viewpoint will give some role to the other push-or-pull factor of course, as Chapter 1 indicates). In the innovation research literature the cruder versions of these models have been replaced by more complex ideas such as 'selection environments' and 'technological trajectories',[5] which tend to correspond more closely to our structuralist perspective.

The argument in these more elaborate models is that firms do not choose under conditions of perfect information and within static market or technological environments in the real world. Rather they select from a limited spread of technologies on offer at a particular time, the limits of which are imposed by their particular set of operating circumstances. Similarly the technologies on which they can draw are not absolute but emerge from a supply side in response to market and other environmental conditions and are shaped in response to those conditions. Over time the dynamics of this process mean that certain forms and configurations of technology will come to dominate and establish a technological trajectory.

In the case of IT, therefore, it is important to remember that the emerging technological trajectory is not a simple extrapolation of technological possibilities but the product of interactions between shaping forces in the user and supply side environments. These are complex forces, and include the regulatory framework (for example, in establishing standards); the relative experience (or lack of it) on the user side; the different supply side groupings and their interests; the influence of competitor's strategies on technology adoption; the international race in development of technology (especially technologies seen as being of strategic national importance); and the role of different actors such as trade unions, employers and government in promoting or retarding different options.

This brief discussion should be sufficient to caution us against assuming that the way in which IT is shaped in the various sectors of the economy is just a product of the core and peripheral tasks that are involved in these sectors, and the speed with which innovators within sectors recognise the applicability of technological potentials manifest in other applications. The shaping of technology is a product of the interactions of many actors. We cannot hope to trace all the subtleties of this process. Our analysis of main IT applications in the sectors of the formal economy is based on our evaluation of the forecasting literature, our analysis of current trends and developments, and the experience we have gained in our research in the field. Naturally we shall present a structuralist view of the developments that are likely in different sectors: we thus take into account the obstacles to innovation stressed by the continuist viewpoint, which tend to suggest that change will continue on established paths at relatively slow pace, with most sectors changing relatively slowly; and also the technological opportunities that are indicated by the transformist perspective, which draws attention to the possibilities for all sectors to leap forward into the use of new integrated systems.

AGRICULTURE, FORESTRY AND FISHERIES

This is the first of the sectors we shall consider, and is not among those in which we anticipate greatest change associated with IT. In the near future (up to say 1995), the relative lack of IT awareness, and of skills devoted to applications in this field, allied to the high capital costs of advanced equipment embodying IT, will probably mean that the uptake of IT in the sector will be small compared to that in other sectors. Nevertheless the pace of change for those within the sector may appear to be quite rapid. Many applications already exist; for example information systems on weather, price trends, and so on, for farmers (such as the viewdata service 'Farmlink' which runs on the UK Prestel system, and parallels in several other European countries) or automated aids for feed control, herd management, milking parlour operations, and so on. There has even been substantial research and development in the field of robotics, for example for sheep shearing applications in Australia. Such IT-related innovations will undoubtedly be improved in terms of cost and effectiveness, and are likely to continue to diffuse so that they become used in widespread fashion by the mid-1990s.

By this time newer applications such as portable scientific instrumentation for monitoring conditions, and sensors which can provide information on soil chemistry and mechanics (for example to help make decisions which require knowing the amount of damage which will be done by allowing grazing or vehicles on a particular piece of land), will be available. Expert systems are also likely to become more prevalent in their own right, especially as decision-making aids which can accept data inputs direct from sensors such as those mentioned above. (Thus IT applications may be synergistic in practice, and also support each other's diffusion.) In similar fashion software for decision support will help farmers to decide how to optimise the mix of foodstuffs to make best use of surplus products, and to plan crop mixtures for the future. Management and information support for agriculture is likely to be an area with significant export potential, for example in 'turnkey' packages in farm, fisheries and forest management.

These applications are not likely within our timespan

to involve much integration of physical processes, as opposed to flows of information alone. Although it is probable that individual items of equipment will be enhanced with IT, the concept of an 'automatic farm' remains rather remote. This reflects the heterogeneity in the organic/biological material which farmers (and similarly fisherpersons and foresters) work with, and the relative unpredictability of the behaviour of such 'raw materials' and the environments associated with them.

Several factors are likely to influence the rate of diffusion of this technology. In most developed countries agriculture in particular has experienced extensive productivity growth over a long period; most of this has been achieved by continual substitution of capital or energy for labour. In the UK, for example, productivity grew by 160 per cent between 1953 and 1975 while employment declined by 50 per cent. Most of this productivity improvement came about through a combination of mechanisation, improvements in farm management and organisation and increasing scale economies.[6] Thus productivity in agriculture is already high and likely to grow only slowly in the future with further replacement of what little labour remains. (Agricultural employment in the UK currently accounts for only about 2 per cent of total employment.) The application of IT is likely to have only a minor impact on this, acting mainly as a reinforcement to trends already established by extensive mechanisation; its labour displacing characteristics are not likely to have a sudden or significant new effect. Where the technology does have a labour-displacing effect this will be in areas where whole systems are replaced with automated equipment, for example in produce handling or feed regulation and distribution. The implications for skill levels are also likely to be small, emphasising the long-established trend of substitution of 'traditional' skills (such as those associated with weather lore, animal husbandry, and so on) by those concerned with the increasing use of technology (in new equipment, chemical and biotechnological aids, and so on); moving the overall skill require-

ment away from farm labourers towards farm technicians
and managers.

Of greater significance is likely to be the growing
concentration in the sector, particularly among the OECD
countries. Larger farms are capable of greater levels of
capital investment and are liable to require more in the
way of coordination and communication functions, for
example to provide closer links to suppliers and markets.
In the longer term other activities such as veterinary
services or financial and technical advice may be obtained
via online communications networks rather than present
personal contacts. Even the operation of the seasonal
labour market may shift to a telecommunications base
rather than the traditional word-of-mouth approach.
Early adoption of the range of IT-based equipment and
techniques is thus likely to be concentrated around this
group of large and relatively advanced farms.

A related factor is the vertical integration with suppliers
of farm materials and equipment, or with the major food
manufacturers. This may take various forms: direct
ownership and control via farm managers installed by
the parent company; franchising systems; or the 'tied
farm' model used by some transnational corporations in
the Third World, whereby farmers retain ownership of
their farms but sign contracts requiring them to produce
certain kinds of products (whose purchase is strictly
quality controlled) and to use company-recommended or
supplied seed, fertiliser, pesticide, and so on. Such
vertically integrated systems lend themselves to linking
to farm networks, taking advantage of advanced communications. This raises questions about the types of
initiatives likely to be needed to move the traditionally-
oriented farming community towards new modes of
working which can exploit the potential in new communications technology.

The above factors suggest that change in the agricultural
area will be relatively slow and the application of IT, at
least in the near future, largely confined to its more
peripheral activities: that is, in the management and
coordination of operations and in the provision and

collection of control information, rather than directly in the growing/breeding/harvesting processes involved. The rate of change will also be affected by the general lack of awareness and skills, particularly in the context of applying IT to specific agricultural problems. A short-term practical point is that the demands placed on equipment and the typical farming environment will call for considerable 'ruggedisation' of any control equipment used in the farm – and this will tend to emphasise 'indirect' communications/information applications.

It seems likely that the diffusion of IT in this sector in a regional context will show a marked difference in impact between industrial and Third World countries. For many farmers in the latter countries production is still labour-intensive and often operating at subsistence level only. Certainly IT has the potential to effect an agricultural revolution through its ability to offer improved management of resources, better communications, more accurate forecasting, use of expert systems and remote sensing, and so on. But the short-term lack of skills and capital, allied to the fundamental problem of the need for land reform in many countries means that this is unlikely to happen.

The early experience of the so-called 'green revolution' in the 1960s provides a still-relevant illustration of the problems posed by attempting to apply a 'technological fix' to the problems of agriculture. This too was based on the belief that advanced scientific knowledge – in this case based on biology and genetics – would result in dramatically higher yields. By and large the new High Yielding Varieties have in fact led to significant increases in production. However the expected widespread benefits failed to materialise for all but a small proportion of farmers – those who could afford the strictly timed inputs of water, pesticides and fertilisers. In some areas this approach was highly inappropriate to the needs of the community, resulting in the loss of smallholdings to the larger landlords who had little difficulty obtaining the necessary credit. Unequal access to the no doubt honest endeavours of the scientists led to increases in production but also to an intensification of rural inequalities.

One last point in considering the agricultural sector is that here IT may well be overshadowed by biotechnology – the cluster of technologies and techniques associated with controlling the behaviour of living organisms. Already breeding of plant and animal strains is widely diffused and new approaches, such as the production of foodstuffs via low energy biological routes rather than through processing plants, are under development. This is not to say that IT will have no role to play in the predicted 'biotechnology revolution'. It is likely that successful biotechnological processes will require advanced monitoring and process control capabilities which IT would be able to provide; for example in controlled fermentation and culture growth. Use of new strains of plant or animal breeding stock requires careful monitoring and control, often coupled with extensive historical documentation; again fields in which IT is likely to be an important aid. It is also likely that the legal and regulatory environment for foodstuffs manufactured using biotechnological routes will require strict adherence to standards – and IT is bound to be used extensively in the monitoring process.

IT support is also essential in the complex process of genetic engineering, where the relevant genetic codes and 'blueprints' can only be unravelled with the aid of computers. Communication between researchers in this field is also of critical importance in order to maximise the use of information collected in research projects throughout the world; in some of the most recent work on genetic engineering major advances in understanding have been achieved through the use of international databases. The problems being examined are now so complex that it is unlikely that a single team would have all the information available to solve them. However by concentrating information about experimental results it becomes possible to detect patterns and to move the scientific base of this field forward.

A further influence on agricultural development with uncertain (but probably reinforcing) implications for the

Table 4.2 **Applications of IT in agriculture**

— remote sensing (to identify patterns in weather, animal or pest migration, etc.

— farm management aids (including expert systems for optimal control of factors like food mixes, fertiliser concentrations and distribution, planting cycles, diagnosis of crop disease, etc.)

— communication systems facilitating remote operations

— mobile communications

— portable instrumentation (e.g. for soil analysis, chemical, moisture, etc.), blood tests for livestock, etc.)

— permanent sensors distributed around the farm to provide monitoring and security information on livestock, buildings, etc.

— simple robotics and control systems for various operations including milking, feeding, picking and harvesting, tractor work, watering and soil management, sheep shearing, etc.

— viewdata and database systems (for market, marketing intelligence, brokerage on agrichemicals, farmer/fisher networks with suppliers and buyers, etc.)

— integration of farming and food processing (e.g. on-farm cheesemaking, wine-making, meat curing, etc.) which utilise IT-based control and monitoring systems

— educational activities (farm schools, leisure holidays, 'natural world' type theme parks) exploiting IT as an educational medium – video, interactive video, etc.

Sources: Miles *et al.* (1986); Bessant and Cole (1985)

use of IT is the growth of social values supportive of such concepts as 'animal rights'. There has been considerable articulation of sentiment in favour of reversing the trend towards 'factory farming', in which, as the name implies, an effort has been made to treat animals

as standardised raw materials who do not need to exercise
any autonomy in, say, exploring their environment or
choosing feeding times, and in which considerable
constraint or at least restriction upon movement has been
imposed. In this context it is interesting to note that in
the UK at the time of writing, computerised feeding is
being suggested to be an economically competitive
alternative to the current 'dry sow' method of pig rearing,
for example. In principle IT offers scope for more variety
in animal care, and could support a move away from, or
change within, factory farming. (In the latter case it could
also support changes in regime, such as those in which
indicators of animal welfare – based on monitoring of
stress levels and behaviour patterns, for example – are
used to set standards for care.) However if changing
social values are articulated in the form of pressure to
return to more traditional farming practices, it is possible
that the application of IT in agriculture will be inhibited
– although there is no reason in principle why an increase
in electronics on the farm should not also be accompanied
by a decrease in chemicals usage.

EXTRACTIVE INDUSTRIES

Within this sector we include mining, oil and gas and
other industries which involve exploitation of natural
resources by extraction. The sector is highly concentrated,
both in patterns of ownership and in physical operations,
and the trend is towards even higher levels of integration,
both within the marketing and distribution operations
and in the production areas. Consequently the potential
impact of IT is considerable, particularly in the organisational and management information systems that are
needed to operate what is often a geographically widespread complex of activities. Some extractive industries
– especially the massive petroleum firms – are among the
world leaders in the use of advanced telecommunications
systems, online databases, remote sensing, expert systems, modelling, and other IT applications.

However when it comes to the 'core tasks' of the sector, the nature of extractive industry activities remains unpredictable. For example, environmental conditions vary widely and pose new and unexpected challenges (such as deep sea mining, offshore oil prospecting, sub-zero temperature work, and so on). Similarly the nature of the raw materials varies and can sometimes pose particular hazards or technical problems. Thus the routine component of the 'core' activities in extraction (for example physically getting the material out of the ground) is limited; and with it the scope for applying information-processing technology has been limited, at least until recent generations of IT became available. As with agriculture, the main applications have come in the 'peripheral' activities such as coordination and communication; and we expect this pattern to persist for some time, despite important exceptions.

For example, the petroleum industry is already a major user of IT systems, such as expert systems in prospecting work; computer-aided design of oil and gas rigs; computer simulation and communications for scheduling and routing of tankers; marketing and general communications networks, and so on. It already makes use of a variety of online communications facilities including local and wide area networks and can be expected to continue to take advantage of new communications possibilities to increase its ability to control and manage such a large and diverse business. Associated with such increases in scale is the use of much development of communications systems to facilitate moves towards greater concentration of key decision-making at the centre with less control at individual production or distribution sites.

In production and finishing operations the scope for IT applications is now growing. The financial resources of the sector mean that more R & D can be devoted to developing such applications here than in agriculture, although a number of short-term problems need to be addressed before fully-automated mining, for example, becomes viable. Projects already under way, such as the Japanese heavy duty robot programme (which looks likely to lay the foundations for automated mining), will probably take ten to fifteen years to produce suitable technologies for industrial application. Similar work on undersea mining, remote sensing and monitoring and integrated management systems is also under way; but again suitably developed systems will probably not be widely available until the late 1990s. An important incentive for such technological evolution is the hostile environment surrounding many valuable resources: this creates hazards for human workers, and often makes it impossible for operations to be carried out other than by some sort of remote control, but of course it places stringent requirements on the technology itself.

Further IT applications are also likely to emerge in support of other energy industries such as nuclear, solar, tidal and wind, particularly in those cases where accurate control and economic operation can only be guaranteed by advanced systems. For example, the use of wind power depends critically on being able to adapt to differing wind conditions while providing a constant output from a generator system. This requires a degree of 'intelligent control' within the system which can only be provided by IT. Similar requirements for accurate load management control exist in the field of hydro-electric power, where IT, significantly, has not only enabled the efficient operation of large-scale dam systems but also of a new generation of 'micro-hydro' plants suitable for application in the Third World.

Productivity in this industry is already generally high, reflecting its capital intensity, so IT is not likely to have a major impact on price competitiveness in terms of dramatic reductions in unit costs of production. It may well play an important role in improving the efficiency of distribution – for example of energy supplies. Its main contribution is likely to be to reinforce the trend already established by extensive mechanisation over the past twenty-five years. In addition the competitiveness of extractive industries does not only depend upon the efficiency with which resources can be obtained; as the collapse in oil prices has shown, external factors can have a much more powerful effect.

That said, the application of IT, particularly in its integrated system configuration, is likely to have some impact on employment. Although mechanisation has taken much of the direct labour out of such industries in the extraction operations, there is still considerable potential for labour-saving in the finishing areas. For example, in coal mining the proportion of employment underground has dropped sharply over the past twenty years due to increasing mechanisation and automation. But employment in operations such as coal cleaning, storage management, loading and distribution management, and in surface support areas has remained fairly high. Forecasts suggest that implementation of integrated systems may lead to labour reductions, although these will be phased over time, with employment falling as old capacity is exhausted and new highly-automated plants are opened up.

An indication of the scale of this potential displacement of labour can be seen in the UK's MINOS project, which is being implemented by British Coal. MINOS (which stands for Mine Operating System) is an integrated mining and processing approach, which aims to halve the number of face workers required, to reduce transport and other underground support workers by a similar amount and cut the preparation and finishing operations requirement by between 25 per cent and 30 per cent. While these figures sound substantial it should be stressed that the level of this quantitative impact is slight in comparison with that of the rationalisation of capacity – such as has taken place within the UK coal industry.

Qualitative changes in employment however are likely to be more significant: we anticipate a growing shift in the pattern of skills that will be required. In order to operate a sophisticated system such as MINOS, for example, there will be a need for overall high levels of skills (with emphasis on IT support and maintenance), deployed within a small and flexible team with considerable autonomy for local operational decisions. For this reason it seems likely that unskilled/semi-skilled manual workers will increasingly be replaced by a multi-skilled shift team carrying out supervision and maintenance of

Table 4.3 **IT applications in the extractive sector**

— remote sensing (e.g. identification of likely deposits)

— expert systems (for prospecting and extraction management, including assessment of engineering, legal and financial circumstances associated with proposed and existing operations)

— advanced computer analysis and display techniques for mapping, prospecting and guiding construction and extraction operations

— computer-modelling techniques to match supply and demand and provide accurate production planning forecasts

— mobile communications

— IT-based management and distribution systems

— advanced process monitoring and control

— communications systems for both exploratory and normal operations

— integrated systems such as for mining, combining extraction and finishing operations

— remote and automatic extraction from hostile environments (undersea, deep mines, etc.) via robotics and other special-purpose devices

— advanced safety features

Source: Miles (1986); Bessant and Cole (1985).

a largely automatic set of direct operations.

The rate of change towards the use of IT systems will be influenced by the technological problems mentioned above, and by the high capital costs involved in such integrated systems. This again emphasises the problems in applying IT in core activities which are complex and unpredictable, as opposed to the more controllable and routine nature of most peripheral activity. Table 4.3 lists some of the major IT applications within this sector.

UTILITIES

In the case of utilities, the range of applications of IT is very wide, covering both the production of a service (for example electrical power) and its distribution. In this sector IT in the form of data processing of distribution and billing information has been in widespread use for some time, and the main changes likely to emerge here are in closer integration. Associated with this is the trend towards higher levels of automation in data collection, for example by replacing manual reading of meters for electricity, gas or water by 'intelligent' systems which can record consumption and transmit the information back to a regional or central office computer system. In this respect utilities seem to be following the example established by the telephone system (an information service), where such billing methods have always been the pattern, and where current trends are likely to be precursors of the pattern that will emerge across the range of utilities. Once again this reflects the pattern we have seen in the preceding sectors, where the coordinating and communicating activities peripheral to the core production are those most affected by IT.

On the 'core' production side, IT applications are increasingly in the area of automated and integrated control of plant, and that of better management of resources through more accurate monitoring and the generation of more control information; for example in the area of water conservation through better flow metering, more accurate valve control, faster response times, and so on. This will probably lead to a trend in demand for skills similar to that in manufacturing (see p. 133), that is, for fewer people with higher level and broader-based skills working in increasingly automated plants. In these instances the relations between techno-

Table 4.4 **IT applications in utilities**

— information collection and management associated with administration, customer management, etc.

— improved monitoring of distribution networks and faster fault-finding

— improved maintenance procedures via remote control, for example sewer repairs by robot

— improved resource management through more accurate information and control and self-optimising systems

— improved customer service and information flow via networks of 'intelligent' meters linked to regional centres

— modelling and simulation for load management and optimisation under fluctuating demand conditions

— weather forecasting to enable supply/demand management

— mobile communications

Sources: Miles *et al*. (1986); Bessant and Cole (1985).

logical development in extractive industries and construction are likely to be mutually reinforcing.

IT also plays an important role in improving the utilisation and conservation of resources. Through more accurate monitoring and control it is possible to balance loads optimally (for example those of power station operations), even under conditions of rapid or unexpected fluctuations in demand. At the same time the provision of information to the consumer – for example via a local 'intelligent' meter – helps encourage conservation and more efficient use of facilities. (We return to this point in Chapter 5.)

A major new application area for IT is in the monitoring and maintenance of what are often geographically widespread and complex distribution networks. Here remote sensing, telemetry, robotics and expert systems are all finding increasing application in fault-location and remote repair activities.

In terms of industrial structure these sectors are already highly concentrated in many countries – often by virtue of monopoly or near-monopoly supplier status. IT is likely to facilitate the decentralised operation of such organisations since it offers the opportunities of networking, and, as such, opens up the possibility of reducing the entry costs and problems for possible competitors. It is also worth noting that IT provides support for the trend towards the use of in-house utility production within larger organisations, since it enables accurate control and management information and experience to be packaged within a reliable control system.

CONSTRUCTION

In principle construction could be a major application area for IT systems and equipment, particularly those developed in the extractive industry (with which it shares the problem of conducting operations in diverse environments). Examples are the use of expert systems for planning and management, mapping and geophysical analysis equipment, remote sensing and site investigation systems and advanced communication and management information systems. However the extent to which the sector does make use of IT will be influenced by its diverse structure (involving many small businesses) and the informal nature of many of its management practices. While the large firms may well be in a position to exploit the integrated communications and control systems described in the context of the extractive industries, small firms may be restricted to simple and discrete applications in the office or in 'intelligent' power tools and measuring/ calculating devices.

In terms of our distinction between core and peripheral activities, construction is a particularly interesting case. On the one hand it follows the pattern noted in the preceding sectors: that is, the main applications of IT come in the peripheral areas such as coordination and communication rather than in the core activities (here, actual building structures); but on the other hand IT also facilitates considerable potential product change, with the moves towards 'intelligent buildings', or, on a larger scale, intelligent or 'wired' communities.

'Smart' buildings are currently an area in which large construction firms and builders' federations are investing considerable resources in R & D and standards-setting. Such systems exploit IT in integrated applications such as security systems, air conditioning, environmental monitoring, integrated communications (via local area networks), energy management systems, and so on. Installing such systems would place IT alongside the other basic structural materials − bricks, scaffolding and plumbing − in the building process and are likely to involve changing working methods and skills profiles. This would also involve changes 'upstream' in the design and architecture area, where techniques such as computer-aided design and the use of expert systems are beginning to diffuse.

Another innovation involving both product and process change is the growing field of prefabrication, particularly of modular units which can be configured by the customer. Here the possibilities of simulation (via some form of CAD system), to allow exploration of different options, represents an important new application area for IT − and again it signals a change in emphasis in the sector away from a one-off 'bespoke' product and towards an 'off-the-shelf' approach. The implication of this for the way in which buildings are produced is also significant; as the pattern moves towards variations on standard modules, so the possibilities for assembly-line-like production emerge and the sector begins to resemble manufacturing. In turn this has implications for the skills structures since such production line work can be automated or at least de-skilled – again through the use of IT-based control and management systems.

One important point here is the impact the expansion of demand for IT may have on the fortunes of the construction industry. The need to develop a new infrastructure by installing cables; or constructing 'intelligent buildings' incorporating high capacity cabling, local area networks and environmental/safety/energy monitoring and control systems; or the installation of road or rail communication, monitoring or control systems, will

Table 4.5 **IT applications in the construction sector**

— computer-aided design in cartography, architecture and engineering with enhanced graphic representation, computer-based estimating and costing for materials, project planning, etc.

— expert systems for project management

— IT-based management and distribution systems

— computer-aided fabrication of sub-assemblies and sections

— on-site and inter-site communications facilities

— IT-enhanced power tools

— simple robotic construction and assembly equipment for prefabricated parts and in levelling or laying operations

— IT-based surveying and geographical/geological analysis

— weather and environmental monitoring

— mobile communications

Sources: Miles *et al.* (1986); Bessant and Cole (1985).

all have major implications for the construction industry. It seems likely that as this trend develops so the IT supply industry will move closer to the construction industry, and the traditional craft and unskilled labour pattern will be replaced by a more technical orientation.

Table 4.5 lists some key IT applications in this sector.

MANUFACTURING

Much of manufacturing involves information-related activities – in controlling, in monitoring, in planning and scheduling, in record-keeping, and so on. These activities include:

• movement of materials, components, sub-assemblies
• control of process variables
• monitoring at all stages in the production process
• quality assurance and control via inspection and testing
• planning and control of material flow and usage throughout the plant
• design and pre-production planning and preparation activities
• inventory management
• organisation of manufacturing operations to make optimal use of inputs such as labour, materials, energy, and so on
• formulation of strategy and plans.

As before, we can see clearly the 'peripheral/core' split in IT applications. Many of these areas have already been affected by the use of IT to improve the operation of various discrete stages in the manufacturing process and it seems likely that the short-term trend (up to 1995) will essentially follow this path (rather as the continuist perspective would suggest). These are essentially applications to the peripheral activities which support the basic producing core activities such as mixing, moulding, cutting, drilling, shaping, welding, and the like.

In these core areas there has been far less penetration of IT to date – although the falling cost/increasing power characteristics of the technology have opened up significant new possibilities in the control field. The diffusion of IT in core manufacturing applications, while by no means as revolutionary as some enthusiastic commentators in the mid-1970s were predicting, is now well advanced. For example, a recent three-nation study of France, the Federal Republic of Germany and the UK found that on average 50 per cent of all manufacturing firms had some form of IT-based automation in their core processes.[7] One of the major barriers to further diffusion is in the area of sensor technology, where the absence of suitable devices to interface IT to the core processes limits its application – again an illustration of the basic problem of applying IT to essentially unpredictable processes, where operations have to be continuously or frequently modified in the light of features of the raw materials being worked into manufactured goods. Examples here include the difficulties of handling cloth in textile and garments automation and the lack of sufficiently accurate vision and touch sensors for robots to permit automated assembly.

As we saw in Chapter 3, however, there is a movement towards what is called computer-integrated manufacturing (CIM) and this philosophy is likely to dominate all sectors of manufacturing in the longer term (in line with the transformist perspective). This moves the emphasis away from applying IT to discrete elements of the production process, towards using it as the common thread with which to bind these elements together. In essence CIM involves the linking together of all aspects of the manufacturing business – commercial and technological – via computer networks drawing on common databases. Significantly, implicit in this is the blurring of the distinction between core and peripheral activities, since both become central to a CIM facility.

Such convergence (as noted in Chapter 3) has begun to happen in areas such as design, where computer-aided design systems have brought together many traditional drawing office, design office, and pre-production planning and customer liaison activities. Similar

trends are found in computer-aided production management, where integrated suites of software are already
available covering most of the key production management functions, such as inventory control, production
scheduling, purchasing, and so on.

Many examples also exist of convergence between
these key areas, such as CAD/CAM (computer-aided
design and manufacture) or flexible manufacturing systems (linking computer-aided production management
automation with machines and transport/handling systems under overall computer supervision).

The pattern is more advanced in the process industries.
Here the tradition of capital investment has been much
stronger; and, crucially, the core activity has been more
a matter of continuous large-scale transportation of bulk
material through a variety of physical and chemical
process stages, which require accurate monitoring and
control of often interdependent variables like temperature
or pressure. Automation of some stages of these activities
has long been among the more advanced applications of
electronics, and now microelectronics, to manufacturing.

Batch manufacturing, by contrast, has relied in the past
on less automated methods because of the complex and
interrupted nature of the flow through the system. The
core activities here involve many different types of
processing, some of which remain very skill-dependent;
thus the traditional pattern in batch-based industries was
essentially dis-integrated. IT facilitates radical changes in
this structure, enabling much closer approximation to
the 'flow' characteristics of the process industries.
Through the integration of design, manufacturing, and
coordination in computer integrated systems, it becomes
possible to produce even very small batches without the
characteristic interruptions and delays of conventional
batch manufacturing.

This change in batch manufacturing can have a number
of major effects on competitiveness; for example, by
smoothing the flow through the works, much of the
inventory carried as work-in-progress can be reduced,
saving on working capital. Computer-based scheduling

means that utilisation of equipment is kept high and thus efficiency is increased. The lack of delay and interruption within the system means that lead times – that is, the time taken to respond to customer orders or to develop and introduce a new product to the marketplace – can be cut dramatically. Further, as utilisation increases and flow through the plant can be optimised even for small batches, so the ability to respond flexibly to changing customer demand patterns (as in fashion markets) and particular needs is enhanced.

Thus IT can be applied in batch manufacturing to transform both core and peripheral activities, which partly explains why there is such strong interest in CIM at present. However we would caution against transformist expectations of a universally rapid move to new systems of production. Given the widely different nature of the materials handled, the processes used, and the final products themselves, the pace and pattern of change will vary considerably. Relatively advanced branches of manufacturing, such as electronics, have already moved a long way along the CIM route. Others, such as garments or metal castings – which deal with difficult and unpredictable shapes of material – are moving at a much slower pace.

Nevertheless the foundations for advanced and integrated automation, even within such traditional sectors, are often already there. For example, CAD is used in garment manufacture for optimising the use of material and in foundries for tool and die design. The move towards a CAD/CAM linkage has already occurred in the garment industry, where CAD-generated information on optimal material usage is linked to CNC cutting, and we anticipate a CAD connection to casting machinery within the next five years.

One of the main barriers for many firms in these sectors (which are dominated by small firms) is likely to be cost, and thus diffusion may take until the end of the century. Alternatives may be established, for example the setting up of central shared facilities for capital-intensive equipment. Equally the costs of some systems have already fallen considerably: for example a two-dimensional CAD system can be implemented on a microcomputer for less than £10 000 (as one commentator put it, for less than the cost of a company car) and many examples exist of successful and profitable innovation of this kind amongst smaller firms.

Another option, already being used to great effect within the Italian textile industry, is to link together such small producers as satellites of a central facility handling production management and control, product planning and distribution. Here the patterns of demand in the fashion clothes market, for example, can be fed back from retail outlets to the centre which then organises highly flexible and responsive production by small units. In this way inventory costs are kept to a minimum and many of the traditional problems of batch manufacturing are reduced or eliminated. The evolution of such cooperative structures will be further facilitated by the development of an advanced telecommunications infrastructure, which will make networking much simpler and reduce the need for physical proximity between production units and distribution centres.

The impact on industrial structure of integrated IT-based systems has been the subject of extensive debate. On the supply side there is evidence of the concentration of resources producing and packaging IT (see chapters 2 and 3). On the user side there is a growing debate about whether further concentration and emphasis on scale economies is likely to take place, using the power of IT to control and coordinate; or whether, as some commentators argue, we have reached a 'new industrial divide', that is, a point in manufacturing history where the rules of the game change.[8] The former viewpoint is clearly more in line with continuist thinking, the latter with transformism.

The argument behind the more transformist view is that the most likely development involves moving from mass production and scale economies to smaller scale production, exploiting what have been termed 'economies of scope': that is, small plants providing a measure of both flexibility and productivity and thus able to enter into market niches. Such 'flexible specialisation', as it is termed, would support the 'small is beautiful' philosophy regarding firm size, since it implies that the relative size of plants will become less important (as small plants can now produce as efficiently as large ones).

Our structuralist view suggests that caution should be observed in trying to extrapolate from what are undoubtedly significant opportunities opened up by the conjunction of current technological and market conditions. First, the ability of firms to obtain economies of scope through the use of flexible technology will depend on how that technology is used within particular firms. Several recent studies have in fact suggested that the contribution of advanced technology (in the form of computer-aided systems) to manufacturing productivity improvement is far less than the contribution due to organisational and managerial changes required to support the technologies. For example, in research on flexible manufacturing systems several studies report that the majority of the benefits – 50 per cent, 60 per cent and even 90 per cent – appeared to come from the organisational rather than technological innovation involved.[9] That is, implementing such systems requires changes in a number of areas, such as plant layout, design practices, product range rationalisation, links to other machinery and the use of group technology, inventory management practices and the skills profile at all levels from the shop floor to senior management. The role of technologies such as FMS can be seen as catalysts for these changes since they force innovation: without it their high capital costs could not be recovered since the systems would fail to produce the significant benefits claimed for them.

Indeed there is a growing recognition that IT-based systems, particularly in more integrated configurations such as FMS or CAD/CAM, do not offer an instant 'technological fix' to basic manufacturing problems. The considerable benefits available come either from 'greenfield site' plants or those plants which have developed a highly integrated approach to organisation and management to support the technologies.

This is often in contrast to the tradition in most western factories, which have evolved organisation and management approaches based on the models Ford and Taylor developed in the 1920s. These emphasised features like increasing specialisation and differentiation between functions, high division of labour and de-skilling of many tasks, high management hierarchies, bureaucratic decision-making structures and mechanistic operating procedures. Over time, and in response to environments characterised by more actors and greater uncertainty, the use of these models has led to increasing complexity within organisations and a growing number of barriers between elements in the production process.

Such models are inappropriate for effective computer-integrated manufacturing, which requires close functional integration, multiple skilled and flexible staff at all levels, rapid and flexible decision-making structures, and an 'organic' approach to enable it to adapt quickly to changing environmental conditions. The lessons from Japan, where post-war reconstruction led to the development of simple alternative approaches to many western practices in areas like inventory and quality management, have begun to be applied to good effect in many firms, where they help develop more suitable organisational foundations for CIM.[10] One recent report on CIM argues that the basic strategy should be: 'simplify, integrate and then computer integrate'; this summarises the basic challenge to effective exploitation of what the transformist perspective correctly identifies as a major technological opportunity.[11]

Integrated IT-based systems will thus probably be the key technological trajectory for the 1990s, with full CIM as the long-term goal. Issues like quality, delivery, design and other non-price factors are of increasing significance, to which IT – used in the context of an integrated organisation – has much to offer. The main question here is the route taken to reach this goal.

The transformist perspective suggests that the technology is powerful enough to solve long-standing problems in manufacturing. Such views underpin much of the considerable strategic investment now going into CIM, especially in some of the more visionary 'concept' factories, such as General Motors' Saturn project. But although such potentials are widely recognised, early experience with IT-based systems in, for example, inventory management, suggests that such technology-based solutions are often sub-optimal, and, in extreme cases, can actually reduce further the efficiency of the firm.[12] This view is also reinforced by recent surveys of users of various IT-based components of advanced manufacturing technology which indicate a growing disenchantment with their ability to deliver the promised benefits.[13]

These apparent problems with IT would be interpreted by the continuist perspective as representing the typical learning curve difficulties common to any new technology. They will only be overcome in the longer term, and will be exacerbated by efforts to achieve quantum jumps in industrial organisation; thus progress towards full CIM is likely to be slow. Successful strategies are likely to involve more incremental progress, gradually building up to full integration from a series of 'islands of automation' within factories based on more conventional technology. The advantage of this approach, it is argued, is that it permits the firm to move along the learning curve and evolve ways of dealing with the problems posed without jeopardising the continuing manufacturing programme.

A structuralist perspective would see these issues as evidence of a more fundamental requirement for a period of structural adaptation, with the need to evolve alternative ways of organising, staffing and managing factories which emphasise parallel technological and organisational innovation. Production of goods in a computer-integrated facility is likely to differ enough from conventional manufacturing to require new ways of looking at the whole process: new training systems and organisations of work, new approaches to assessing efficiency of production and achieving quality control, and so on.

There is considerable scope for different patterns of evolution in features such as the scale of operations in manufacturing. There is an argument which suggests that, while the optimal size of actual manufacturing units may decrease as a consequence of the move to flexible specialisation and economies of scope facilitated by IT, the scale of *total* manufacturing operations – that is, including marketing, the financial management system, administration, distribution, and so on – will actually increase. Since IT permits more 'federal' structures of industrial organisation, it is possible that large firms will exploit its communications and coordination potential to move into new global markets, operating transnationally, carrying out the actual core manufacturing in small sites which have a high degree of local autonomy, but drawing upon common services (such as R & D, marketing support and merchant banking); control resting in a powerful central headquarters group.

Another possibility – perhaps characteristic of other branches of manufacturing – involves coexistence of both large and small firms, with the former retaining control over volume markets and the latter providing highly specialised products and services within defensible niches in the market. The idea of increased decentralisation through the use of IT – with the prospect of an 'electronic cottage' industry at the (transformist) extreme – is, to a limited extent, feasible. However a more likely picture would involve planned location of future industrial complexes (which may well involve fewer and smaller plants) away from city or suburban areas – an approach being actively pursued in Japan at present.

Whichever pattern of external industrial structure emerges, it is clear that IT has major implications for organisation and operations within the firm. Productivity in manufacturing is likely to continue to rise, albeit more slowly than transformism suggests, but this will be less due to labour savings than to improvements in the way other factor inputs are used. Manufacturing employment accounts for only 10–15 per cent of the working population in many countries and is expected to continue to fall.

Current interest in the new IT-based technologies of CIM already places greater emphasis on factors like reductions in inventory, or improvements in machine utilisation, than on direct labour savings. In several factories the proportion of costs attributed to direct labour involved in manufacturing is now so low (below 5 per cent) that these are being considered as part of the general overheads rather than a separate category. IT-based systems offer considerable new opportunities here since the flexibility and range of applications mean that other kinds of savings and 'strategic' improvements in competitiveness (such as increased flexibility, better delivery performance, shorter lead times for new product development) can be made.

Although the overall pattern is one of decrease in the number of people likely to be employed in manufacturing there is also a major shift in the composition of labour required. In particular the trend is likely to be towards higher and broader levels of skill and for greater flexibility in the way in which skills are deployed within the firm. This increase in the demand for multi-skilled flexible workers can already be seen in areas like maintenance, where IT-based systems require a range of disciplinary or craft skills. For example, maintenance of industrial robots requires diagnostic and repair skills in the fields of electronic, electrical, hydraulic, pneumatic and mechanical systems, plus a grasp of software programming and debugging. Such demands may well lead towards more of a team-based approach to work organisation, in which semi-autonomous groups of highly-skilled staff take responsibility for whole plants or at least large sections thereof. In many ways the precursor of this pattern can be found in the large-scale process industry plants of the present. As such teams take responsibility for operating and maintaining automated plants at a basic level, so there may well also be a growth in services such as specialist maintenance or applications software development.

Significantly, few industrialists or researchers now see much future in the prospect of fully-automatic factories with very low manning levels, largely because of the very high software costs and associated risks in trying to design-in sufficient reliability and flexibility. Instead the trend is towards the use of unmanned third-shift working ('lights-out' manufacturing), and of higher levels of indirect support workers rather than direct operator intervention. In the future it may be possible to control an increasing number of plants remotely from a control room linked via networks and telemetry to the plant itself, and many of the management and administrative support functions associated with traditional factories could be carried out at a considerable distance, again utilising networks and advanced communications.

Although the technological trend is one of convergence between functions and operations in manufacturing,

Table 4.6 **IT applications in manufacturing**

— computer-based production management systems (embracing monitoring, planning, control)

— computer-aided design

— computer-aided manufacturing (via CNC, DNC, FMS, hierarchical monitoring and control systems, etc.)

— computer-aided testing and inspection

— expert systems for project management, plant optimisation, production scheduling, etc.

— computer-based automated storage, retrieval and transport systems

— computer-based automated manipulation systems (robotics, AGVs, intelligent conveyors and pallet systems, etc.)

— integrated inter- and intra-site communications

— factory automation networks

— computer-integrated manufacturing.

many patterns of work organisation in the sector have remained essentially static for the past seventy years. There appears to be growing concern about the increasing inappropriateness of the 'dis-integrated' pattern of organisation to underpin IT-based change such as that towards CIM; but there is an equal difficulty in effecting rapid change in the culture and practices which have dominated manufacturing for so long.

For this reason we expect the main barriers to diffusion and implementation of IT-based systems in manufacturing to be organisational rather than technological. Other barriers are likely to include the problems already mentioned of technological standards which will allow interfacing of different items of IT within factory automation networks, and the slow evolution of fully-configured 'turnkey' packages for industry – particularly in the less glamorous sectors such as garments, footwear, metal castings, and so on. Perhaps, however, we should not see these features as 'barriers', but more as 'features of the industrial terrain' which channel the development of IT applications in particular directions, so that visions of the factory of the future advanced by IT suppliers will prove to be poor guides to the systems that eventually emerge.

Table 4.6 indicates some of the key areas of IT application in manufacturing.

SERVICE SECTORS

The tertiary sector is really a collection of quite distinct sectors with very different types of demand, product and organisational structures. There is considerable variation between services in the balance between the application of IT to 'core' and 'peripheral' activities. In information-based services (such as banking, insurance, broadcasting, telecommunications) core activities already involve much IT; but in services that are more concerned with physical processes and with goods (for example maintenance, transport, cleaning) or with people (for example health and welfare services) IT has been most important to peripheral tasks of administration, coordination and communication. As in some of the sectors discussed earlier, this has reflected the diverse properties of the goods and properties involved in the more physical services, and the even more diverse characteristics and needs of the individuals processed by people-centred services: in both cases they resist the sort of standardis-ation required for much use to be made of traditional data processing on mainframe computers.

Technological change across practically the whole range of services is now likely to be rapid, and will be the more apparent in that the sector starts from a low base line. Investment in services has tended to be in plant rather than equipment, and they tend to remain strongly labour-intensive. There are of course some exceptions to this pattern; those service sector industries with information activities as their core, and with large-scale bureaucratic operations such as health care and central government administration, have already made extensive use of computers and networks.

Although there has been quite a rapid tendency towards concentration in these sectors, most services are still likely to rely on small firms and self-employment to a notably greater extent than other sectors. Smaller firms are in general perceived as being less able to undertake the larger investments required for complex IT systems (unless they can function through some sort of federal structure). Significantly this pattern of small-scale service firms appears to apply as much to professional services which use personal computers and other advanced technological aids as to traditional personal services such as catering and hairdressing. This reflects the fact that some services are heavily involved in knowledge-intensive activities (like architecture, accountancy, law) where experts bring to bear specialist skills and archival material on ever-changing problems, while others are much more involved with activities like cleaning goods or properties or preparing them for consumption. In the former case there is much shared interest in developing IT applications to relieve the more routine aspects of the tasks (preparing standard letters and contracts, inserting standard components into designs, and so on), and new innovative firms are often started as spin-offs from large firms – sometimes even those from the IT sector. But even in these cases, the small scale of firms may restrict their opportunities for IT investment.

In general the entry costs to use of IT in this sector are much lower than for manufacturing and thus a faster initial diffusion rate is expected. But while this holds for discrete items of equipment such as word processors or electronic point-of-sale terminals, it is far less the case for integrated configurations such as automated teller machine networks or online databases. Nevertheless the central role of information in the service sector, particularly in those fields where information activity is at the core, coupled with the widespread availability of suitable technologies suggests that IT systems will be diffused widely by the early years of the third millenium.

One feature that may well accelerate the diffusion of IT in services is the presence of many service sector activities within other parts of the economy. For example, all sectors have their own 'internalised' office functions, and thus office automation is likely to be significant everywhere. Its significance will of course be very different in sectors where office work is a central function and those where it is 'only' contributing to the design and coordination of other activities. Equally there will be differences in importance between sectors dominated by large organisations with extensive bureaucratic functions, and those where office work is already just one of the many functions of the small-scale entrepreneur. But technological development in specialised office service firms, in well-resourced large organisations with extensive office functions, and in firms where highly skilled professionals are in close contact with office functions, will exercise a significant influence on the availability of office IT applications throughout the economy.

As in manufacturing, however, the key element in the

use of IT is the integration of processes which are currently separate. In the office-related part of the information-based service sector a continued 'mechanisation' of individual labour-intensive service functions is likely to dominate the trends until the 1990s. Integration is not likely on any large scale until the next century although larger firms in the service sectors (and elsewhere) are likely to have advanced office automation systems by then.

In services whose core functions are basically information-processing ones (we include banking and related financial services here, as would many of the industry's own commentators, our reason being that a major part of the operation of these services is the manipulation of symbols rather than physically storing coins or notes), IT-related change has been more rapid – in some cases quite spectacularly so. In banking, for example, extensive systems have already been established 'behind the scenes' to facilitate cheque clearing (BACS – Bankers Automated Clearing Service); settlement between banks (CHAPS – Clearing Houses Automated Payments System); and international money transfer (SWIFT – System for Worldwide International Funds Transfer). Home and other telebanking systems based on viewdata and similar networks (including speech recognition) are also emerging.

Perhaps the most advanced and integrated systems in the information service sector are in the financial services operations linked to the money and securities markets, where massive investments have been made in international information and communication networks. IT also makes it possible to provide a wide range of services – financial, information, and so on – which are tailored much more to the particular requirements of an individual customer. In many respects this mirrors the trend towards smaller batch, flexible production beginning to emerge in manufacturing. How far this represents a real counter to the previously observed trend towards the 'industrialisation of services' is difficult to predict. Here a structuralist viewpoint would propose an alternative to the continuist expectation that (with the grudging exception of a few glamorous services) IT will only slowly find applications to services, and those to support their industrialisation, and the transformist vision of a rapid leap toward teleservices and automated service provision. We would draw on the recent analyses of the 'reverse product cycle' in services, which argue that there is a learning process in which IT is first used to substitute for existing processes of service production, and only gradually comes to be exploited for its ability to improve quality and offer new and improved services. Some services, especially finance, are much further down this learning curve than others, where IT applications are much more novel.[14]

Many commentators believe there will be a short-term proliferation of services taking advantage of the opportunities offered by IT networks. These will pose a minor threat to large organisations but in the longer term the use by major actors of IT to improve networking and use of resources will enable them to retain a dominant position. There may however be increased international competition in tradeable services – as we have seen in the aftermath of the 'Big Bang' in the London financial markets[15] – and IT may facilitate entry of major new players and concentration at the international level, possibly at the expense of national monopolies.

The rapid and extensive diffusion of advanced IT systems in the information services sector can be explained by the centrality of fairly standardised information-processing activities to its operation.[16] By contrast, while people-centred services certainly do require the elicitation and use of considerable amounts of information, this is often very person-specific, and of a sort that has previously required too much in the way of dialogue between client and service provider, and the application of technical knowledge and social skills, to be handled by machines.[17] Thus the bulk of IT application has focused on the more peripheral activities, especially those associated with administrative coordination and communication. Further, in the public sector, which contains many of the key people-centred services, there are specific problems for IT innovation, including:

- restrictions on capital expenditure and public investment due to government efforts to limit public sector
expenditure
- procurement policies that restrict public sector organisation's freedom of choice to suppliers that may be
approved for political purposes rather than because of
their appropriateness for the task
- the split between local and national government and
between different branches of these
- the person-to-person nature of many of the services
involved, such as education, health care and social welfare
provision
- concerns about the privacy and civil liberty implications of increased access to, and integration of, databases containing masses of personal information on clients
(health, welfare, educational, police records, for instance)
- the weight of bureaucracy and its tendency to develop
its own corporate goals
- the existence of powerful interest groups who may
obstruct efforts to change working practices in order to
preserve job conditions or defend professional expertise
(both trade unions and professional associations are very
strong in most public sectors)
- problems in recruiting, training and retraining technically skilled personnel (often at uncompetitive pay rates
in comparison with the private sector).

So far most IT-based innovation in public services has
involved rationalisation, but we believe that, in line with
the 'reverse product cycle' idea, as more administrative
functions are being reshaped we are also beginning to
see more innovative applications. Thus, following a
technological trajectory in which there has been a shift
from mainframe administrative computing to distributed
processing using microcomputers, some local authorities
are now implementing a model in which centralised
databases serve distributed intelligent terminals, with
the aim of 'getting closer' to the communities they are
meant to serve, and thus being able to respond more
quickly to their needs. This allows for an integration of

services (as well as technologies) although doing so raises questions about privacy and confidentiality within the context of delivering such services, as noted above.

Another step in this trajectory, and one emphasised by the transformist approach in particular, involves a shift to the provision of the information components of services via online or portable computers and databases. This development of 'teleservices' has already been tried out (with mixed results) in the case of banking and shopping, as well as (more clearly successfully) for corporate information and financial services (online databases of scientific and financial information, Electronic Data Interchange, and so on). But there are also hopes that it can be applied to person-centred public services, both to their clients and to support voluntary and advisory organisations – for example to keep information on claimants' rights, legal precedents and case law, debt management packages, produce standard letters, and so on. (These organisations are expected to take up the relevant IT faster than end-users themselves, especially where there are the impoverished, elderly, and so on.) We shall consider such applications further in Chapter 6.

In the case of private services, some traditional activities occupying a middle ground between goods-based, physical activities and person-centred, psychological/biological activities – hospitality industries, tourism, and so on (but not domestic service, which also typically combines these features) – are undergoing more substantial change, with the gradual blurring of the distinction between their core and peripheral activities as more integrated systems are installed. For example, fast food restaurants already embody several of the advanced automation and organisational features associated with manufacturing, while the hotel, catering and tourist industry is beginning to look beyond simple booking and accounting systems to those which involve growing integration of information operations. In the latter case there seems to already be apparent a shift to more 'customised' services using these technologies as an alternative to the 'industrial' mass

package holiday system that has evolved over several
decades.[18]

Goods-based services such as retailing and physical
distribution are likely to benefit further from improvements in materials management, which arise from IT
application in optimising planning and scheduling systems, inventory control systems, routing systems, and so
on. With the growing emphasis on reducing levels of
stock held in all stages of the distribution and retailing
chain has come an interest in so-called 'just-in-time'
principles like those taking hold in manufacturing. In
this case the idea is that goods should arrive just in time
for them to be sold or passed to the next stage in the
chain. Such approaches will depend increasingly on
sophisticated planning and scheduling systems based on
IT: for example by bar-coding all items and monitoring
their flow through the system and relating this information to an overall supervisory computer. Moves
towards EFTPOS systems linking banks and retailers
more closely will require a much higher degree of
responsiveness as the improved information flow from
the point-of-sale permits more accurate ordering and
forecasting of requirements.

The pattern of employment in services is likely to
change significantly in the longer term as IT applications
become more integrated. At present many service sectors
are still growing in terms of employment (albeit gradually
in all but a few cases, and the employment growth is
not in proportion to the overall expansion of the sectors;
for example banking has been characterised by a long-
term pattern of 'jobless growth'). But in the longer term
the information-intensive nature of many service sectors
will inevitably mean that greater substitution of capital
for labour in performance of these functions will
take place – within expanding sectors the scope for
redeployment rather than redundancy is much increased.
Thus emphasis may be placed on greater 'front-office'
personal attention while the traditionally informative-
intensive 'back office' activities will be automated via IT.
This pattern, already apparent in some large supermarkets
which have reintroduced elements of personal service

(such as fresh breadmaking, specialist food counters, and so on), is likely to be particularly associated with the implementation of integrated IT systems which impact on the core as well as the peripheral activities of service sector operations.

In terms of qualitative changes the pattern is similar to that which obtains in manufacturing, with a decline in basic information handling and routine clerical activities (analogous to unskilled direct operations tasks in manufacturing) and an increase in the need for higher level skills, breadth and flexibility in their deployment. IT may automate the 'labouring' involved in information work but it will not necessarily help in deciding what to do with all the information generated, processed and stored by the new technology. Many commentators mention the growing need for 'information management' skills within service sector organisations, and the analogy here is again with manufacturing, whose requirements for organisational and managerial adaptation to support and direct the application of integrated IT have already been discussed.

At the level of professional skills, the emergence of expert systems may pose significant employment challenges in the future. Forecasts in this area are very speculative since there is still little agreement about how far and how fast developments in artificial intelligence are going, although the sheer amount of investment under programmes such as the Fifth Generation Computing programmes in Japan, the USA and Europe is likely to yield some usable commercial applications. Many professional jobs could, in principle, be performed better with the help of AI and the likely application area is very wide. In services this is likely to have most impact in those areas where professional advice is available on an expensive consultancy basis – for example, in the legal and financial services area – or in those applications where the volume of work is too great for the individual to carry it through efficiently: for example in routine medical diagnosis and screening or in some welfare applications.

Another important feature of the employment pattern

associated with IT in the service sector are its implications for participation of different groups in the labour market. IT could be used to provide a much wider spread of opportunities for disabled people – for example in the field of programming. Equally the substitution of IT for many basic clerical and information 'labouring' jobs is likely to have a disproportionate effect on women since it is traditionally in these areas that women have sought part-time work.

The transformist perspective has laid great stress on the prospects associated with the application of IT to service production and the arrival of advanced communications networks for widespread 'teleworking': that is, working from home or from a convenient local base. Telework is seen as particularly appropriate for many office and professional services. The advantages of telework include savings in office space, travel costs and the opportunities for individuals to schedule their work to suit their own particular requirements. However the continuist approach makes rather a compelling case that organisational obstacles will inhibit the growth of telework. These include, for management, reduced contact with and direct control over workers, and for workers the risk of loss of social contact in work, and the usual difficulties of sustaining dual roles of domestic and child care as well as a formal job. Nevertheless we are aware of growing interest in telework, despite some negative reaction to the initial hyperbole with which the practice was introduced. There have been a number of experiments with 'mixed arrangements', such as using community centres as locations for terminals, so that workers are able to maintain social contacts (and escape from home!) without travelling long distances to work.

While these experiments do not seem to have met with great success, they point to what is probably the most substantial conclusion to be drawn from the telework debate. This is that 'remote working' in a great many forms is enabled by IT: whether it be from one's home (as in the case not only of the teleworker, but also of the washing-machine repairer who transmits data on the machines serviced that day and recorded during the working day on a portable terminal); the use of computer-communications 'in the field' (for example by insurance sales staff who call into their company systems in order to tailor policies to the clients they are visiting); or the use of mobile communications in many service jobs. Even the journey to work can be integrated into the working day: for instance, in Sweden the ASEA company has its own carriage on the main railway line from Stockholm; this means that employees who prefer to live in the city can begin work *en route* to the company's plant two hours' train ride away in the south. This tendency to reduce the spatial linkage between the formal workplace and the site at which the work is performed is paralleled, in services, by the increased ability for consumers to obtain services remotely (for example teleservices, online systems), where the linkage between the site of the service supplier and the site at which the service is provided is weakened. Additionally there is weaker linkage in time as well as in space – thus automated teller machines can be used outside banking hours, telebookings can be made while theatres are closed, and so on. We take up some of the implications of these developments for consumers in later chapters.

Table 4.7 indicates the main service sector applications of IT.

INTERNATIONAL DIFFUSION OF IT

We have now completed our overview of IT applications in major economic sectors of the formal economy. Although the vast majority of discussion of the application and impact of IT takes place within the 'developed' countries – and our own analysis has so far been overwhelmingly oriented to the circumstances of these already-industrialised countries – there are naturally significant implications associated with the technology for the Third World. Let us briefly consider these.

There are diverse views on the way in which the technology is likely to affect patterns of participation in world trade and industrial development. Some commentators have suggested that the application of IT will reinforce the present high level of dependence on the developed countries and widen the gap between rich and poor nations. In the extreme case, it is argued that specific applications of IT in the advanced countries will

Table 4.7 **Main service sector applications of IT**

Information services

— office automation technologies, combining processing, storage/retrieval and communications of data, text, image, etc. in integrated and stand-alone configurations

— local and wide area networks

— automated operations in banking (via automated telling machinery and electronic funds transfer at point of sale (EFTPOS)

— expert systems for database search and retrieval and overall management

— new types of library and information retrieval service via online access

— electronic mail, computer conferencing

— viewdata (including interactive systems)

— advanced telecommunications (message forwarding, cellular radio, DBS, novel local/mobile communications)

— home computer-based service access (to financial services, electronic mail/fax terminals, etc.)

— new display devices (wide screens, high definition TV, etc.)

Person-centred services

— new types of record bearing and personal identification systems (e.g. laser cards)

— expert systems for aiding professional services decision-making – e.g. in medicine or education

— computer-aided instruction

— computer assistance in routing and optimising systems – e.g. for ambulance/fire services, appointments
scheduling

— computer-based self-service facilities to aid welfare
clients (e.g. in establishing benefit entitlements, type
and availability of jobs, courses, facilities, etc.)

— administrative record keeping systems

— availability of some services via videotext and other
interactive telecommunications systems (teleservices)

— communications with staff (e.g. intelligent 'bleeper'
systems)

Goods-based services

— advanced materials management systems with optimal routing, planning and scheduling to support just-
in-time delivery and minimum inventory operation

— integrated point of sale and inventory management
systems

— bar code and other online inventory management
information systems

— viewdata or telephone-based networks for teleshopping

enable them to improve competitiveness to the extent
that they can recover markets 'lost' to Third World states
in fields like clothing and footwear, where developing
countries have some competitive advantages based on
low labour costs.[19] While we would classify this as a
transformist view, there is a very different reading of the
evidence from the same perspective. At the other end of
the spectrum there are commentators who see IT as a
powerful new opportunity for at least some developing
countries to 'leap-frog' in their developments because
their relative lack of established industrial infrastructure
means that there are fewer institutional barriers to adoption of advanced systems based on IT. This 'alternative'
transformist perspective is seen as being particularly
relevant to the newly-industrialising countries of South-
East Asia and Latin America.

A third (and less readily classifiable) school of thought
sees the possibilities of applying IT as an 'appropriate'
technology by exploiting its malleability to develop
applications which are suited to the particular environments of the Third World. Such 'blending' of new and
traditional technology is essentially applied on a local
and small scale but can help deal with some of the key
problems of developing countries such as lack of skills.
Examples of 'blending' applications of IT include small-
scale hydro-electric power systems, microelectronically-
controlled load management systems to provide energy-
saving generators, and the use of portable computers to
collect and maintain records on agriculture, medical and
other aspects of rural life.[20] This would seem to be more
in line with a structuralist perspective, but structuralism
will also direct our awareness to the fact that so far the
success of many fine-sounding 'appropriate' technologies
has been very limited, in large part because they do not
meet the need of powerful interests behind national
technological development.

In practice the pattern of IT application and its
associated implications in the Third World is likely to
vary enormously. For example, it is important to separate

out different groups of 'developing' countries with different levels of resource endowment, industrial development, educational infrastructure and participation in world trade. On this basis at least four different groups can be identified, ranging from the newly-industrialising countries such as South Korea or Brazil (some of which have very good prospects of being able to exploit IT to advantage), to the resource-exporting countries and the centrally planned economies, and to the very poor countries which are only just beginning the process of industrialisation, such as some of the African states. For this latter group it is fairly clear that IT will at best be only a peripherally relevant technology and its introduction will depend in large measure on the actions of external actors such as the aid agencies.[21]

In very broad terms three scenarios can be identified for the Third World in relation to IT.[22] The first, which the continuist perspective will tend to see (regretfully) as highly plausible, sees IT largely applied in the developed world to the disadvantage of the majority of Third World states – the exceptions being some of the more advanced NICs. The second possibility, favoured by the transformist perspective, is one in which there is rapid and widespread adoption of IT by the newly industrialising countries, along, perhaps, with several other states. This would lead to their improving their competitive positions in certain fields, to greater participation in world trade and to more rapid development for some countries – although the poorer states would still be considerably disadvantaged by the technology. A third possibility involves the blending approach, mentioned above, being used to provide sufficient measure of small-scale and appropriate application of IT to help poorer states, in particular, to achieve some measure of independence from the developed world in certain areas. From our structuralist perspective, and drawing on our observation of power relationships within and between countries, we would tend to see the likelihood (but not the order of preference) of the three scenarios as descending from the first (most likely or most dominant in the overall mixture) to the third (least so). However we would stress: (1) there is no inevitability to this – if there is political will, and the appropriate deployment of expertise, a better combination of trends can be achieved; (2) there is always the possibility that such change in political will may be brought about by social movements and challenges to existing power relations; (3) power structures are not monolithic, and in practice some mixture of the three scenarios is highly likely. We return to this issue in the concluding chapter.

SOCIAL AND ORGANISATIONAL ISSUES IN IT INNOVATION

We have sought to provide an overview of the application of IT across the main sectors of the formal economy, and in different world regions. Is IT different from other major technologies in its pattern of innovation? We have already pointed to its pervasiveness, and its differential relevance to the core tasks of different sectors. In addition we should note that a number of other general characteristics of IT are likely to affect the rate and direction of its application within different sectors. These include the following:

● It is a 'black box' technology for many users, especially among smaller firms, more traditional sectors and within the developing countries. That is, it is not transparent in its style of operation, it requires new skills to use and even to purchase it, and it is not easily repairable by users.
● It is a malleable technology which can be used in a variety of different ways to suit different organisational or national environments. This places emphasis on new skills in the design and configuration of systems in order to achieve the best fit between system and organisation.

- It is essentially an integrating technology and acts as a catalyst for the integration rather than division of labour within organisations at various levels.
- It is a powerful technology in stand-alone configurations but its full potential benefits emerge when it is used in integrated systems form.

These characteristics pose a number of problems which can act as barriers to diffusion. The black-box nature of the technology requires the evolution of new skills on the part of users, coupled with the provision of suitable support facilities on the supply side. This is complicated by the fact that IT is not a single technology but a broad and (partly and increasingly) integrated field, so that experts in one branch may not be able to deal with another: for example computer programmers and telecommunications engineers.

Problems also emerge in configuring systems to suit particular user needs, since the supply industry (which knows about the technology) frequently has no clear idea of user needs or even of their operating environments. This can lead to the development and installation of inappropriate systems, which may perform in suboptimal fashion to say the least; in the extreme case this may lead to subsequent rejection of IT by the user.

The need for new skills is not confined to operating and maintenance skills; as we saw in Chapter 3 management skills, particularly in the area of information management, will be of central importance. Such skills focus on the design, configuration and implementation of IT systems in such a way as to exploit their full potential not only to handle larger amounts of data faster and more cheaply, but also to produce useful information from this.

In the short term it is likely that the introduction of IT systems will lead to a variety of conflicts within organisations. Indeed there are already many examples of this: new groups set up to implement organisational and technological innovation have clashed with established interest groups such as the data processing department over the specification, decision-making and control of resources. (We know cases within the IT industry, too, where the clash involves several interest groups: the firm's own suppliers seeking to exploit their internal markets, the DP department with its own philosophy and preferred systems (often IBM), and the 'networkers' who are concerned with corporate communications systems and the like.) As we observed in Chapter 3 the successful application of IT is likely to require considerable adaptation on the part of both user and supplier organisations.

The continuist perspective views the pattern of development as one in which IT simply reinforces and facilitates long-term trends in the development of the economy, for example in the growth of the service sector or the decline of agricultural employment. Thus there is a continuity, for example, in the pattern of the demand for skills in industry and the evolution of suitable new skills to match it, which is subject to short-term fluctuations but will remain in balance in the longer term. Similarly the evolution of new industrial structures is seen as a gradual process which IT facilitates but which is not determined by it. Or again the possibilities for reorganisation in ownership patterns and industrial concentration are likely to move towards greater centralisation, along lines already well-established during earlier periods of industrialisation and development. The likely outcome for the Third World will also be similar to the present situation, with heavy dependence on the developed nations for technology and technology-based products and limited opportunities for participation in world trade. Indeed the role of IT may be primarily to recover some of the lost ground in markets where developing countries have enjoyed a small competitive advantage based on low labour or materials costs.

The policy implications of this school of thought are essentially *laissez-faire* (in the West, at least). That is, the process of development is assumed to be broadly similar to that which has gone before, and thus 'tried and tested' policies will be appropriate to its management.

By contrast the transformist perspective sees a step change resulting from IT application. Ways of operating are dramatically changed and with this comes radically new structures of skills, employment, industrial organisation, and so on. For example, this perspective portrays the possibility of a polarised society in which productive work is carried out by a small number of people supporting a highly automated network of machines and computers. Within such a group there will also be considerable polarisation of skills requirements, with a few low level or unskilled occupations remaining and the rest belonging to a form of technocracy. Patterns of work organisation will shift dramatically with a major reduction in traditional Taylorist approaches to production organisation, if not the elimination of all direct labour from certain areas of manufacturing and their replacement with robots. Transformism tends towards an optimistic interpretation of these developments: working hours are likely to be substantially reduced (thus redistributing employment and maintaining employment levels, at least in part), the benefits of highly productive industries will be widely shared, working life will become more meritocratic as skill becomes more important, and so on.

Traditional industrial structures may be replaced by networked federations of small semi-autonomous plants or 'electronic cottage' industries, although the communication and coordination power of IT may well lead to high levels of concentration of final ownership – the 'mega-corporations' described in some science fiction literature. Regional distribution of industry and commerce may also change radically, for example with relocation of production plants to remote and otherwise undesirable areas but with operation and management by telework. These transformist expectations have significant policy implications; such radical transformation is likely to require equally radical policy decisions in order to bring about the required degree of social and organisational change. But for transformism the emphasis is placed strongly on the development and production of IT and its applications but far less on the user side – the question of how it is used, and by whom. The assumption is often made that investment in IT applications equates to being able to obtain the full potential benefits, and little is made of the need for organisational change and adaptation in parallel with technological innovation. And political and value trends complementary to the ideal pattern of technological development are expected to arise more or less spontaneously: there may be a clash between old and new waves of political actors and social movements, but the urgent task is really to accommodate to the latter.

Our structuralist view stresses the complex inter-relations between structural change (and stability) and the human action involved in exploiting the opportunities and minimising the problems posed by IT application. In general the structuralist position in policy terms emphasises both the supply and demand sides of technology policy, that is, a concern not only for the development of IT applications but also for the context in which those developments will be applied.

As we have already remarked, the pace at which IT is evolving and the opportunities now open for advanced and integrated forms of operation (such as CIM or EFTPOS) are outstripping the ability of even sophisticated organisations to cope with them. New structures cannot be assumed to follow from the technology, especially when, as we have seen, IT is characterised by the relatively wide range of choices about structures and systems design which it offers. Consequently it is necessary to invest time and resources in determining what structures are most appropriate for the range of interests represented in organisations, and in planning and timely development of these in the light of the options implied by technological development.

In terms of policy implications the areas in which such structural change might be needed include:

• education policy (to ensure an adequate supply of skills, to develop the necessary mechanisms to identify needs, to establish flexible delivery systems, and to empower disadvantaged groups in terms of access to information resources)

• telecommunications policy, aimed at establishing coherent standards and a suitable infrastructure (such as ISDN) to provide the basic 'information grid' on which advanced network systems can be developed

• employment policy, to ensure that the necessary adjustment mechanisms to minimise dislocations in the labour market associated with a shift away from manufacturing employment and towards an information/service economy are in place

• international trade/aid policy, to ensure that rapid development and application of IT does not further disadvantage and even impoverish developing countries, particularly those on the lower rungs of the industrialisation ladder. (The risks attached to such imbalances can be seen in the problem now confronting many banks over Latin American debt repayments.)

A further important point in the structuralist approach is the disaggregated view of emerging trends. That is, we do not expect the rates of change or structure of implications around IT in different sectors, occupational groups, or national economies to be identical. And for this reason we do not expect simple blanket policy prescriptions to be effective. Much will depend on providing relevant and targeted information to policy-makers (including 'informal policy-makers' in social movements and business organisations) on the specific issues involved in specific sectors.

NOTES

1. For more detailed discussion of individual sectors and IT application a range of useful references and indications for further reading can be found in Whitaker *et al.* (1988).

2.   Examples of such IT-based innovations throughout the developed world are regularly reported in the *Microelectronics Monitor*, a technology-awareness bulletin published in Vienna by the United Nations Industrial Development Organisation.
3.   See, for example, Schonberger (1986).
4.   Examples of this kind of analysis can be found in Langrish *et al.* (1972).
5.   For a fuller discussion of these terms, see Georgiou *et al.* (1985).
6.   See Rothwell and Zegveld (1979).
7.   Northcott *et al.* (1985).
8.   Piore and Sabel (1985).
9.   See Bessant and Haywood (1985).
10.   See Schonberger (1986).
11.   Mortimer (1985).
12.   An example is the case of TI-Raleigh, which reported in *New Technology* (1984) that 'the changes in computer control systems have not only failed to produce improvements but caused a serious loss of production efficiency'.
13.   See, for example, New and Myers (1987).
14.   See in particular Barras (1986) for a discussion of the reverse product cycle in services.
15.   The term 'Big Bang' refers to the October 1986 liberalisation of the trading practices at the London Stock Exchange, removing barriers to new entrants. The change was particularly characterised by introduction of automatic clearing and stock broking systems.
16.   Information-processing services typically involve standardised information processing for the following reasons: some of these services are based on repetitive operations with data of very limited kinds (for example financial data, with common currency metrics), while communications services carry very diverse types of information but do this in standardised ways (for example mass broadcasting, telephone networks). Some other services however are more creative ones, involving the production of fresh information (as in consultancy and entertainment).
17.   But there has been considerable non-IT innovation in some core activities: for example in pharmaceuticals and medical equipment. More recently IT is being used to enhance such equipment (or even make it possible, as in computer-aided tomography), and to follow through treatment regimes.

18.   See Poon (1988) for a detailed discussion of the implications of IT for the structure of tourism.

19.   For example, see Hoffman and Rush (1988).

20.   For a fuller discussion and more examples of blending, see Bhalla *et al.* (1984).

21.   For a detailed analysis of the prospects for IT application in different Third World economies and sectors, see Bessant and Cole (1985).

22.   See Bessant and Cole (1985) for a fuller description of these scenarios.

5. Living with IT

We have examined likely directions of IT-related change within the formal economy, discussing their implications for formal work – full or part-time employment and self employment. Formal work has become of central importance to most aspects of everyday life: it is a major determinant of income distribution, availability of free time, people's social networks and places to live, and other such features.[1] Thus it is important to review the implications of IT for formal work in this light.

Forecasts of the consequences of various IT applications for formal work are numerous – perhaps more so than any other issue covered in the literature – with estimates of future employment levels evoking much controversy. Studies of the use of IT in most *established* branches and sectors of the economy tend to forecast reductions in employment levels, or jobless growth at best. Studies drawing on macroeconomic models tend to predict lower levels of job loss than do sectoral studies; this is largely due to compensatory effects (increased demand associated with cost reduction). Some of these 'macro' analyses, even while accepting that IT is liable to be linked with major increases in labour productivity, suggest that those countries which are in the forefront of innovation may well experience some employment growth (at least within the IT sector itself). These empirically-based studies cannot really come to grips with the transformist notions that the main hope for future employment is not in the buttressing of *existing* activities but in the creation of new areas of economic activity – whole new branches of industry and groups of occupations.

Though the controversy about future employment

levels is a lively one,[2] three well-established trends are on the whole agreed upon across our three perspectives:

1. continuation of the long-term shifts of the preponderance of employment from the primary to the secondary to the tertiary sector
2. continuation of the reduction in core manual and production occupations, with a relative increase in ancillary, administrative and professional jobs
3. continuation of the reduction in lifetime working hours.

Beyond these three points there is more disagreement. Referring back to the framework introduced in Chapter 1 (Figure 1.3), any quantitative changes in formal working numbers or practices will be dependent upon demand. Demand levels, in turn, can be influenced by the cheapening of existing products or services on offer through the use of IT. Furthermore they are shaped by the creation of *new* IT-based products and services (and of course other non-IT-based products and services). The extent to which a quantitative reduction in employment materialises, therefore, is a function of broader economic and social innovation – new products and ways of life – and the demand associated with such innovation.

Significant lowering of employment numbers only translates into a reduction in working hours if the work that exists is redistributed amongst the active labour force. Linkages between the distribution of working time and the resultant distribution of income will, to a large extent, determine the nature of final demand for both familiar and new products. Again 'social innovations' – in working hours, leisure activities, continuing education, remuneration systems – are of importance.[3]

The principal focus of this chapter is the final demand for information technologies, in the home or the community, and their influences on ways of life. Here we shall consider the broad set of implications associated with specific ITs within three broad (and often overlapping) areas of social life associated with final demand. As outlined in Table 5.1 we have included housework,

Table 5.1 **Areas of social life to be considered**

Category	Examples
Housework, safety and security	Cleaning, maintenance, household goods, clothing, meals preparation, shopping, gardening, do-it-yourself decoration, alarms, etc.
Sport and personal care	Exercise, active leisure (participatory sport, games, hobbies), health maintenance, child care, rest, etc.
Home entertainment and communication	Use of mass media, spectator sport and performance, hobbyist and game home computing, music, personal communication, etc.

safety and security; leisure and personal care; and home entertainment and communication. (It is not a coincidence that these closely parallel the distinction drawn in Chapter 4 between goods-based, person-crentred and information-based services: these are the informal equivalents of the three service types.)

These are followed by a section on the integrated home and community of the future which addresses the question of the 'delivery' of these three categories of applications. We shall attempt to identify the ITs likely to be most relevant to the area, the main medium- and longer-term implications of possible technology developments, and those issues which we believe require special attention; and we shall also seek to indicate the approaches taken by the continuist, the transformist and the structuralist perspectives.

The application of IT to domestic equipment – and the creation of new consumer goods and services based on

IT – is now widely termed 'home informatics'.[4] Of course in large part the development of home informatics is due to the cheapening of microelectronics; so much so that it may well be cheaper to use digital controls and displays than mechanical or electromechanical ones, and the cost of 'informatising' an item of domestic equipment is very low relative to the cost of the equipment.

While a continuist perspective might well be sceptical about home informatics and regard this incorporation of cheap microelectronics into household goods as gimmickry, it should be recalled that there is already much information processing in the home, and that this offers scope for IT applications. Indeed much consumer electronics involves precisely this purpose.

Another significant related change occurring in these information-processing goods is the digitalisation of domestic goods and services. In line with some of the broader developments of digitalisation discussed in Chapter 2, we can see significant steps toward digitalisation of the information functions performed by domestic equipment (see pp. 35, 61, 181). Digitalisation is the foundation on which many new products and services will be built. Just as the compact disc player has facilities that go well beyond the conventional record player, so new generations of radios, TV – and even cookers and washing machines – are being developed with significantly new features.

In many cases drawing on applications transferred from their development in industrial settings, IT will offer advantages (Table 5.2) which are liable to appeal to consumers, and which will move the trend from the present improvements in control and displays incorporated in domestic equipment to the addition of improved and radically new functions,[5] which may more properly be labelled 'home informatics'.

HOUSEWORK, SAFETY AND SECURITY

Private households have been steadily increasing their 'capital-intensity' by accumulating over recent decades a

Table 5.2 **Advantages offered by IT applications to household technology (home informatics)**

Remote control	infrared switches eventually leading to multi-remote devices operated by a single controller, and tele- or distance control
User-friendly	voice control, menu displays providing more informative and realistic output displays and voice synthesised messages
Programmable	ability to fit current user requirements, and automatic control which takes into account, for example, energy tariffs, the weight and nature of the food or clothing being processed, etc.
Informed	memory to recall previous programming and data inputs, ability to interface with other devices to optimise performance and with external information sources
Portable	smaller, more personal devices which permit greater mobility (cordless devices for convenience of use), devices for fitting into small places or providing economies for single people
Safe	warning indicators, automatic cut-off and fail-safe controls
Maintenance	easier repairs, auto-diagnostics
Energy conservation	more energy-efficient devices, ability to take into account changes in environmental factors such as temperature or energy tariffs

wide range of consumer products. Many household technologies have their roots in industrial applications, with the now commonplace equipment such as washing machines, vacuum cleaners and water heaters having all first found application in the formal economy. Given the origin of much of these technologies, perhaps we should not be surprised that consumer durables have increasingly made the home not merely a site of consumption and personal support but also a site of informal production. Self-services have become important in various forms of housework: washing machines and automobiles instead of laundries and buses, to name two familiar examples.

Nor is it entirely surprising that strong analogies can be drawn between the predicted degree and direction of change in home technologies and those in the formal sector. Microelectronics is already being incorporated into many of these consumer products and thus into the 'processes' of household activities includi. g domestic appliances, alarm and safety equipment. As is the case in industry, the fall in the price of semi-conductors has led to the replacement of mechanical and electromechanical controls with microelectronic controls in nearly all these product areas. In many instances these can be dismissed as mere gimmickry although, as indicated in Figure 5.1, serious applications in heating, cooking and cleaning technologies are on the increase.

This is not to suggest that the trajectories of domestic IT equipment will precisely or faithfully mirror those in industry. Different motivations and availability of financial resources have already established markedly different technological trajectories. Domestic sewing machines, for example, are often much more flexible (in terms of switching between stitches) but much less robust than industrial sewing machines. Home computers used primarily for games are hardly in the same category as the computers used in industry – though they may compete with office systems. However characteristics such as portability, programmability, power conservation and 'user-friendliness' will, in our opinion, contribute to a movement towards greater integration of functions in

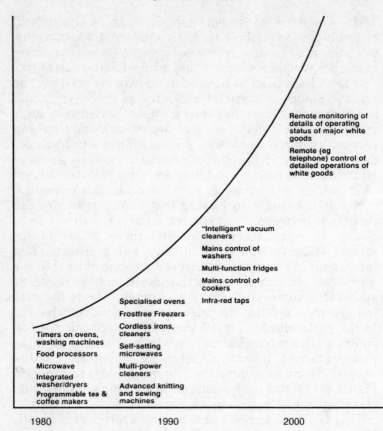

Figure 5.1 **IT applications in housework**

Note: The chart indicates the approximate period at which these items of consumer electronics are likely to be widely retailed and in use; indeed most of them have already been developed at least as experimental models.

domestic goods – as has been the case in industrial applications.

Applying IT to existing household activities is one thing. For new activities to emerge a change in the core equipment may be necessary. Some of the more dramatic household innovations will also depend upon a change in the way they are delivered (infrastructural change) as well as social attitudes towards their use. To some extent this is analogous to changes in industry which depend upon new working practices and forms of social organisation.

Differences between the three perspectives we have been contrasting throughout this book are perhaps even more pronounced when it comes to final demand in the 'household sector' than they were in regard to the sectors of the formal economy. The continuist viewpoint sees little reason for the long-term trends in consumption patterns to change – and stresses the stability that lies behind these trends. The home of the future will then be one which has evolved gradually, and levels of housework will be slightly reshaped in line with, for example, growing interest in do-it-yourself or specialist cookery. Thus IT will be mainly used as a fashionable gimmick (yuppie toys, IT as YT) in status-conscious households; its serious applications are liable to remain few, and people are unlikely to welcome hi-tech solutions to everyday problems. The success of earlier household technologies has been based on their reducing the physical labour involved in cleaning, and so on: but information processing is more of a feature of the social life of households, and no one will want IT to reduce this. It would be fine to have bed-making robots (though where would we store them when not in use), but until that far-off day IT has little relevance to the home.

The continuist perspective would stress this point with respect to the application of IT to various aspects of domestic life. Some innovations are evidently attractive – baby and fire alarms, emergency buttons for the ill or elderly, for example. Increased perceived threats to personal and home security, increased concern about health problems and hazards are liable to promote further developments along these lines – better monitors of foetal and infant health (related to fears of 'cot-death') and, perhaps, of domestic pollutants, improved intruder detection, more energy conservation. These are however 'more of the same' rather than major changes.

The transformist perspective, in contrast, sees the development of home informatics as liable to revolutionise housework. Assuming a redistribution of working time in the formal economy, transformism projects more availability of free time for domestic work, and shifts in values which would encourage more sophisticated self- or community servicing. Furthermore increased proportions of the working population are liable to be engaged in telework, and this should result both in increased time spent at home and in massive improvements in domestic computer-communications. IT is seen here as being productively incorporated into almost all forms of domestic equipment, as portrayed in Figure 5.1. As well as upgrading the quality, efficiency and usefulness of individual household items, these stand-alone items are liable to be steadily integrated into 'smart houses' or interactive home systems (see p. 192).

Kitchen equipment, such as the microwave oven, provides a good example (in terms of the transformist perspective) of how new technologies can be rapidly accepted, if they are designed well and accord with trends in social values (in this case freeing individuals from the tyranny of collective consumption, food preparation, and hard work). New models are becoming increasingly 'userfriendly', for example by reducing the need to pre-weigh the food and adjust the oven accordingly. Conceptually this is not far from an automated oven: the microwave, or more conventional cookers, could be equipped with sensors which weigh the food, detect and measure the vapours emitted, and determine internal temperatures via probes. In fact advanced models are already on the market: one model is capable of storing a large number of different sets of cooking instructions.

Similar facilities can be envisaged for most other items of domestic equipment. Many are already being introduced as top of the range products: transformists see them as rapidly becoming standard features. Washing machines will have touch-panel controls and self-adjusting dryers which regulate the heat and air flow by weight of load and fabric characteristics. Self-diagnostics and safety features (after all most accidents occur in the home) will tell us when the fridge door has been left open or the power supply is disrupted. Fridges, already self-defrosting and supplied with ice-crushers and other built-in tools, will (in a typical transformist scenario) be able to tell the shopper what items are near spoiling and require consuming soon or being disposed of, or, courtesy of the bar codes and simple readers, what items we are running low on. With the prospect of linkages to a microcomputer with a menu planner program, it is not difficult to imagine a larder or freezer which not only indicates its contents but suggests various dishes which could be prepared – according to your dietary requirements.

Timing devices have been available for many years, permitting the automatic turning on-off of electrical devices and thus taking advantage of off-peak tariffs, increasing convenience of use of a range of domestic equipment, and so on. Microelectronic controls add the possibility of remote control, through the telephone or portable communication devices, of anything from cookers to washing machines. A logical next step is to combine control (remote or otherwise) with monitoring and display of information (for example in a 'window' on the television); or linking control with sensors – which adjusts to changes in temperature, the presence of occupants or intruders, or pollution levels.

There is hardly a household task to which microelectronics could not conceivably be applied.[6] Skilled activities such as sewing already have electronic control units, although some tasks such as ironing and vacuuming require complementary advances in sensor technology. Water taps turned on and regulated by the proximity of a hand as indicated by infrared detectors, ovens that require an adult-sized presence to work, tape measures which provide digital readouts and calculate geometric areas are all well within the transformist vision. The list is limited more by failure of the imagination than by what is technologically possible.

One of the first areas likely to experience a rapid rate of innovation is security and safety equipment, particularly in those parts of society which are highly status-conscious or where social inequalities increase insecurity. We have already mentioned a range of equipment here: indeed there is a proliferation of stand-alone devices for fire and intruder detection. Local authorities have been assessing the value of emergency systems in homes for the disabled or elderly in which buttons activate remote services by telephony. Detectors of different types can (and have) been connected to centralised computer and telecommunications facilities which not only relay emergency calls to the required services but can provide necessary medical details on the individual (for example whether there are particular disabilities or reasons for concern; who is the responsible doctor, and so on).

Information technologies applied to security devices are also likely to transform the humble door lock. Already electronic locks can provide information on unauthorised intruders or tampering. Microelectronic keys are available in business applications. In the longer term, in domestic as well as business environments, conventional keys are expected to be rendered obsolete by personal laser cards, voice activated commands ('open sesame') or through pattern recognition (capable of face or fingerprint identification). As we move from the keyhole to the keyboard, 'intelligent doors' and 'smart locks' will not only be less draughty but could relay information to the visitor (such as when would be a more convenient time to call) or to the home occupier, by providing information to the resident (thus allowing the resident to avoid commercial pedlars or Jehovah's Witnesses). Programmed doors themselves could deny entrance (or even communication) to certain classes of visitors – which gives rise to two types of speculation. First, that various official bodies might press to have regulations governing such equipment-programming (for example making it illegal to refuse to talk to the police or to open up to police with warrants or to social workers who are responsible for assuring the well-being of children). Second, that confidence tricksters and enthusiasts of all kinds might develop means of confusing intelligent front doors, fooling them into permitting access/communication. (However we would expect some of the entry to be accomplished remotely, by telecommunicating one's sales pitch to residents rather than bothering to call in person.)

In the movement from industrial application to domestic use, to which we referred earlier, perhaps the best example is found in the transfer of technologies developed for energy process control. The time-scale for the introduction of IT-enhanced energy systems like heat pumps and solar heating are, however, largely determined by political factors. (These include pricing policies for different forms of energy, the availability of subsidies for large-scale conversion of the housing stock, and public support for what may be high initial research and development costs for non-conventional energy systems.) In the long term some transformists expect a significant movement towards IT-operated solar heating, with private householders even selling excess electricity back to the public power-generating authorities. (This practice already exists in Denmark, where some colleagues of ours live in collective housing projects which sell windmill-generated power back to the grid.)

In the more immediate future, both continuist and transformist perspectives envisage that a wide range of domestic appliances will be rendered more energy efficient, particularly through the use of timing devices and digital displays of expenditure and tariff charges. Considerable interest has already been generated by energy suppliers in 'mains signalling' techniques. In these techniques, existing electrical wiring, installed for power generation, is used additionally to convey simple information. The energy authorities see the usefulness of meter information being supplied in this way, which reduces labour in conventional means of collecting energy usage details. Furthermore it is possible to use mains signalling to relay changes in tariffs, which could be used, in turn, to control domestic equipment. Thus, for example, households would reduce energy costs by using power-intensive equipment when tariffs are low (for example washing machines that turn on at night). This is in the energy utilities' interest, since it smooths power loads and reduces the need to keep stations ready in stand-by for peak periods. Mains signalling has evoked considerable interest among electricity companies, but other techniques such as wireless control of meters and telephone metering are also under study.

While energy conservation may be principally motivated by cost considerations, financial saving is only one of several incentives for IT-based home energy management systems. Health issues arising from domestic pollutants and ecological concerns are likely to become increasingly prevalent as more airborne carcinogenic agents are identified (for example radon from natural sources, organic chemicals, pollutants associated with new furniture and adhesives). As self-service and do-it-yourself activities increase, people have more knowledge and self-interest in getting the job done well. Heat, moisture and pollution monitoring and control, linked to automated ventilation and dehumidifier systems, would seem a likely development. Further linkages could be made to alarm and back up systems (to cover the event of a power failure). These might converge around, for example, a programmable heat pump – if this technology can be developed cheaply for mass domestic use.

The continuist perspective proposes that people will largely reject the intrusion of 'soulless' technology into the home and everyday lives. A transformist view, in contrast, considers that the familiarisation (of people with technology) and simplification (of technology for people) will continue to march hand in hand. The attitudes that currently render baby and fire alarms acceptable, for example, will increasingly facilitate the application of IT to other aspects of domestic activities (and as we shall see, personal care). The current rather gimmicky prototypes of the electronic bathroom and bedroom are thus treated seriously by transformism – not as necessarily providing accurate images of the future, but as demonstrating the vast changes that are possible in the home.

Our structuralist perspective leans mostly towards the transformist view of rapid change in, and enhancement of, household appliances. But we remain more sceptical of the degree of consumer enthusiasm for teleshopping and similar innovations. In Britain viewdata-based teleshopping has not proved successful, except where it has been supported by public authorities as a social service to the elderly: we wait to see whether France, with a large population of Minitel terminals, proves differently. In the USA, interestingly, the linkage of TV advertisements and telephone shopping has taken off rapidly but this reflects (a) cultural differences (such as geographic dispersion and the 'catalogue' tradition); and (b) far less of a technological leap. Nevertheless the computerised ordering systems developed for such applications provide a basis for more advanced computer-communications teleshopping, so perhaps we should not be too sceptical.

Nor are we convinced that there really is a large untapped public demand for new information services (other than entertainment services), at least not one that will be manifest in the near future. Technological change in the home will be facilitated or impeded by the rate of development of standards in home communication systems, and by that of advanced telecommunications facilities (ISDN, broadband communications, user-friendly interfaces). Without standards (as we saw in Chapter 3), there are problems in getting different items of equipment and applications to work together. There is less assurance of 'future-proofing' – as people who invested in the wrong type of video tape-recorders have learned. Without improved telecommunications the range of services on offer will be restricted.[7]

Cultural factors also mediate household applications of IT. By this we refer particularly to the sexual division of domestic work, and the associated social evaluation of housework as an onerous duty or as creative leisure. The degree to which certain applications are favoured will be affected by the size of families and availability of formal services such as crèches and nurseries; and by the physical layout of apartments and houses, the proportion under private ownership, and the rates at which the population moves and at which new houses are built. We expect a considerable proliferation of new domestic equipment in homes over the next few decades. But this will constitute a slower development towards the more advanced home systems than the transformist perspective seems to indicate. And even if homes in different countries possess similar equipment (which they may not; microwaves are not equally successful around Europe) they may well differ considerably in the house-work strategies that are employed.

A number of social issues are raised in this context. One concern frequently expressed is that the 'automated home' will lead to greater social isolation – telework reduces social contacts at the workplace, and teleservices do the same for activities like shopping. While such concerns are probably overstated it is quite plausible that some groups are more vulnerable than others in specific contexts: for example mothers with young children, who are already often isolated and depressed; or the elderly.

The continuist perspective would suggest that these concerns in fact constitute one reason for the slow uptake of home informatics. In contrast, a transformist view might well be that IT can help resolve these problems, allowing for better communication between people; for example enabling the parents with small children to share their worries with each other, to organise mutual child-care arrangements, and the like. Our structuralist view inclines us to consider that the issues are really very uncertain: just as the advent of TV has had a complex and multifaceted set of implications, so too will the emergence of home informatics interact with existing trends and conflicts in everyday life. At this point all we can really do is to highlight a number of topics on which we suggest that research and social movements need to focus:

• problems of privatisation and isolation
• changes in the sexual division of labour (can new technology be implemented so as to ease existing inequalities?)
• relations between generations (parent-child relations, care of the elderly, etc.)
• the possibility of a reduction in people's experience of variety and diversity as it is constituted in interpersonal interactions (including those with strangers and people of other cultures), with a concomitant increase in experiences based on the manufactured diversity of the fantasy world of mass entertainment and computer games.

But the last point on the list moves us away from IT applications to domestic work, and towards issues around entertainment and communications. Returning to domestic work, a second set of issues concerns the consequences for certain formal services of increased home working and self-servicing. Just as the washing machines reduced demand for laundry services, and the vacuum cleaner enabled middle-class households to evade the escalating expense of servants, so current innovations may support a shift from services (for example domestic cleaners) to goods (for example vacuum cleaners); or from a traditional service (for example cinema staff) to a new service (for example broadcasting staff).[8] The employment implications of a shift to, for example, electronic mail or teleshopping are hard to estimate but are potentially very significant. Some new jobs are created (in software development, in administration, in delivery of goods, in training) but these are typically fewer than in the traditional service. But freed labour can be used to improve service quality or provide new services, so the extent of job loss is by no means as overwhelming as might first appear.

Related to the employment issue, the structuralist perspective suggests that dualism with respect to formal work (see Chapter 4) may be mirrored in the world of work and home. Those who are most productively engaged in the formal economy may also have the most productive domestic equipment and as a result be more competitive with odd-job workers when it comes to do-it-yourself, and so on.[9]

Finally it is plausible that concern expressed about 'hacking', invasion of privacy, unauthorised surveillance of computer operations, fraud and data protection will also be raised with respect to the automated household. Unless parallel developments occur to secure computer systems, there will always be the possibility that nosey neighbours, the police, or tax inspectors, could inspect home accounts and records. Kids (and adults) could go wild, just as they now do with telephone bills and credit cards, burglars could reprogram front door systems, and separated spouses could take revenge. None of these actions would represent anything out of line with current forms of human behaviour: the technology merely offers new ways of continuing old conflicts.

SPORT AND PERSONAL CARE

Many of the points made concerning domestic work also apply to the social activities of sport and personal care. (We put these together because (a) there is a degree of convergence in the use of the IT to satisfy the demands of a wide range of activities subsumed under these headings; and (b) for many in western society today sport has become equated with personal care, health and fitness.) Certainly some of the initial applications have been aimed at the specialist or to activities currently in vogue among those with more ability to gain money than to think of sensible ways of occupying their time. The continuist perspective might place running shoes with built-in microprocessors (available now) within this category. Jogging enthusiasts, or those bitten by the more recent craze for serious 'walking' apparently do find a use for such 'informed' shoes. It is unlikely however that cobblers will have to familiarise themselves with electronics, as such applications hardly represent a radical up-grading of these activities and are unlikely to find mass appeal. Being able to transfer data from one's shoes into a personal computer to record one's walks, to set exercise schedules, and so on, is not a significant requirement of most people.

Nevertheless a wide range of equipment used for specific leisure activities – sports vehicles, clothing, exercise machinery, games and toys – is liable to incorporate IT for not dissimilar ends. In other words IT will be used for monitoring performance and providing training advice, for closer simulation of reality in training or other settings, for convenience and for sheer fun (Figure 5.2). Currently available computer software compares the individual's performance on various exercises with previous attempts and sets a standard to aim for. IT has already been incorporated into rowing, cycling and running equipment and it hardly requires a flight of fancy to foresee the linkage of these with a video recorder, allowing the sports enthusiast to run the Boston Marathon or have a round of golf at St Andrews from the comfort of the home (if the home has room for such energetic activities, and neighbours are prepared to put up with the associated thumping).

Sport is increasingly being linked to health and the future demand for health monitoring equipment is likely to coincide with that for exercise equipment. Associations are made between a lack of physical exercise and a wide range of ailments from heart disease to premature senility. The somewhat excessive behaviour of individuals seemingly addicted to activities such as jogging or 'pumping iron' has also led to an increase in sports-related injuries (previously restricted to tennis elbow); and control equipment incorporating IT will increasingly be used to monitor physical limits of the individual enthusiast. Similarly diet has been recognised as an important factor in both good health and physical performance. Tennis champions and track stars are among the newest recruits to turn to diet as a means of improv-

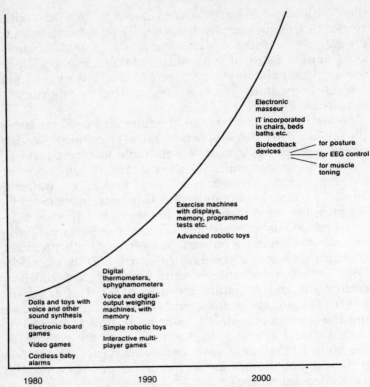

Electronic masseur

IT incorporated in chairs, beds baths etc.

Biofeedback devices —— for posture
        —— for EEG control
        —— for muscle toning

Exercise machines with displays, memory, programmed tests etc.

Advanced robotic toys

Digital thermometers, sphyghamometers

Dolls and toys with voice and other sound synthesis

Voice and digital-output weighing machines, with memory

Electronic board games

Simple robotic toys

Video games

Interactive multi-player games

Cordless baby alarms

1980   1990   2000

Figure 5.2 **IT applications in sport and personal care**

Note: The chart indicates the approximate period at which these items of consumer electronics are likely to be widely retailed and in use; indeed most of them have already been developed at least as experimental models.

ing performance. The connection between diet and health is of course nothing new, but again the application of IT to the individual's ability to receive advice, to monitor and receive feedback on the nutritional adequacy of diet and exercise regimes is already under development.

IT allows simplified use of many medical devices and there is already a market for digital thermometers and pulse meters as well as others listed in Figure 5.2. Already available in Japan is the IT toilet. While you sit on it, it measures your heart rate, and so on, and gives you a health check (making 'spending a penny' the best value since having your fortune told when stepping on the scales!). What is currently a specialist market for biofeed-back devices for meditation and relaxation could also find wider demand – either in stand-alone products or integrated with exercise and sports equipment into 'lifestyle assessment systems'. The transformist perspective would suggest that what has begun as aids to the medical services is likely to find its way into the home. We would thus see expert systems for self-diagnosis or monitoring equipment linked to remote diagnosis by one's doctor. However as structuralists we would express concern that the growing dualism in access to medical services (epitomised by arguments about resources available within private and public health facilities) could be exacerbated as a new 'health' market develops which caters more to the well-off healthy than the invalid or the infirm.

HOME ENTERTAINMENT AND COMMUNICATIONS

Although many of the devices portrayed above may have relatively limited or specialist appeal, a considerable number of developments (Figures 5.3, 5.4), particularly within audio and video equipment, together with the linked home computers and video games, have been taken more seriously and generated significant demand. Many of these products and services represent an increase in quality on previous generations of equipment, or provide mass access to information services which were previously restricted to the very wealthy.

The developments which are taking place are occurring on two different levels. One direction of development has been for smaller, lighter and more robust equipment which provides access to the services to anyone anywhere. The personal stereo is a good example (one can listen to

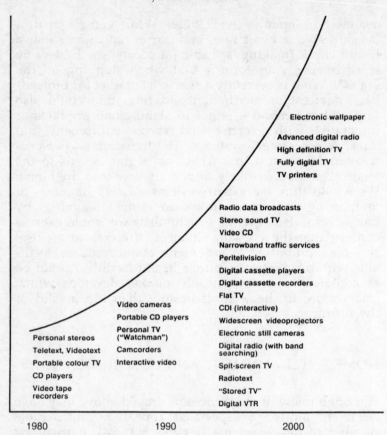

Figure 5.3 **IT applications in home entertainment**

Note: The chart indicates the approximate period at which
these items of consumer electronics are likely to be widely
retailed and in use; indeed most of them have already been
developed at least as experimental models.

music hall performances while going roller-skating); and
new generations of cassette (digital audio tape or DAT)
and compact disc (CD) players provide facilities and
quality which heretofore have only been available on
extremely expensive 'living room' systems. Developments

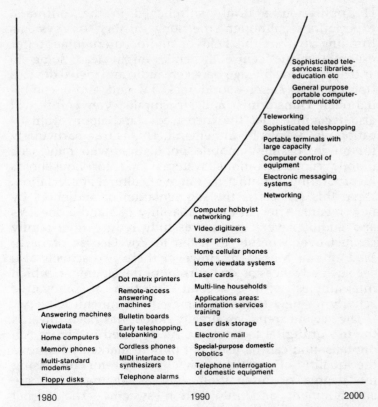

Sophisticated tele-
services: libraries,
education etc

General purpose
portable computer-
communicator

Teleworking

Sophisticated teleshopping

Portable terminals with
large capacity

Computer control of
equipment

Electronic messaging
systems

Networking

Computer hobbyist
networking

Video digitizers

Laser printers

Home cellular phones

Home viewdata systems

Dot matrix printers   Laser cards

Remote-access   Multi-line households
answering
machines   Applications areas:
                               information services
Answering machines   Bulletin boards   training

Viewdata   Laser disk storage
                    Early teleshopping,
Home computers   telebanking   Electronic mail

Memory phones   Cordless phones   Special-purpose domestic
                                        robotics
Multi-standard   MIDI interface to
modems   synthesizers   Telephone interrogation
                                        of domestic equipment
Floppy disks   Telephone alarms

1980   1990   2000

Figure 5.4 **IT applications around home computing and
telecommunications**

Note: The chart indicates the approximate period at which
these items of consumer electronics are likely to be widely
retailed and in use; indeed most of them have already been
developed at least as experimental models.

in complex liquid crystal displays and flat screen technology will provide a boost for efforts to miniaturise TV,
and fit well within this general trend of sophisticated (or
portable) stand-alone equipment.

Such stand-alone applications can be found within the
visions of all our three schools of thought. This form of

IT application is firmly entrenched in the continuist expectations, although the long history of 'systems thinking' within the field of audio entertainment (for example music centre systems) might lead some to anticipate some linkage between audio and visual devices (for example stereo-sound rack TV and audio combinations). Transformist and structuralist viewpoints will also recognise that the increased stand-alone sophistication will always be in demand. This is true particularly for an increasingly mobile population who may seek mobile communications systems; and for households incorporating a conflicting range of cultural appreciation. What this reflects is the segmentation of audiences by new media. After all the availability of stand-alone TVs and audio players can successfully reduce inter-family conflict over whether to listen to Boy George or Bach; Madonna or Messiaen. However these two schools also see such advances as one current of development, which intermingles with a second direction of innovative activity for new forms of home entertainment delivery.

The second trend, as already noted, has been towards the use of digital technology. As depicted in Figure 5.5, digitalisation can be used not only to markedly improve the quality of reproduction, but also for increasing the degree of integration and 'packaging' of home entertainment and information systems. The digital revolution is already being felt through the development of CD players – which are widely recognised as providing higher quality reproduction than all but the most sophisticated (and high-priced) conventional analogue record players. Depending on the rate of development of digital cassettes they are expected to dominate the market within a decade. Digital audio-tape and video-tape recorders have a potentially enormous capacity for the bulk storage of visual and audio data, though compact discs seem better for the rapid location of material.

CD technology allows for the storage of massive quantities of data. Instead of the hour or so of hi-fi music on the conventional audio CD, it is possible to store the contents of a multivolume encyclopaedia, or thousands

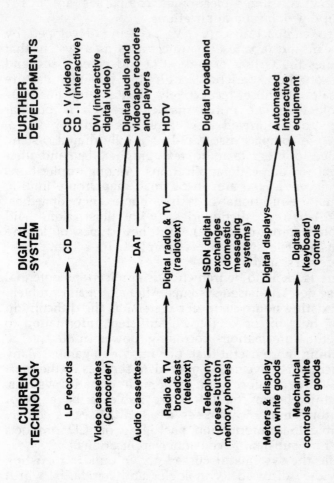

Figure 5.5 Digitalisation of domestic technology

of facsimile pages of manuscript (or 35mm photographs). CD-ROM has emerged as a significant data storage technology for business applications, especially where there are substantial archival components of the work. But now consumer electronics companies are busily developing domestic applications.

Video compact disc (CD-V) is being developed by European and Japanese manufacturers as a system that combines the virtues of audio CD and video discs (and builds on the experience acquired in the manufacture and sale of these respectively digital and analogue technologies). The initial market foreseen is popular music – an improved mix of records and pop video. Interactive compact disc (CD-I) is a fully digital system, intended to integrate audio, text, graphic, data and other material for domestic applications. Among applications currently envisaged are: in-car road maps/route finding systems;[10] educational aids like home encyclopaedias, foreign-language dictionaries (with illustrations and exemplary pronunciations); and new types of leisure gadgets (music synthesisers/samplers, on-screen 'painting' devices, and so on).

There is likely to be tremendous applications potential in these new CD-based systems. After all a major problem with existing home computer systems is the difficulty in getting hold of (or keying in) sufficient information to make the information-processing power applicable to something more useful than playing video games. Many commentators have seen online data services as the most likely source of information for home informatics systems. (And thus home computers are liable to be a major boost for communication services.) But it seems equally plausible that information packaging on CD products could find substantial consumer applications.

While the systems discussed above build on existing and widely diffused technologies and standards, which would typically be recommended from a structuralist perspective, it should also be noted that some firms are taking a more transformist approach. One well established consumer electronics firm in the United States has been pressing ahead with interactive digital video (DVI), a system that utilises advanced methods of data compression in order to cram vastly more quality video information on a disc than can be achieved with CD-V. This involves more of a 'quantum jump' however: it requires completely new decoding/decompression devices and thus involves a new generation of equipment altogether.

It is also worth noting that a similar contrast of strategies is apparent in the area of high definition TV (HDTV). Japanese manufacturers are working towards HDTV systems that make a complete break with existing TV studio equipment, transmission systems and TV sets. (They have, incidentally, won considerable support from TV producers and film makers in the United States, who have been impressed by the quality of the new kit with which they have been allowed to play.) The European industry, in contrast, is pressing for systems which build incrementally upon current TV technology – so that one would only have to acquire a new set to receive the broadcast in high definition. For those without the new sets, broadcasts could still be received in their conventional form on a standard TV. The stakes in this case (as in CD systems) are high, with the system that triumphs capturing a large world market.

The success or failure of these different strategies is not just a matter of whether continuist or transformist or structuralist prejudices are the correct ones. Certainly the dynamics of consumer acceptance of new technologies will play a decisive role. But in large part these dynamics and the associated issues of standards-setting, availability of services, and so on, will depend upon the policies of leading actors. How major industrial companies act, and bring pressure to bear on governments, will shape the trajectory of both these areas of home informatics. The one thing we can say for certain is that major developments of new consumer goods and services are highly probable in both areas.

The movement to digitalisation is well under way. Teletext is already digital and some TVs have already

incorporated RAM chips which can store many pages.
Other developments which consumer electronic firms
expect to diffuse widely in the not too distant future
include features such as split screen facilities for multi-
channel viewing, zoom and freeze frame, and so on.
Some of the facilities are already available on TV sets
and videos, and others such as wide screen and high
definition are likely to find ready markets. (This is one
reason why HDTV standards are such a contentious
issue.)[11] We can see enhanced TVs being the heart of
domestic messaging systems, of electronic wallpaper, and
of fax-newspapers which print out the items one wishes
to retain. But the linkages between systems can be
difficult.

The high data transmission requirements of quality
sound and vision (see Chapter 2) mean that the integration
of TV with other products and services will require rather
more advanced small area networks than those supporting
the conveyance and integration of energy management,
alarm and emergency, and household systems. Such
networks would require integration with home computers
and enhanced telecommunication devices. Telephones
have already been the subject of considerable innovative
activity during the 1980s, with, among other advances,
the introduction of auto-dial and answering facilities,
cordless phones, visual displays, and so on. In some
countries residential PBXs (private branch telecommunications exchanges) have begun to find a market. They
may well play an important role in permitting access to
information services such as viewdata, and the spread
of services such as teleshopping without tying up lines
for long periods, preventing conventional telephony.
ISDN systems will permit voice and data channels to
come together down the same cable at the same time.
Simple devices to permit simultaneous use of a domestic
phone line for several purposes are already available.

Turning to further innovations in telecommunications
equipment, voice activated telephones can already be
installed in automobiles and the possibilities exist for
'smart phones' which can identify the source of a call

and filter out unwanted callers. Advances in answering machine technology should see newer models which provide a range of information on request as to the availability of the owner or where he/she can be reached. By the year 2010 we would expect the concept of the 'portable communicator' – a battery or solar operated communications device which the individual can easily carry anywhere he or she likes – will become a reality as cellular radio systems evolve and become more sophisticated. The difficulties involved in developing a pocket- or purse-sized communicator should not be underestimated. If, as some commentators foresee, a conveniently mobile computer/communicator would incorporate all the features of a filofax (and more) then the visual display alone will have to be of considerable sophistication. Nevertheless with added facilities such as automatic re-dial, the ability to search alternative numbers for particular individuals, and a capacity to receive and send written text, such a device makes a mouth-watering prospect for any transformist.

The main advances however will be in the convergence of computing and telecommunications. Until recently most home computers have been used for their game-playing entertainment value (although many were purchased by parents who were convinced that their children's education would be hampered without them – this was capitalised on by manufacturers). Now they are becoming increasingly popular for such activities as controlling music synthesisers and text processing. No doubt game-playing will remain popular, especially as software realism continues to increase, leading to new 3-D graphics, better sound (voice synthesis, and so on) and more sophisticated scenarios. But it is its potential for providing new or enhanced information services at low cost that home computing will come into its own. As high-intensity domestic data storage and retrieval (through CD-ROM and CD-I) and data communications (to online services) become available libraries, dictionaries, encyclopaedias, catalogues, and so on, will be a button touch or spoken word away.

Computer communications are becoming increasingly popular in Europe and North America. The French Teletel (viewdata) system was launched with a large-scale promotion and has achieved wide popularity. A policy decision to distribute unsophisticated 'Minitel' terminals free of charge helped win the acceptance of a public which already numbers over two and a half million subscribers. (Furthermore people were effectively forced to use it, by having their own access to an important service – phone directory enquiries – provided through viewdata.) This system, in addition to providing services ranging from holiday bookings to astrological predictions, offers the user an anonymous (if so desired) means of making contact with large numbers of people (known as *messagerie*). And indeed it is communications, rather than access to databases, that has become the booming activity on Teletel.

The UK Prestel system initially suffered from a degree of user-unfriendliness and has been slower in its rate of diffusion to domestic consumers (business applications took off rapidly). It has proved popular with hobbyists and currently offers a wide range of services (Table 5.3). The quality of text and graphics has a long way to go on any of the available systems; photo-videotex is cumbersomely slow even on ISDN systems although with broadband, or broadband transmission, appears a better solution. It should not be long before systems offering 'hard copy' (via laser printers) become available, eventually followed by 'magic slates' (portable, probably foldable, displays with storage).

As we have argued, the continuist viewpoint sees the sort of home information services discussed above as unlikely to take off on any scale in at least the next few decades, while the structural and transformist viewpoints expect progressively rapid developments. This perspective is quick to dismiss some trends, such as video games and home computers, as short-lived fads. The video tape-recorder, enabling improved use of TV (but little in the way of new entertainment activity), is for them more typical and likely to be a more enduring domestic

Table 5.3 **Computer-communication services**

Teleshopping	currently best equipped to handle consumer durables for national chains but still requires backup from other information sources for sophisticated graphics
Telebooking	inspection of programmes and timetables and the ability to check availability of facilities (e.g. sports halls) on required dates, opening hours, special offers, delays, and running times (buses and trains)
Telebanking	opportunities to inspect accounts, transfer funds, make payments, speculate on stocks and bonds
Electronic mail	includes regular electronic mail and facilities for sending telexes and telemessages
Telesoftware	facility to 'download' software
Bulletin boards	wide variety of small and large-scale boards offering opportunities to talk, request advice, make contacts, transfer information on special subjects
Telegames	conventional computer games, computer chess, or multi-user role-playing adventure games
News	specialised and generalised up-to-minute information on weather, events, etc.
Databases	on-line search of bibliographies and factual databases
Interpersonal services	chatline, agony aunts, viewdata art galleries, graffiti boards, advertising
Computer networks	conferencing, multi-contributor discussions

innovation. They would thus anticipate the steady diffusion of improved 'brown goods' such as flat screen, teletext, wide screen and high definition TV, digital tape and video tape-recorders, radio data services and radio text, advanced telephones, and the like.

The transformist perspective tends to stress developments around computer systems and new information services. The wide screen TV may be used with appropriate graphics software as 'electronic wallpaper' which could be linked to new types of ambient music based on digital sampling devices and synthesisers. But TV screens will also be used to access computer-communications networks such as viewdata, bulletin boards, multi-player telegames, and text, audio and video libraries. These networks, illustrated in Figure 5.6, will service leisure and entertainment requirements directly, and also support improved access to existing services via telebooking.

From our structuralist perspective we accept that considerable change is likely. But its pace and precise directions are liable to be set by a host of social and cultural factors. It is insufficient to see all developments here as driven by a long-term trend of demand towards more individualised, more sophisticated leisure. Leisure activities are related to cultural traditions (including emphasis on family or other social networks); to work experiences (including the organisation and level of hours of work, as well as skills and exercise of autonomy at the workplace); and of course to the availability and comparative price and quality of various goods and services. One of the most important enabling/constraining factors is the organisation of telecommunications infrastructure, with interactive cable systems presumably promoting more rapid and decentralised innovation.

The new IT-based equipment allows for considerably more local and even self-service production of video, radio, music, and the like. Whether this leads to a revival of participant entertainment or one of community leisure services is an interesting question, and one where national differences may well emerge. In Japan, for

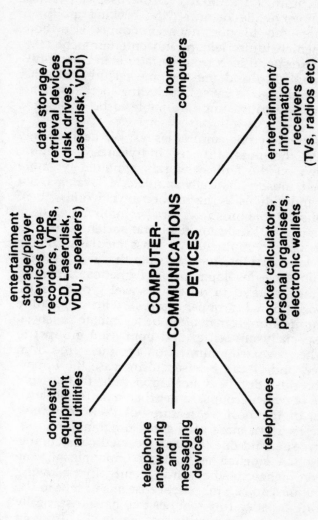

Figure 5.6 **Convergent computer-communications technologies in the home**

Source: Miles, Rush, Bessant and Guy (1986).

example, IT is already used for 'voice-enhancement' (for example recordings are filtered so the user can replace the lead singer while retaining the backing group) in singing-bars – but this does not seem popular elsewhere. The form which future leisure and entertainment takes may well correspond to current variations in community group membership and out-of-home leisure. In either case some traditional services, including, perhaps, some forms of mass broadcasting, are liable to be challenged severely.

This raises numerous cultural issues. We have already touched on the possibility of individuals becoming more fixated on the fantasy worlds provided by more personalised, more realistically simulated IT systems. But as well as individuals living in their own worlds, there are also considerable prospects for IT reinforcing existing cultural divisions. While multicultural societies are rich environments, and multicultural mass media are liable to expand our horizons, it is possible that new systems could support the development of IT ghettos: programming regimes tailored to different social groups (ages, ethnic and regional groups, classes) with very little intercommunication. It may often be legitimate for social groups (especially minorities and oppressed groups) to organise their own communication channels free from interference, and IT can be used to increase the opportunities for this. But it is not impossible that greater divergence between groups, rather than a more collective affirmation of the positive features of their identities, will be the result of more segmented programming.

Another issue, and one that has received considerable airing, is often labelled as 'cultural imperialism'. The proliferation of new media, while in principle allowing a diversity of choice, in practice seems often to be undermining broadcasting regimes that have historically managed to preserve something of national culture in the mass media. Around the world there is concern that an 'Americanisation' of news and entertainment services is now under way, and that there is also likely to be an erosion of audiences for public service broadcasting with the high standards that, at its best, it has achieved. To this debate we can add little that is fresh: it seems to us as structuralists that the problems identified are indeed significant, even if the scale of the threat is sometimes exaggerated.

SMART HOUSES, HOME AUTOMATION AND INTERACTIVE HOME SYSTEMS

We have often referred to the potential role of IT as an agent that can integrate previously discrete activities or pieces of equipment. In earlier chapters we argued that the real significance of IT will not really be felt in industrial applications until these extend beyond 'islands of automation' to whole systems innovations like FMS and CIM. Home informatics has similar features. We can look beyond the discrete innovations discussed above to the development of integrated systems in home informatics. And indeed manufacturers are doing so, under the labels of 'smart house' (in the USA and Japan) and interactive home systems (in Europe).

To the continuist perspective an integration of home informatics, as in the home energy system or in the remote control of domestic appliances, is not foreseen until well into the twenty-first century, if at all. Certainly IT may be applied to consumer goods and different goods may be brought together. But this is better described as aggregation than integration: equipment such as stereo and television are placed into the same housing and perhaps given shared controls; but beyond this few functions are shared. Given the pace of change already witnessed during the early 1980s, the continuist vision may be extended to incorporate the convergence of several different pieces of equipment around IT. In the face of radio alarm clocks, and so on, it is no longer difficult to see the sharing of more controls, output, or methods of data processing where there is already close physical and functional proximity of the previously discrete activities.

The transformist vision will be more ambitious. It is here that we find conceptions of the 'home of the future' that require a leap of imagination much greater than needed in jumping from a phonograph to a 'hi-fi rack' system or a 'music centre'. What is foreseen is a combination of central and distributed 'intelligence' to give truly 'smart houses'. Before 'smart buildings' are commonplace in even leading industrial environments, visionaries are busy imagining their diffusion to ordinary households. Systems such as those proposed for alarm and security or energy management would be distributed from a central point. On the other hand there are reasons for audio and visual entertainment technologies and personal communications to retain the facility to be detached into portable devices.

A structuralist perspective will point to problems in achieving such integrated home systems. Most are linked to patterns of expenditure on household goods and the age of the housing stock in many countries. Unless available in modular form it is only the wealthy who are likely to be in a position to purchase complete systems and to have their homes rewired. The need to introduce systems which can be easily up-graded or extended, as well as the different infrastructural requirements, will result in a staged introduction of systems starting with those mentioned in earlier sections – including home entertainment, home security, and home energy management.

As in the cases of CD-I and HDTV, we come upon a competition between European 'continuism/structuralism' and US/Japanese 'transformism' in respect of strategies for home information. European efforts around interactive home systems are going into developing standards which would allow consumer goods to communicate with each other and with central controls (or not, as the case may be) via a variety of media. In other words the strategy is an incremental one, aimed at giving goods the capacity to integrate or to be stand-alone; and if integrated, to be via whichever is the most appropriate medium (for example mains signalling, optical fibre, radio, infrared, and so on). In contrast the US and Japanese 'smart house' approaches start from fundamentals – whole new methods of house design and wiring of consumer equipment.

Figure 5.7 illustrates the staged approach as we envisage it. A major constraint, mentioned above, is that each of these systems tends to use different means of transmission. High data flows associated with home entertainment and information systems (particularly audio and video) will require cabling or wiring which allows multiple transmission to any part of the house. On the

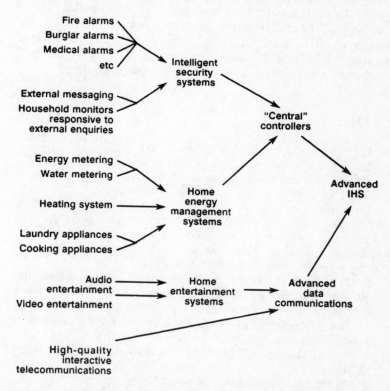

Figure 5.7 **The networking of household functions**

Source: Miles, Rush, Bessant and Guy (1986).

other hand both security and energy systems can be introduced with the electricity networks already in existence: mains signalling will allow for the remote reading of meters and the remote control of a wide range of domestic appliances. In the not too distant future it will probably be as inconceivable to build new homes and public buildings without incorporating some form of low data-intensive systems within small area networks (SANs) using optical fibres, as it would be today to construct buildings without plumbing or electricity.

The next stage of development – systems with the carrying capacity for data-intensive systems – seems likely only to derive sufficient impetus from the availability of high-quality information services from public or private sources. The pace of development will be, to a large extent, dependent upon the speed at which national telecommunications infrastructures are digitalised.

NOTES

1. See Jahoda (1982); Jahoda and Rush (1981).
2. See Bessant *et al.* (1985); Freeman and Soete (1987).
3. For one approach to social innovation, see J. I. Gershuny and Miles (1983).
4. Miles (1988).
5. We could easily elaborate disadvantages alongside the advantages we have cited: easier maintenance means 'non-user repairable' or 'throwaway'; portable means 'intrusive'; programmable means 'fiddly', and so on.
6. For illustrations of both prototype and commercially available equipment, see *IEEE Spectrum*, (May 1987) an issue devoted to hi-tech in the home.
7. See J. Hartley *et al.* (1985) for an illuminating discussion of these points.
8. J. I. Gershuny (1977); and J. I. Gershuny and I. D. Miles (1983).
9. R. Pahl (1984) makes this point forcefully.
10. The city of Houston (and soon London) already has a computer-taxi system in which the dispatcher feeds in the location of the request for travel and the computer indicates

which taxi is closest to the destination and available to pick up the fare. In addition a car rental company in California offers a reception desk computer service which maps out the best route to the travellers' destinations, and several public police and ambulance services already use a form of in-vehicle road map to speed up response to emergency calls.

11. See A. Watson Brown (1987).

6. Acting on IT

Chapter 5 noted the tendency towards a convergence of some aspects of leisure and preventive health care, with the new emphasis on sports, exercise and diet. The transformist perspective, in particular, will take this as a trend which can only be amplified by the application of IT in everyday life.

A similar trend is also apparent in the convergence of certain aspects of educational and entertainment activities. These activities involve supplying information (and information organised as knowledge) to clients. In the case of education and training, such information is usually in large part standardised (for example textbook, lectures, multiple choice tests) and in part individualised for particular clients/students, or somewhat interactive (for example seminars, personal tutorials, feedback on essays). Again the IT-based availability of interactive services, information utilities, mass data storage and expert system software may enhance this convergence. Education and entertainment can be delivered through the same media – TV, VTRs, computers, CD-I. And they may use similar formats and require similar skills in their preparation – teaching programs based on video games, for instance.

In addition new telecommunications systems in principle allow for new forms of social participation. While a more one-to-one situation is possible in education and entertainment, as opposed to mass distribution of standard fare – even if one end of the exchange is an expert system or database rather than a teacher (or textbook or soap opera) – IT also allows telecommunications to move away from its classical one-to-one format. Using electronic mail, computer-conferencing, viewdata and other systems, a variety of formats are possible: one-to-one, many-to-one, and many-to-many telecommunications.

Not surprisingly the potential emergence of new forms of social interaction and participation that build on these possibilities have been widely discussed. A few efforts at establishing community networks have already been made, and there have been many speculations about 'electronic town halls' and 'computer democracy'. In this chapter we discuss the IT-related trends in social participation, education and final demand for services.

These three topics span issues that we have already begun to approach in Chapters 4 and 5 (especially in our discussion of IT innovation in services; and new household activities). They have several features in common: they all involve what are conventionally classified as service activities, they are important areas in respect of human development and social change, and they deal with aspects of the relationship between individuals and the wider society.

SOCIAL PARTICIPATION

As illustrated in Table 6.1, the term 'social participation' covers a wide spectrum of possible activities. As well as conventional political activities such as voting and (more or less active) membership of political parties, it includes:

• membership of voluntary welfare organisations (whose activities may be focused on particular segments of society such as the elderly or physically handicapped, or on particular social problems like child abuse or homelessness)
• membership of groups centred on a wide variety of forms of cultural action, from agit-prop to community entertainment and social clubs (gardening clubs, sporting and theatre groups, and so on)
• working with political groups dedicated to social change (such as local chapters of anti-nuclear or anti-

Table 6.1 **Areas of IT application in social participation**

Outreach	using IT to develop newsletters, videos, etc.; targeting potential audiences; and for delivery of messages (e.g. broadcasts)
Networking	computer-communications within and between groups (email, bulletin boards); access to databases
Internal	collection of membership lists; finance, organisation, etc.
Decision-making	aids to cooperative working; access to expert systems, expertise and technical or historical information
Direct action and publicity	using IT in political activities of various kinds (e.g. new media publicity, counter-surveillance, 'hacking for peace', mobile communications, etc.)
Welfare activities	expert systems for counselling and advice, calculation of benefits, formulation of official or legal documents by citizens' advice groups, etc.

apartheid organisations, women's action against sexual violence) and some groups who might be considered as dedicated to conservation (for example some environmentalists, historical building protection societies, and so on), but who would probably represent themselves as being at heart concerned to change some destructive tendencies in our societies.

In terms of community and political affairs, as in the household, the continuist perspective sees little role for IT, whose main applications are seen as being industrial ones. However some concern is expressed on the issue of privacy and surveillance associated with data banks and new telephone systems. Until recently many 'alternative' political groups (not by any means continuists in many other respects) were averse to using computers for membership lists and the like on the grounds that it would be easy for authorities or political opponents to access their records: since people have gained more familiarity with IT and found that their paper-based records have often been practically public documents, these concerns have diminished. Another reason for rejecting microcomputers by such groups – that they were 'masculine' technologies or would entail the creation of technical élites within groups – has also faded as experience with home computers has diffused.

It has been suggested too that some familiar media may be rejuvenated through IT. Desktop publishing and new print technology make possible local or group newsletters and papers; cheap camcorders have brought with them home-made videos; low-powered broadcasting enables local TV and radio to develop, and so on. The transformist perspective suggests that political (and cultural) activity will flourish, using such IT means of getting messages across. Our structuralism leads us to be cautious: we note that broadcasting freedom has only exceptionally resulted in community radio rather than muzak, and that the new papers (at least in the UK) are in general of low quality and feature limited local content.

Both the transformist and structuralist perspectives anticipate that many interest groups (social or political) will be liable to employ new media of all kinds (computer-communications as well as printed texts and videos), both for internal communications and for reaching new audiences for their messages. In this they would be simply following the lead of business organisations – and often drawing upon skills developed in business or public service applications. There are tendencies resisting new technologies among such social movements: as noted, IT is still seen in some quarters as liable to increase the role of experts and decrease the importance of grass roots mobilisation, and this concern is not entirely misplaced; there are significant dilemmas in determining whether, for example, to 'tailor' one's messages to specific groups or to concentrate outreach efforts only in those areas where the response is likely to be most positive. But, contrary to their presentation in cartoons in the popular press, activists are often technologically literate. Thus the rejuvenated peace movement of the early 1980s was able to make considerable use of the first generation of home computers in organising membership lists, producing leaflets and newsletters and communicating news rapidly; and Citizens' Band radio to coordinate demonstrations and chases after Cruise missile convoys; viewdata to announce forthcoming events and promote appeals; videos to explain the case for specific activities like non-violent direct action, and so on.

The structuralist perspective may anticipate considerable experimentation with viewdata and similar information services for local communities, but tends to see the main users of IT for community purposes, in the foreseeable future, being active members of political parties and social movements. An example of this is the Geonet computer-communications network, used internationally by 'green' and Labour movement groups for electronic mail and information exchange. This system used an online bulletin board as a means of rapid collation and distribution of information on the Chernobyl disaster, and at least one international magazine has its contributors around the world send their texts electronically. Technically these activities are not surprising, since commercial and scientific organisations have now been using them for years; our point is simply that the application of IT in these ways *is* taking place, despite scepticism from many sympathisers and opponents of such groups.

The transformist perspective, of course, looks far beyond this. Numerous authors have outlined what they see as the scope of these new media for creating a more participatory society, in some visions with regular referenda and consultation exercises being employed, especially at local levels. At the very least IT will be used, in these accounts, for more interactive articulation of political concerns, more rapid formation of interest groups, and greater attention from governments to popular pressures. But it is also likely to be applied to creating new systems of democratic participation: new ways of sampling opinions and obtaining votes, new occasions for public consultation, new modes of access from citizens to their representatives.

In the institutions of local government we are already witnessing a move towards the provision of electronic community bulletin boards; these may include council minutes, notices of local activities, and so on. Access to one's local representatives in some parts of the United States is now being made available in this way (where it is possible to email one's congressperson or senator). The transformist perspective proposes that the same technology could be extended to increase public participation in local and even national government by collecting ideas, canvassing opinions and gathering priority ratings of goals and objectives from the population at large or from specifically affected groups (for example local residents of a major technological installation). This might be seen as promoting a form of 'flexible politics' (drawing on the model of flexible manufacturing systems). Citizen participation would be encouraged at an early stage of the policy-making process, and the role of government would become more that of allowing social interests to be articulated, and of resolving the inevitable conflicts, rather than the conventional mixture of bureaucracy and élitist decision-making. Ideally such systems would not only allow for electronic referenda (through home computer-communications systems) on major issues but also participation in the setting of priorities, decision-making criteria, and even the division of responsibilities from the outset of the policy-making cycle.

The continuist viewpoint sees such speculations as

utopian dreaming, while from the transformist perspective they indicate the nearly inevitable culmination of
changes that are already afoot. Our structuralist viewpoint
would lead us to agree that there are considerable
potentials here, but that they are likely to be realised
only to the extent that popular movements press for
them.

More sceptical commentators, in line with these structuralist perspectives, wonder whether new modes of
political participation might not be manipulated (by
careful phrasing of referenda questions and managing
of discussions, for example). Would they support participatory democracy, or something more akin to either
populism or corporatism? (After all, the new mass media-
style political leaders in the USA in particular do not
bode well for the link between the mass communications
technology and mass politics.)

Another line of scepticism would be to ask whether,
within current systems of representative democracy, new
modes of participation would not contribute to the
supposed 'overloading of democracy'. Here it is suggested
that political leaders are finding that their ability to make
far-sighted and effective decisions is impaired by having
to deal with a press of trivial issues: entrenched interest
groups who exploit the democratic institutions to make
their case heard and whip up media sympathy; gullible
bleeding-heart liberals; dangerous currents of xenophobia
that underlie the national psyche; litigatious professionals; political opponents. (Electronic referenda, if
binding, could lead to the return of capital punishment
in many countries, and the use of nuclear weapons in
conflicts.)

Certainly IT can dramatically increase access to all
sorts of public information; some commentators see
information overload as a major challenge for national
political systems. We would be inclined to view much
recent talk of the 'overloading of democracy' as a
combination of (a) economic crisis making it harder
to reconcile diverse interests and (b) organisational
difficulties in coping with new political demands and

movements.[1] But we would accept that IT can increase the pressure of information, from mass mailings, exposure to large volumes of documentation (especially where technical issues are raised, as in nuclear power politics) and what we might term 'automated lobbying'.

A more immediate concern for some commentators has been the use of IT by highly organised pressure groups – such as the so-called 'moral majority' religious fundamentalists – for more systematic, selective and effective fund-raising and information dissemination (for example tailoring attacks on local candidates who do not support the objectives of the organisation, and the known attitudes and prejudices of readers and viewers). While these techniques were intially viewed with some abhorrence by political opponents, similar techniques are already being adopted by many mainstream political parties and their supporters – and even by less conservative pressure groups where they have been able to raise sufficient financial resources and/or technical expertise.

One area where IT is often supposed to reduce difficulties in political communication is the development of machine translation. This is widely heralded as a means of reducing problems associated with language barriers. However the broader implications of advanced machine translation capabilities are rather mixed.[2] In multinational societies it is possible that individual groups, despite gaining more access to national culture, would become more insular. The result would be less effort put into mastering other languages and engaging in less informal contact with members of other groups. At the same time intercultural information flows should increase, but it is still likely that native speakers of those languages which it is initially most economic to translate will be advantaged relatively to others. In the longer term, with machine translation applied to expert systems and other tradeable information services, fears about cultural imperialism could find a new focus.

An issue already raised (Chapters 4, 5) concerning formal employment and household activities – the problems that would be likely to follow upon a growth in dualism in society in general, and the differential access to information systems and skills that this would imply – will be particularly important to the future development of social and political participation. While optimistic transformist views have it that the cheapening and increased power of IT will mean more open government (and corporations) and widely-based social mobilisation, if past experience is any guide the benefits of IT are unlikely to be conveyed evenly across regions or across social groups. (Even now telephones are unevenly distributed and are too expensive for poorer people to afford.) To the extent that the broader areas of cultural and political life are mediated through IT, then new forms of disadvantage may accrue, perhaps to the already disadvantaged.

It may be recalled that an innovation that provided greater physical mobility – the private motor car – has led to a worsening of public transport facilities for non-drivers in many areas. Could IT, while creating greater information mobility, have similar tendencies? This may seem unrealistic – after all, IT infrastructure will not mean lead and carbon monoxide pollution, and it will not require a driving licence to gain access to it. But it is not hard to think of new inequalities that could appear. For example, some traditional media may deteriorate (newspapers and even public service TV may be drastically reduced) and it may become harder or dearer to shop for those left reliant on paper money. There are bound to be some gains and losses associated with IT, as we shall argue at greater length in Chapter 7. This does not mean complacency or impotence however: it means that we should look for ways of countering inequalities. Training and computer literacy schemes, community resource centres, and broadly-based systems design are among the means that are most often suggested as ways of avoiding further dualism.

The development of social dualism is in part a function of trends in the formal economy – partly a matter of using IT in ways that polarise the workforce and displace large groups of labour, for example; but also a matter of other managerial strategies as to industrial organisation and location. In part too it is a function of wider developments in the political economy such as regional, welfare and income (re)distribution policies. Applications of IT alone, or even efforts to 'fine-tune' the technologies and broaden social access to them, are bound to be only a small part of the total efforts that are necessary. But this does not render these approaches irrelevant.

Furthermore we should not neglect the possibility of IT being used to offset some inequalities, for example those based on physical disabilities.[3] IT systems that have been developed for specific groups include:

• for hearing-impaired people, means of using telephone-type communications (for example phones with screens, with amplifiers, with links to email services), subtitles (as teletext services) for TV programmes
• for vision-impaired people, aids in reading texts (for example systems that can read printed material out loud), and aids to navigation such as 'sonar'-like detection of objects around a walking person
• for those with motor disorders and paralysis more sensitively controlled wheelchairs and prosthetic devices.

Such applications have been the focus of considerable attention, in part because they are worthy and sometimes inspiring, but also perhaps because they help offset the negative image that, say, military and labour-displacing innovations lend to IT as a whole. Do they provide pointers to the use of IT in empowering the socially disadvantaged more generally? They certainly do in the sense of dramatically illustrating the malleability of IT, its application to the most diverse ends. It would be interesting indeed to see if an effort to bring the technology to address the problems of political and informational empowerment could achieve such dramatic results.

EDUCATION

The degree to which social participation incorporates IT (or is indeed promoted by it) will depend in considerable part on the educational and training infrastructure. Education is important in familiarising people with new technologies – and not just as private consumers. By providing an understanding of how systems work it can help people identify new applications and be critical (in an informed rather than destructive way) of the limitations of established ones. Subjects like media studies can also help students gain more awareness of the social construction of cultural and technological products, and of how and why they achieve particular effects.

The history of computers in schools, as in many other public services, goes back to the early 1960s when mainframe computers were brought in to help with educational administration (for applications such as student records and financial control). On the 'core' teaching side, however, computer-assisted learning has had a chequered past. Immature technology was heavily promoted by advocates of 'programmed instruction'; and as a consequence computers became associated with rigid and tedious multiple-choice questions presented on ugly screens or in teletype print. Students were isolated from teachers and from each other, and the equipment was relatively expensive. Much of the use of computers in education has followed what is known as the 'bucket' approach to learning – with students as the receptacles and the computer replacing the teacher as the tap.[4] A major factor in this has undoubtedly been the tendency for the design and development of software to be undertaken by computer professionals, with little or no participation by educationalists.

Fortunately the increasing capabilities of computers, particularly their improved graphics and larger data storage capabilities, together with increasing computer literacy among professionals, have begun to change this situation. Software has been developed, for example, based upon student-centred philosophies of education which recognise that human learning processes are not the same as formal problem-solving methodologies (although a large proportion of educational software, it must be admitted, is still of mediocre quality.) For example, simulations are now available which enable students to play an interactive role in situations which would otherwise require considerable exercise of imagination and discipline – such as operating a nuclear power station, acting as Finance Minister in a government, or making economic and social decisions as a French gentleman living in the reign of Louis XIV.[5] These simulations are sometimes criticised as reducing students' acquisition of imagination and discipline, but we are far from convinced that this is actually the case.

Even more ambitious systems are under development. 'Hypertext' presents knowledge in the form of a web of interlinked topics (as opposed to the serial representation in books and most other media). Each student is able to explore a subject by following whichever links he or she chooses. A student using a hypertext on English literature could choose to study a Shakespeare play, following very flexible links so as to move at will between the text of the play, a glossary, historical and biographical details, and the views of critics.[6] Perhaps audiovisual access to excerpts of different theatrical interpretations of the drama, elaborations of it in other media (opera, film), and outlines of critical debates could also be available.

In higher education the spread of television, together with a desire to provide wider access to 'élite' knowledge, led to the successful establishment of the Open University in the UK in the 1960s. Many countries now feature similar institutions. In the United States IT is being used as a medium for extension of this approach to form the 'electronic university'.[7] Course materials are supplied by mail, but assignments are delivered and submitted over the telecommunications network, which also provides an electronic mail facility for communication between students and staff. Teleconferencing allows students to form small study groups, or to participate in a seminar discussion with an academic tutor. The British Open University is well along the route to offering a computer-communications mediated course itself as we write. (Not surprisingly the topic of the course is IT.)

With the reduction in computing costs and the increase

in concern (computer literacy being seen as a necessary
condition for economic competitiveness), governments
in many advanced industrial nations began support
programmes for the diffusion of microcomputers in
schools. The publicity given to these schemes by governments and manufacturers has led many parents to fear
that their children will be left behind in the race for a
'good' job (or indeed any job), and to splash out on a
home computer.

The school system has not had an easy time in adapting
to the emergence of IT. On the one hand many of its
pupils were familiar with microcomputers at home, even
if only as games machines; and on the other hand the
hyperbole about 'missing out on the IT revolution' that
was fuelling the rapid uptake of home computers could
not but have an impact on teachers. The idea of 'computer
literacy' had gained currency in the early 1980s but
was subjected to various interpretations. Views roughly
ranged along the continuum from 'knowing how computers work' (from integrated circuits through to the
fundamentals of programming) to 'knowing what computers are used for' (from being able to use simple
programs to studying applications in business environments). To some extent the confusion reflected teachers'
own unfamiliarity with IT – some of the training for
teachers themselves left a great deal to be desired – and,
in part, a real uncertainty about what skills were going
to be in demand in the information age.

One of the most interesting developments in this area,
which we include as an example of how educational
philosophies might be influenced by IT in the future,
has been the use of LOGO as more than just a
programming language suitable for very young children
to learn (but still sophisticated enough to keep many
adults happy).[8] Here the task of education is seen as the
promotion of (among other things) cognitive development; and cognitive structures are developed through
our interaction with the phenomena we are seeking to
understand. While LOGO can be used for text processing
or musical composition, the most innovative use has

been to encourage children to use the language to guide 'turtles'.

'Turtles' can be of two kinds. They can be simple wheeled robots, whose speed, distance and direction of movement can be controlled by commands from a computer. Or they can be 'turtle graphics', drawn on a VDU screen as if the turtle has been leaving a track behind it. Either way they allow the cognitive structures of the program to be tested interactively in an appealing and striking fashion – the child can see directly what shapes have been created as a result of a set of instructions. Has the pattern been drawn as expected? Has the turtle been navigated out of the maze?

LOGO allows children to develop understanding of problem-solving methods and the fundamentals of programming, and can be applied to teach formal mathematics, geometrical and other skills (although the principal application to date has been in simple testing). The core insight is that interaction with media that may include standard textual and cognitive material but may go beyond this to draw on physical movement, simulation, video imagery, and so on, is a powerful educational tool. (Thus turtle graphics reflect Piagetian child psychology's recognition that abstract understanding is generally built upon an earlier acquisition of principles through more concrete experience.) This insight underlies many other applications of IT in educational settings (Table 6.2).

Concurrent with cost reductions in hardware there has also been a shift in educational philosophy towards more interactive and self-paced learning. Hardware and software are being developed to meet the needs of an expanding market, both within the formal education setting and for home learning or 'distant' learning. With the use of viewdata and telesoftware, networking of students and tutors, interactive video, and so on, a transformist might see the world of the correspondence course student (or the hobbyist) as being turned from the poor relation of education into the vanguard of a new educational era in which the computer is becoming a surrogate teacher and more. Their line of thought further

Table 6.2 **Some applications of IT in education**

Example	Notes
Microcomputer	used as host and control for most other applications. Medium for gaining language and arithmetic skills (word processing, spelling and number games); basis for computer literacy, teaching programming skills
Interactive videodisc	medium for storing and displaying text, graphics, sound and video information. Beyond substituting for film and slides, enables greater realism in simulations; can be used as multi-media hypertext
Simulations	makes it possible to 'experiment' with otherwise inaccessible historical, geological, biological, clerical, physical, technological, etc. systems
Hypertext	allows self-directed exploration of material that may be text only or multi-media
Robotics (turtles etc)	used to illustrate practical applications of programming and systems thinking; believed that transliteration of program instructions into real world aids learning by adding perceptual dimension to cognition
Networking	allows access to remote sources of information, collaborative preparation of materials, tutorials to be extended over time

speculates on the application of artificial intelligence to education, enabling development of sophisticated IT teaching tools for simulation, tutorial programmes, dialogue and expert teaching systems.[9] The electronic university would form the basis for the replacement of formal educational institutions by 'learning webs', through which anyone could participate in courses as either student or tutor.[10] Eventually these webs would extend to span all types of education, not just that of adolescents and adults.

Not surprisingly many commentators adopt what we would call a continuist viewpoint here. They doubt that many children can be motivated to learn outside the traditional classroom, and point to the role of schooling as a system of discipline (if not just as a massive child care institution). Resistance from members of the education profession is seen as inevitable, at least until more teachers are themselves computer literate. Furthermore, even in countries with active programs for computers in schools, there will often be only one micro for each one or two hundred students, with limited funds available for software. (The much-vaunted success of these initiatives has, perhaps rightly, been compared to that of a program to encourage cookery education which installed one oven per school and provided a year's supply of potatoes.) In terms of quality of education the continuist perspective would echo teachers' doubts about the extent to which the human contact between teacher and pupil (and among pupils) should be mediated through a computer.

As structuralists (and educators) we sympathise with some of the points made in the continuist critique of IT in education, although we consider educational institutions to be more heterogeneous and open to change than suggested in the preceding paragraph. In some schools, for example, the ratio of students to microcomputers is already approaching respectable proportions. Yet this suggests an additional educational problem may be developing due to the unequal access to IT in society. The more computer-intensive schools are generally those able to raise additional funding from private sources. Children from higher-income backgrounds already tend to do better in terms of educational achievement. The extent to which they receive parental stimulation and help (or extra paid tuition), and the number of books they have at their disposal, already makes a marked difference in terms of grades or advancement into higher education. When we consider the application of IT to education (such as CD-I based encyclopaedias, teaching aids, dictionaries, maps, special software to assist with the revision of typical courses) potential for unequal access to these technologies at home will result in even greater inequality in school performance.

Nevertheless an increase in IT applications in the other areas of social activity discussed in previous chapters is likely to fuel demand – not only for applications in schools but also in continuing and vocational education. As working patterns shift (or unemployment increases) the market demand for software will also accelerate, with concern over the quality of the product added to that of availability and access. And while increased choice in the delivery mechanism for education will be welcomed by structuralists there will be concern over the confusion of the content with the package. It has already been noted by some commentators that although IT has been applied to school catering for menu development and nutrition planning, the taste has yet to improve.

FINAL DEMAND

In this chapter, and the preceding one, we have argued that home work, leisure, entertainment, communications, education and social participation – huge components of everyday life – are all likely to be considerably altered over the next few decades. So far in this chapter we have been focusing on the implications of this for social participation and education. Now let us turn to another aspect of the relation between individuals (and households) and wider society: patterns of final demand for goods and services; or rather the balance between domestic production and consumption and the purchase of services from the formal economy.

As a result of improvements in the quality of consumer goods, and the range of activities which they catered for, the value of household 'capital equipment' is liable to increase substantially in the medium to long term. This is liable to lead to changes in the location of production and consumption. Just as current domestic equipment has been associated with shifts into the home of some production (for example washing clothes in washing machines rather than laundries) and some consumption (for example gaining entertainment via TVs rather than cinemas), so new consumer goods may be associated with further shifts. In some cases this may result in the replacement of a previously bought-in service with home production; just as the washing machine has previously taken its toll on the hand laundry. The discussion above about educational technology, for example, raises the possibility that more education will be carried out in homes rather than schools.

For the continuist perspective such changes are liable to be slow ones, in which substitution involves relatively little change for the client-consumer: examples might be electronic mail replacing overland post or electronic newspapers substituting for the paper and ink variety (once cheap, good quality printers and efficient user-friendly delivery systems are available). For the transformist perspective change will capitalise on the opportunities of advanced IT: for example the medical expert system and online link to the doctor's office would be seen as increasingly replacing visits to the GP except in real emergencies.

The extent to which individuals participate in various activities is also likely to change. TV, and now video tape-recorders and cable TV have already led to significant increases in the amount of time spent in 'consuming' the performing arts and viewing sports at home as compared to visits to the cinema, the theatre and the stadium. But this sort of cultural consumption has grown in absolute terms; as time spent at formal work has decreased so 'passive leisure' has increased. However a range of action leisure pursuits has also become more popular, and within domestic work some routine activities have declined (partly in consequence of more productive domestic technology).[11]

As well as entertainment, news and mail, new information services could be important in supplying information more widely, but this is currently of restricted circulation owing to the cost or difficulty of making it personally relevant. Access to various information services may well mean, for example, that a wide range of counselling and advisory services, many of which are currently available to only a small segment of the population, will become more widespread – and available at home rather than in 'front offices'. For example, most countries have been actively computerising their employment services, either through 'job banks' which attempt to match job seekers with employment opportunities, or vacancy circulation systems. The next step for many countries is the movement of terminals from the offices providing services to the unemployed to various public places including libraries and supermarkets. The transformist perspective would relate this to viewdata systems like Teletel; as they become increasingly popular such information could just as easily be piped into the home. The structuralist perspective would place more emphasis on the time scale necessary for such services to be brought within the financial reach of the supposed client populations (for example unemployed people), and on the political will of governments to subsidise the costs needed for rapid take-off (although, as noted above, the French government has done that with the distribution of free Minitel terminals).

So far we have tended to stress developments in consumer goods, and thus in the activities which they are, or may be, used for. Change in these activities may adversely affect the final consumer services that conventionally support them – 'self-services' like private transport undermining public services like buses; 'electronic services' like TV undermining traditional services like theatres. But, as noted in Chapter 4, the application of IT will affect the production and nature of final services too, just as it is busily reshaping household products.

In goods production computer-integrated manufacturing has brought a shift from manufacturers' preoccupation with economies of scale towards more concern with economies of scope, and away from 'just-in-case' planning to 'just-in-time' systems. (Of course we should not exaggerate the extent to which this change has worked through: but we have identified it as a substantial part of the new technological trajectories and organisational paradigms in manufacturing.) By the same token providers of final services will be able to move towards more flexible provision of their activities through use of IT. The potential for decreasing standardisation – restoring an element of personal service to clients – while at the same time holding or even reducing costs, could result in a return from some self-service activities back into the formal sector. In addition to cost-reduction, 'customisation' and increased flexibility, IT-related innovations can improve the provision of final services through better scheduling, simplified equipment maintenance, and even customer design facilities (Table 6.3).

For the continuist school the likely pattern of use of IT in services is probably exemplified by the rationalisation of the administrative functions of existing services (especially 'back office' functions). Little more than this is expected. In effect the strategy is one of doing what is already done more efficiently, and of being thus able to respond to increases in demand on the services – welfare of the elderly, health care, the maintenance of public buildings, or law and order – without dramatic resourcing implications. In private service provision concern over systems costs may be less – or be expressed in different ways – but there are still constraints upon information. These include in particular fears about security, reliability, and liability in the case of theft or fraud.

The transformist perspective would stress benefits such as those listed in Table 6.3. These are seen as providing stimulus enough for a shift from the current emphasis

Table 6.3 **IT-related innovations in final services**

Cost-reduction	the automation of manual activities in final services (e.g. bank tellers, ticket sale and collection, provision of timetable information etc.), electronic funds transfer reduced the need for (and costs of) processing cash
Quality improvement	use of database management systems, routing and scheduling systems, queue management to reduce delays, save costs and make more efficient use of time. Use of expert systems-type decision aids to allow wider access to professional skills and knowledge. Better displays (more information, more attractive, more interactive)
Customer design	computer-aided design can be used so as to increase customer/client design choice and enhance the decision-making process in public and private services
Client-centred	transport services can be adjusted to meet customer requirements, with more flexible routing and timing, provision of goods in shops can be based on individual demand; appointments can be made and adjusted so as to minimise delays and maximise convenience
Self-service	involving the customer or client in some work previously carried out

	by service workers (usually in dialogue with customer); this has proved popular in many circumstances due to opportunities to exercise choice at one's own pace
Ease of maintenance	repair is a service, and the reliability of IT equipment is an important component of its success in final services; the development of modular and auto-diagnostics will lead to equipment requiring less maintenance than electro-mechanical devices
One-stop shopping	services at home as teleservices; multiple services in one service outlet (e.g. online financial services in bank front offices)· communications available in previously isolated locations (trains, planes, waiting rooms)

on rationalisation to considerably more augmentation and the creation of new services.[12] While many new business services have appeared recently (for example online databases, remote monitoring of buildings, trade data interchange), it must be conceded that new consumer services like telebanking and teleshopping have been generally slow to take off, at least in the more advanced versions (using home computers rather than push-button telephones, for example). Technological enthusiasts (transformists, as we have labelled them) are undaunted. They argue that it is only a matter of time for new services to become acceptable. And the services will be

boosted by the development of an advanced telecommunications infrastructure, which will reduce costs
further and allow for more rapid interaction with high
quality video displays.

As structuralists we see also the potential of technological advances in final services. Indeed the application of
IT to enhancing services, or to meeting existing needs
in new ways, is of particular significance. In many
respects the final service sector could be in a position to
lead innovation rather than follow changes occurring in
industry. The difficulties that are faced by services partly
reflect the pace of technological development. While it
is rapid, in some respects expectations can outrun
practicalities. People used to high quality graphics on
TV and home computers are often dissatisfied with the
standard of viewdata graphics. Teleshopping will not
match their aspirations until you can receive pictures of
the items on sale that are so clear that you do not need
to touch them. (And receiving these pictures needs to be
as easy and fast as flicking through a catalogue or running
one's eyes up and down a supermarket shelf.) To meet
such requirements, higher telecommunications band-
width (permitting rapid delivery of high quality images
and even video) and better software (more user-friendly
ways of retrieving and communicating data) are important. Our disagreement with the transformist approach
here is more about the likely pace at which services of
this sort will be available than the importance of such
innovations. Where transformism tends to see emergent
enabling factors, we tend to share a continuist focus on
existent constraints at this point.

But we also share other concerns of the continuist
approach here. In part innovation in services is not just
a matter of technology, it reflects the problems of
changing social attitudes away from the traditional
relationships that exist between the public and those
offering or selling services. And it reflects those associated
with achieving agreements on common standards and
comprehensive tariff structures between the major institutions involved in service provision. There is usually a
learning period required before service providers move

from rationalising their current activities to augmenting them and creating new services. In the case of services, this learning process often demands participation – from users and regulators as well as providers.

Arguably those service innovations concerned primarily with the rationalisation of existing services have greater implications for those providing the service than those receiving it. One important issue is employment: new demand and new jobs are more likely to be created around the provision of new services than around the supply of more of the same (unless it can be massively cheapened and/or improved). But the structuralist perspective would indicate other issues of concern. For example, the issue of access to services arises again, and there is more general concern over who controls the service, what interests it serves (for example does it bolster or undermine expertise, patriarchal attitudes, and so on), the degree of human contact it provides, privacy, and the range of choice available.

We began this section by recalling trends in innovation in domestic equipment, and have gone on to reappraise innovation in final service production. What of the relations between them? The following points should be considered together:

(a)   over past decades innovation in domestic equipment has led to self-service and new supporting services (through new media) displacing a number of traditional consumer services to a considerable extent

(b)   as we have seen, considerable application of IT to household goods is possible, enabling these goods to intercommunicate within and outside the house to an increasing extent

(c)   while in the past innovation in many consumer services has been limited by the inappropriateness of mechanical and electronic technologies to their core activities, IT is applicable to practically all services.

This makes for an indeterminant image of the future. On the one hand goods, services catering for these goods, and associated lifestyle practices are challenging and will

continue to challenge consumer services. As domestic
work, transport and entertainment services have been
challenged in the past, so may education, health and
'law and order' (security services) in the future. On the
other hand services can respond to the challenge by
using IT themselves to reduce costs and increase their
quality. How far these two forces balance out will be
affected by several factors – the inventiveness of consumer
goods; manufacturers (where competition is international); the development of telecommunications systems so as to support different types of new services; the
degree to which service sector innovation is recognised as
an important policy issue; and the extent to which public
services play a constructive role in establishing new ways
of providing services, facilitating social learning about
IT and helping to set standards, and so on.

But this mention of public services directs our attention
to another issue raised in this context. For it will be
apparent from the discussion that new consumer goods
(and associated new audio-visual and software services)
provide a challenge not only to consumer services as
usually understood, but also to public services. As we
have noted in several instances, some of the key
applications of domestic IT are aimed at consumer activity
connected with education and health, areas traditionally
catered for by the public services. Indeed it seems that
there may be something of a convergence of education,
sport, games, lifestyle and nutritional activities in part
fostered by IT developments, in part by increased leisure
time and awareness of health and welfare aspects of
exercise and eating patterns.

Where 'welfare' and public service activities of various
kinds are involved the continuist perspective tends to
project steady process innovation with the formal services.
In contrast it depicts at best a rather slow and sporadic
uptake of new IT in home-based educational and medical
services and systems.

The transformist viewpoint, on the other hand, would
anticipate rapid process and product innovation, both
pushed by technology and pulled by demand. This

perspective would, for example, stress the potential of teleservices to improve the quality of many parts of the educational and medical systems. Clearly some aspects of these activities require close personal contact, but whether or not these are residual features of the service will vary across types of activity. Medical operations are not deliverable as teleservices, but other personal elements (drug prescriptions, health counselling, care of the elderly or children) might be handled by a mixture of technological innovations and community-based services. The continuist perspective is not unreasonably sceptical of the public and professional acceptability of such developments. For example, will teachers, doctors and other experts be prepared to relinquish some of their existing power and expertise to automated systems? Will clients in the public at large be willing to sacrifice their existing personal contacts with experts? Where will the paramedical and paralegal workers come from and how will they be trained? Is it ethical to sell medical records kept on computers to private companies for analysis? Such problems are bound to mean that change will be slow, requiring an extensive learning period.

As structuralists we would tend to agree with the reservations of continuism. But the requisite changes are dependent on the policy decisions and strategies adopted by public service authorities, private competitors, sub-contractors and new entrants, and telecommunications systems providers. In some areas change may thus be more readily forthcoming than in others. Quite clearly major issues of public policy are raised, and some of the actors involved are generally regarded as being rather slow to undertake radical innovations.

Nevertheless ongoing social changes (such as the ageing of western populations) and issues raised by the application of IT itself (for example growing requirements for training and retraining) may provide powerful incentives for experimentation along these lines (an issue we return to in Chapter 7). Furthermore the current political orthodoxy has it that the state's presence in many welfare activities should be reduced to one of standard-setting, while the work should be a matter of private enterprise or community care. Transformism might view this as providing an opportunity for the 'informal economy' to flower. But we see, also as a substantial risk of replacing one form of alienation – bureaucratic and only partly egalitarian welfare services – with an even more dualistic one: high quality combinations of private and self-service in privileged communities; low quality poorly paid 'community' services in underprivileged communities.[13]

In some respects a little healthy competition can be a good catalyst for change, in bureaucratised public services as elsewhere. Innovative ideas for training and health care may well emerge from entrepreneurs (and voluntary groups) experimenting with CD-I, online services, and the like. Innovations in care of the elderly and educating children may similarly be catalysed around technologies like expert systems, home computing, and 'smart houses'.

But such innovations may also threaten public services and lead to new inequalities in social welfare. They might benefit the well-off (and healthy) and leave the poor (and unwell) with second rate, underfunded services. They may reinforce perceptions of public services as inadequate, poor value for money and offering little job satisfaction – which would lead to vicious cycle problems in their obtaining adequate public financing and being able to recruit capable staff. They may allow uses of new IT services to exploit public services unequally – getting more for their children and themselves from education and health services, by coming to them better prepared.

If our argument above is correct, then IT poses a challenge to public services equivalent to that which electronic and cheap motor power posed to conventional consumer services. And this challenge comes at a time when neoconservative politicians are busily redrawing the boundaries of public and private service under imperatives that are more ideological and self-interested than anything else. However with this challenge comes opportunity: IT can be used by the public services (and by voluntary and community associations) to improve service quality and create new services – if they are to flourish in the future – to seize opportunities. This will not be easy, given financial constraints and both electoral and organisational politics. But it will be a key part of the struggle which is necessary, if IT is not to reinforce tendencies towards greater social dualism.

NOTES

1. Miles (1985).
2. Gurstein (1985).
3. See Johansen *et al.* (1981).
4. O'Shea and Self (1983).
5. The Louis XIV simulation is 'The would-be gentleman', written by Carolyn Lougee at Stanford University.
6. The Shakespeare example of hypertext is based on research at Brown University. See 'The difference in higher education', *Byte* (February 1987).
7. Meeks (1987).
8. Championed by S. Papert (1980).
9. O'Shea and Self (1983).
10. Illich (1971).
11. Gershuny *et al.* (1986).
12. In terms of Richard Barrs's analysis (1986), this would mean a more rapid passage through the 'reverse product cycle'.
13. Miles (1985).

7. Back to the Present

In the visions of the future depicted in the previous chapters, information technologies can be seen to be coming to perform roles of great significance in social life – be it in the home, the community, or the workplace. This is something the three perspectives we have delineated agree upon, even while they have many points of conflict. This corresponds to the conclusions we reached in a different type of study, in which we contrasted the views of experts as elicited in an opinion survey. We distinguished a number of different sets of expectations, and noted that 'although the speed and direction of change differs between these groups, even the most conservative of these scenarios provides a vision of the future which implies immense social change.'[1]

In attempting to outline the key features of the three perspectives, and the forecasts that are associated with them, we have placed considerable stress on the role of IT, and have not set out to provide a more 'holistic' view based on an analysis of social change more generally. In doing so it may seem that we have veered towards technological determinism, and we cannot and would not wish to deny that technological development will continue to be a substantial factor in the making of the future. Nevertheless we are not seeking to argue that technology is itself the main force of change. Technology is a product of human action upon the world, and is inextricably part of the web of social interests within which we individual humans and the social groups we belong to are formed.

We believe that it is important to address the features of IT, for these features are sufficiently novel, and the achievements that have been made in this area are so great, that substantial new opportunities for social action are being created. This is less a matter of the 'effects' of technology than of the interplay of human actions, some of which, by changing technological possibilities, affect the scope of future actions. (In the same way great cultural products may change the scope for future actions – we have inspiring leaders, metaphors, and works of art to orient us.)

TECHNOLOGICAL DETERMINISM AND TECHNOLOGICAL FORECASTING

We trust it has been clearly demonstrated that no matter how unique the powers of IT may appear to be, or how malleable the forms that it may be given, this technology is grounded in the properties of the natural world – it is not magic. However amazing IT applications like expert systems, robots and satellite communications may be, these are still far from being the products of unfettered human volition. Our technologies still have to accord with the properties of the natural world, and they build upon principles and practices established through generations of human labour. Indeed most major applications now are only achieved after many person-years of effort devoted to them.

Nevertheless IT applications are designed by human beings motivated by a variety of social interests and pressures. The course of technological evolution is neither arbitrary nor autonomous. It is shaped by social and economic dynamics. The way particular technologies are used and the reaction to these uses are the product of human capabilities and choice.

This process is an extremely complex one, and the way in which technology and other social products and processes are interrelated and interact remains in many respects poorly understood. (Consider the debates about the 'effects' of TV, or about the real interests behind the course of nuclear weapons development.) In spite of, or perhaps because of, the enormous resources devoted to such high profile programmes as the Fifth Generation Computing Programme or the Strategic Defense Initiative (both efforts to make high technology an element of national strategy), the relationship between technology and society is most frequently and implicitly described in formulations of questions such as, 'how can society adjust to these new technologies'; 'what uses will be found for these technological capabilities'; or 'what demand will there be (or what demand can we create) for these potential uses'.

Each of our three schools of thought proposes distinctive conclusions as to the social implications of information technologies: indeed within each perspective there is considerable debate about most topics. This diversity, or cacophony, leads some commentators to throw up their hands in horror. All they can conclude is that the implications of IT could be *either* centralising *or* decentralising; *either* de-skilling *or* upgrading; *either* enhancing *or* threatening democracy, and so on. Table 7.1 summarises the main features of the three schools as discussed in the preceding chapters. Although we have favoured the structuralist viewpoint, we acknowledge that all three bodies of analysis have something to offer. (By the same token all three are open to criticism.) The world stubbornly refuses to sleep in the conceptual boxes we build for it.

For example, too few commentators take into consideration that social life is a complex web of action, reaction and counteraction. Feedback loops may be positive or negative, so that while some activities find resonance through society the echoes of others die quickly, or are smothered. Some innovations help turn the social tide, some only surface as brief fads, and others sink without a trace or stay submerged in the mind of an inventor. Many technological innovations require changes in practice or organisation if new products or processes are to diffuse. These changes may be required to facilitate effective implementation so as to maximise benefits; or to limit opposition by reducing costs. Often both types of change are largely neglected even by informed analysts. Neglect of the first type results in a perception of IT as a mere substitution for previous activities or functions. This in turn leads to failure to observe the implications of system change, the sort of transformation of organisational functioning that is associated with new patterns of integration (or differentiation) of activities, as discussed in Chapter 3 and subsequently. Neglect of the second type of change often leads to anticipation that the use of IT will rapidly lead to drastic consequences, where there is a failure to see the offsetting reactions which stabilise the system.[2] Such an approach was taken, in particular, by many early accounts of the 'impact' of IT on employment, where cataclysmic forecasts were made which failed to note, for example, that word processors might be used so as to increase the volume of output (or reworking of the same output) rather than to displace clerical workers.

Let us consider this second type of change in a little more detail, for there are several different types of reaction to the costs of new technological applications. New social movements (for example environmentalism) may lead to changes in the treatment of externalities, and thus in the use of design of a technology. Fears about the invasion of privacy or the protection of data and intellectual property may evoke a similar response; thus data protection laws and new copyright regulations are being passed or discussed in many countries.[3] Sometimes such compensatory action is very successful, as in the case of some campaigns to protect particular habitats or to reduce air pollution by means of pollution control devices. Sometimes campaigns of this sort are unsuccessful or involve long struggle. They may run up against entrenched interests. And sometimes it is not really possible to recognise the scale of externalities until we are quite a long way down a path of technological development. (We used to have men with red flags to control motor traffic, and now we have traffic lights: but

Table 7.1 **Core assumptions of the three perspectives**

Continuist	Sees IT as part of long-term evolution of technical capabilities, rather dismissive of claims of its 'revolutionary' nature. The social implications can be projected from experience with earlier generations of electronic devices. Main features of society liable to remain unchanged, unless as a result of political upheaval. Forecasts: typically short- and medium-term, based on tried extrapolation and conventional modelling approaches, and often restricted to employment and consumer market issues.
Transformist	Sees IT as a revolutionary development, contributing to a major shift in civilisation as those associated with the agricultural and industrial revolutions. The social implications follow from a complex of changes in values and institutions, and can be identified as 'seeds of the future' in some current experiments and social movements. Forecasts: typically long-term, scenarios only loosely related to present, based on study of leading-edge developments, broad range of social and cultural topics treated.
Structuralist	Sees IT as the basis for a reorganisation of industrial society – part of the core of a 'new technological system', 'long wave' or 'growth paradigm', the social implications generally related to

the components of such a structural change, which can partly be deduced from historical analogies (e.g. with electrification) and partly from studying changes in organisational structures. Forecasts: typically seek to combine elements of the two preceding approaches, but mainly concentrated on industrial and organisational change.

would we have considered these sufficient had we been aware of the future levels of carnage which we – in the present – routinely accept? Some industry commentators have remarked to us that current data protection legislation may be like the red flags.)

But social innovation is not just a matter of social movements and organisations. Individuals may also, more or less spontaneously, change their behaviour so as to compensate for the costs of change: lifestyles appear to diffuse, as well as consumer goods, and these lifestyles both build on the opportunities that new technologies represent, while seeking to overcome any negative features associated with them. This does raise questions of social relations and inequalities: just as it may be another community that experiences the acid rain (and thus has to take steps to minimise the damage) so it may not be the user that experiences the annoyance, or worse, associated with motor cars, portable music systems, and so on.

Thus we are not being complacent at this stage in our argument, but simply pointing out that very often commentators do not raise the question whether social relations will mean that compensatory actions will be limited. Rather there is remarkably little attention paid to compensatory actions at all: forecasts often stop at depicting immediate 'impacts' if technologies were to be applied and nothing else changed in the social system. (This would be a technological deterministic approach indeed.) But there are many complex social actions taken in response to the opportunities and problems associated with new technologies.

Thus when we consider current fears of the isolating aspects of telework and teleservices it is as well to remember that similar fears were expressed concerning broadcast TV. While television has indeed hit some other entertainment services hard (and we can probably all think of individuals where the fears were justified), there has nevertheless been considerable expansion of some other forms of sociable leisure (for example sports, entertaining at home). And, without taking a 'Pollyanna' view, it could be argued that TV has actually helped to overcome what had previously been a gender segregation in the types of leisure and entertainment on offer. (A cynic might describe the change as being from a situation where men went out to bars while women and children stayed home, to one where we all stay home.)

In that it offers the opportunity for more realistic and varied home entertainment, IT seems to have the potential to allow for continuation of this trend. But at the same time the technology enables more individualised and potentially less standardised fare. This may mean less shared experience – even if (as the cynic would note) all that people were sharing was Dallas. Before we extrapolate from this that the 'information society' will mean an atomisation of society into uncommunicating individuals, we would need to consider social reactions that might develop to such a trend. It is not our intention to work these possibilities through systematically, but we want to underline the point that instead of talking about the 'impacts' of IT we should be considering both the shaping of technology and its applications, and the reciprocal reshaping of the social environment in which these applications are nested.

It is certainly hard for forecasters to judge correctly even the first phases of such cycles composed of multiple actions-reactions-counteractions. Indeed, much as is proposed in physics by Heisenberg's law of uncertainty (which suggests that the very process of measurement changes what is being measured), so may social and technological forecasts themselves enter into, or even be part of, these cycles. Efforts to influence the course of events run the risk of disconfirming themselves! Many of the most striking forecasts – works of fiction like *1984*, and non-literary works like *The Limits to Growth* – have been written with this as an objective.

We have set out more to provide a 'road-map' of forecasts and to illuminate the issues they raise, than to engage in our own detailed predictions of future trends. No doubt our own visions of probable and desirable futures (would that they were the same thing!) has been evident – this is practically an inevitable feature of this activity. Although we have aligned ourselves with the structuralist perspective, we have attempted to set out, at least schematically, the views presented by all three schools. It is now time for us to consider some of the points at which they suggest that choice is possible or that action is necessary.

In this concluding chapter we briefly review some of the analyses of that sort. We shall begin by using each perspective as a way of raising important issues in the IT environment affecting national policy-making, first in terms of national differences and the competitive struggle between countries, and then in terms of the scope for action within countries. The former discussion will be organised in three sections, each beginning from the specific issues addressed by one of the three perspectives. We then draw together some of these threads of argument as they apply to the circumstances of Third World countries. In the final section we argue for the need of a regular and highly-integrated role for forecasting in the decision-making process, and for the use of social experiments as a means of promoting a wider debate over the appropriate application of IT and improved decisions about technological development.

CONTINUITY AND COMPETITIVENESS

Advanced industrial nations

For the continuist perspective IT represents an(other) incremental step on a long path of technological evolution. The key factors setting the pace and direction of innovation are familiar ones, as set out in the extensive literature on industrial innovation in 'normal' conditions. For example, these factors include:

- how far technological changes are matched to user needs
- the structure of factor costs and the availability of managerial, technical and workforce skills
- the availability and quality of education and training
- the level of development of the science-technology system and the nature of the linkages between industries and R & D
- the rewards and motivations for entrepreneurial activities which can take the necessary risks to capitalise on opportunities provided by IT.

Case studies have related such factors to the innovation and diffusion of some ITs in specific sectors. Studies of national innovative performance also provide considerable support for their fundamental significance.[4] Even in a technological revolution these factors are likely to remain highly relevant: IT may change the form they take but, if anything, it may intensify their salience (for example training needs may become more acute: new space for entrepreneurship, demanding new skill combinations, may be opened).

The continuist viewpoint leads us to consider the factors that differentiate between countries whose past performance suggests that they are more or less capable of responding to the challenge of new technologies. For example, relevant evidence can be drawn from analysis of trends in patenting and export performance. Using such data it has been concluded by some of our colleagues that Sweden, Switzerland and West Germany have long-standing strong innovative capabilities. Japan has joined this group more recently, while Belgium and France appear to be moving towards it and the Netherlands and the USA seem to be leaving it. At the bottom of the league table of industrialised nations we find Canada, Italy and the UK, who seem to have much less ability to compete across the board – although they may have some strong sectors.[5] In the long term, such trends have major implications for geopolitics and global economics: the economic dominance of the United States may be further eroded, while divergence among countries of the European Community could increase its internal strains. (Both developments are liable to reduce the ability of the western countries to be mobilised by a powerful leader.)

The more immediate problem that the lagging countries face is how to reverse these trends, or at least how to avoid reductions in living standards in the face of them. The problem is compounded by the fact that the usual adjustment policies seem insufficient to create new employment opportunities, since they do not in themselves ensure the growth of dynamic new sectors. (But after all, as we have seen, the continuist viewpoint would not place much stress on this.) This has led to considerable interest in national innovation policies, which have been promoted in many quarters as means of 'breaking the mould'.

But such policies are prominent in almost all countries, not just the laggards; and the initiatives in industrialised countries have been in fact remarkably similar. Thus priority is given practically everywhere to R & D in IT, biotechnology and new materials. Naturally there are national differences. Some countries have attempted to stimulate activities in these fields through tax incentives and other broad-brush policy mechanisms, while others have adopted more selective and interventionist mechanisms such as direct grants.[6] Larger countries have become involved across the board; smaller ones look for niches. In nearly all cases, however, more effort is being put into means of evaluating the direction and effectiveness of research, and into the promotion of closer academic-

Table 7.2 **A schematic view of regional differences in conditions for innovation**

Japan	United States	Europe
Strictly coordinated export policy	'Market-pulled' innovation	Long tradition of scientific research
Politico-economic infrastructure with interweaving of state, banks and industry	Great personal mobility and competitiveness. Many new technology-based firms formed	Lack of entrepreneurship and the formation of new technology-based firms
Aggressive industrial policy, long-term public and private sector strategies	Legislation and education directed toward entrepreneurship	Emphasis on supporting traditional sector
Coordinated policy toward the acquisition of technology	Support for strategic sectors in connection with position as superpower (defence, aerospace)	Relative weakness in product development and marketing, lag in the commercial exploitation of new technologies
Strong emphasis on efficient mass production and on total quality control	Rapid growth of new industrial sectors based on radical technologies	Paucity of venture capital

Japan	United States	Europe
Home market which demands innovation	High availability of venture capital, large home market which demands innovation	

Source: Rothwell and Zegfeld (1985).

industry linkages. The historically less innovative countries do not seem to be at any particular advantage in pursuing such policies – even if their sense of urgency is greater.

Western Europe in general has specific concerns about technological innovation; the perception of the European situation is compared to that of the United States and Japan in Table 7.2. Where production costs are very high (for example chip production), European national markets are often too small for the volume production needed to survive in increasingly global industries and there has been a noticeable failure (with a few exceptions in particular niches) to capture world markets. National research capabilities are too limited to seriously address the whole range of priorities; entrepreneurship is inhibited by various obstacles such as a lack of venture capital. Despite great variations in industrial performance and technical competence within Europe, these problems are widely conceded, and have promoted not only major national efforts (for example Britain's Alvey Programme for fifth-generation systems) but also efforts at collaboration (IT programmes like Esprit, Eureka and Race).

Considerable effort is being put into liberalising trade within Europe, and to harmonising standards (until very recently telephones from one country could not even be guaranteed to work on the systems of another). Despite reluctance from some national leaders, many European Commission officials (especially those from smaller countries) are promoting the idea of a European Technological Community, along with projects such as a European optical fibre grid. Perhaps of greatest significance has been the recent spate of mergers and joint ventures between various electronic companies (in the fields of scientific instruments, medical equipment suppliers and semi-conductor manufacturers) with the aim of creating European companies that will be of sufficient size to capture world markets and bear the ever increasing costs of R & D.

But in addition to the economic divergence already noted there are other factors which continue to impede cooperation, including:

● linguistic differences
● the ties to other regions (especially to the United States and other former colonies) that are partly associated with these; different political constellations and trends[7]
● a lack of trust between companies over agreements to share research results
● other factors mentioned earlier, such as different size, culture, traditions of training and research, and so on.

There are thus good reasons for concluding that continuity is quite likely in the relative performance of Europe as a whole with respect to overall IT innovation.

Attempts to capture particular market niches may meet with some success, as where specific countries – perhaps Sweden and Germany are outstanding cases – have to date shown themselves to establish footholds in manufacturing. But even apparently secure niches may be destabilised in the course of technological evolution (while new ones may be created). The UK's well-established position in certain services (for example aspects of entertainment, education and financial services), though being slowly eroded, is also likely to persist. In the long term those UK services that depend upon language advantages (for example computer software and most information services) may be hit by machine translation, reducing the UK's comparative advantages here. But more significant is liable to be the application of IT to tradeable services in the form of teleservices, new entertainment media (for example high-definition TV) and high quality information and Electronic Data Interchange systems. The countries with most advanced development of the ITs – computer manufacture, supply of HDTV studio and consumer equipment, telecommunications infrastructure, and the software and services that these support – are liable to be the suppliers (or orchestrators) of new services. On the whole it seems more than likely that continuist 'pessimism' will be justified, and that western Europe will continue to lag behind Japan and the USA. (Of course the continuist perspective would not consider this so drastic a problem as we would, from our structuralist viewpoint.)

In almost total contrast to the position in western Europe is Japan's highly coordinated and long-term export policy. Of course there are many myths about Japan, usually introduced as 'well known facts', and we shall not attempt to summarise or dispel the whole rage of these. But some points should be pursued.

As is frequently pointed out by European governments who are loath to increase the degree of government-supported R & D, in Japan the overwhelming majority of funds devoted to IT innovation comes from individual companies and not government. However the nature of the Japanese politico-economic infrastructure, in which there is an interweaving of state, banks and industry, renders such support unnecessary. It is too simplistic to say that in the West governments fund research while in Japan it is the companies. After all much of government funding in the United States or Europe comes from companies as tax revenue. More important than the way in which the funds are raised, perhaps, is the issue of where R & D is best *located* (in industry, academia, or government labs); and where R & D *priorities* are best established and evaluation about progress best made.

Many commentators credit Japan's success to particular psychological and cultural aspects of Japanese society. While there may be some truth in this, and there is no denying that major cultural characteristics of 'western' and 'eastern' societies do differ, there is little evidence to support claims that these as a whole account for differences in economic performance. The continuist perspective is liable to see national differences as enduring features, but this does not move us very far towards identifying which aspects of other societies might be emulated, or which might be difficult (or problematic) to transfer. It suggests that technology transfer from Japan will not work well, or will take a long time, since a slow absorption of practices is possible. In terms of policy implications this perspective is making the point that one need neither look for sudden breaks in trends nor aim to create them, whether in firms or government.

In terms of future economic success the United States is likely to fall somewhere between Japan and Europe. Great advantages are to be found in the massive size of the home market, significant venture capital, and a legislative and education system geared towards entre-preneurship. In spite of the rhetoric of the market economy, there exists in the United States an implicit industrial policy geared to the promotion and protection of its high technology sector. The Strategic Defense Initiative can be seen as just the latest in a long line of defence (and space) programmes which, although having other stated objectives, have been important sources of R & D for the electronics, computer and telecommunications industries.

Protectionism also features prominently in the overall policy with restrictions placed on specific components as a defence (or penalty) against 'dumping'. COCOM (the programme which restricts the sale of high technology products, to Communist countries in particular) is often seen as an example of the use of protectionism as part of the IT strategy. Portrayed as a means restricting access to military secrets and to slow the development of

Soviet weaponry, many commentators (and industrialists) suspect that the contractual limitations placed on the sales of European or Japanese companies which incorporate US-made semi-conductor components in their products, and the delays and inspections of their operations that have often been entailed, constitute the covert rationale for the policy. The elected representatives who destroyed a Japanese computer on the lawn of the White House may have been engaged in a vote-attracting pantomime (and may have been capitalising on racial prejudice to boot). But the contractual restrictions policy is clearly a fig leaf for a 'creeping' protectionism.

TRANSFORMATION AND ATTITUDE CHANGE

The transformist approach tends to put less stress on structures and strategies and more on what we identified as the values and attitudes which are seen as underlying them. For this reason the forecasts and visions of the future that it projects can appear somewhat science-fictional, as little is revealed concerning the process of moving from the world as we know it to the radically restructured information society.

In line with the orientation of this school, there has been considerable research into the 'impact' of IT at the workplace and in the home.[8] But before considering attitudes and values that bear on IT as such, we should note that these studies emerge against a backdrop of considerable speculation about value change in industrial society (for example the erosion of the work ethic, increased value of leisure, environmentalism, distrust of expertise, and so on). A number of commentators have suggested that such long-term value change has on the whole been detrimental to economic growth and technological innovation. Others, in complete contrast, contend that concerns with self-expression and the environment may often facilitate or reinforce innovation. Thus it can be argued that rejection of mass-produced items in favour of more individual goods and services, or opposition to nuclear power and other large-scale technological programmes, would actually support many flexible and resource-conserving applications of IT.

But the evidence in favour of long-term value trends is much less clearcut than is often believed, and the degree of faddishness in discussions of 'new age' consciousness, 'third wave' attitudes, and 'post-bourgeois' values is rather high.[9] A recent review of a wide range of survey results has made a strong case that much less change has taken place over the long term than is generally alleged, and that those more subtle changes that are apparent have not necessarily been economically detrimental.[10]

Thus, despite the popular belief that commitment to employment has declined, it actually appears that having a job has become in some respects more central in people's lives. We still ask new acquaintances 'what they do for a living' and children 'what they want to be when they grow up'. It appears that the importance of paid employment as a source of social and economic resources has grown for women in most western societies, while there is little sign of its diminishing for men (although some subcultures are clearly disaffected from employment – but this may well be a defensive response to failure in the job market).[11]

Whereas employment remains a central value, what does seem to have changed are the rewards people expect from work – and here there are signs of a mismatch between aspirations and reality. Appreciation of work relates not only to its extrinsic features such as wages or job security, but also to its intrinsic aspects such as the opportunities for self-expression or enjoyableness. Corresponding to the increased appreciation of many leisure and recreational activities – typically as complements to, rather than substitutes for, employment – fewer working hours and less physical work does seem to be desired by people in the West. But this is far from a substantial shift to a set of new 'post-industrial' values, and even less does it indicate that attitudes are inhibiting technological progress. (Although this might have been the case if IT necessarily led to less pleasant, less flexible, less skilled work.) Depending on how it is implemented, IT seems to fit these trends well, and thus the transformist suggestion of virtuous circles between social practices and technological change seems to be borne out, provided that the application of IT is carrried out appropriately.

Many studies of 'new values' have set out to examine national differences, even though cross-national survey research is costly and laborious. But concern with the trends in competitiveness of various countries has been a strong incentive for research. As with all cross-cultural surveys, there must be some doubts about precisely what national differences in responses to attitude-questionnaires and opinion polls reveal. Caution must be observed before concluding that differences in responses are really indicative of diverse attitudes to technology or towards work. In some instances they may only be reflecting cultural or linguistic differences in the way people respond to questionnaires. Nevertheless their results can make interesting reading.

As might have been hypothesised, one cross-national survey in the 1980s found majorities of Japanese and American workforces to have high work ethics, with Sweden closely following and Britain – but also, surprisingly, West Germany – far behind.[12] The same survey also reported that West German and Japanese workers were the most enthusiastic for shorter working weeks, and there was also evidence of interest in more fulfilling work. Such tendencies, if widespread, could lead to the development of somewhat different patterns of IT application and industrial relations. Reduced working hours, for example, might form part of a trade-off involving shiftwork and flexible working patterns, such as may be ideally suited to new technology systems. The malleability that is inherent in IT could well prove advantageous in respect of new demands placed on work – although this would require a major shift in the emphasis of systems design. Those organisations (and countries) with more developed forms of worker consultation and participation *might* be better placed to take advantage of this potential. (The same malleability can however contribute to the formation of a workforce polarised by occupational groups and career opportunities, and security of employment. This side of the debate is more usually addressed through the structuralist perspective and will be picked up in the next section.)

Several of these studies have specifically addressed attitudes to IT. Most surveys of public attitudes towards new technology, and particularly of workers' attitudes to IT innovation in the workplace, show them to be generally positive. In at least one study of technology acceptance, however, fears about job displacement ranked high; only in the USA does more of the population focus on job creation as an outcome of applying IT. But in most cases there are positive attitudes towards working with IT systems and undergoing retraining where necessary.[13] West Germany (again) and Japan make surprising exceptions to this, which suggests that such attitude measures may not be reliable guides to workplace acceptance or rejection of technological change. The USA displays high levels of experience with, and positive views of IT. In contrast the Japanese results appear anomalous, although the relatively low levels of reported experience may reflect a slow pace of introduction of microcomputers and word processors (due to problems with non-Roman scripts in most current IT systems). While there was considerable interest in gaining experience with IT, there is an unexpectedly high reluctance to undergo retraining in Japan. Less surprisingly these surveys found younger respondents in all countries to be more positive to IT than their elders, suggesting that the acceptability of the new technologies may continue to grow. Despite perceptions of a threat to jobs and some reluctance to retrain, sizable proportions of the population stress innovation as a way of regaining competitiveness.

Perhaps attitude surveys tap superficial transitory views, rather than more profound orientations which will influence behaviour in important ways over long periods. Certainly one interpretation of these results is that such expressed attitudes to IT could be a product of immediate national circumstance, rather than straightforward expressions of deeply-held orientations. As well as corresponding to national stereotypes of 'accentuating the positive', for example, the American public was here captured at a moment (1985) where growth prospects had taken a turn for the better, and pride in their technology as an expression of national strength was being fostered (propaganda over the SDI being a case in point).[14] And perhaps, despite the FRG and Japan leading the world in some industrial applications of IT, the national experience of the technologies was still limited to relatively few sectors and occupational groups. Placed in the context of their countries' long-term growth performance, some people may be inclined to pay more attention to threats to the quality of working life than to the need to accept innovation in order to maintain competitiveness.

Another recent (1986) set of surveys of employees' views of IT in the FRG, Israel, Japan, Sweden and the USA found considerable similarity in responses across the countries. Evaluations of IT at work were largely positive. More respondents typically agreed that their jobs had become more interesting, responsible, clean and free of stress as a result of technological change, than those who felt they had become more difficult, burdensome, monotonous, lonely and dependent on others. While the ordering of these items is roughly similar across countries, it is notable that Japanese workers stood out in stressing the negative aspects of change.[15] From the same study Japanese workers were more likely than others to describe their jobs as routine and offering little say about workplace affairs; less likely to see their jobs as a source of pride, useful or productive.

If attitudes and values are important in accounting for trends, explaining international differences and identifying the long-term implications of IT, these data hardly demonstrate the point. Perhaps the surveys are not probing deeply enough – perhaps they overlook social relations and other non-physical issues. We would interpret evidence from within the UK as suggesting that the interpretation of workers' attitudes to new technology might not be as clearcut as some commentators initially suggested. Several independent studies during the 1980s have reported a high degree of acceptance in the workforce in the UK of a range of micro-electronically based technologies.[16] What needs to be kept in mind is that for most firms experience with these new technologies is limited to first generation applications, often for discrete activities. However, as the transformist perspective would stress (and as indicated in Chapters 3 and 4), it is the integration of functions which, potentially, will have the greatest impact on firms and their workers. This may go some way to explaining the more negative aspects of the Japanese returns, although not of the paradoxical relation between high levels of innovation and high reported dislike of it.

One corollary of this would be that, if the design of new technology products, and their integration into new technology systems, does not adequately take into consideration requirements for the quality of working life, then the potential for resistance will be increased. This is further borne out by the responses to questions on organisational change. The same British survey, which recorded the most enthusiastic response to IT-based technological change, recorded a high negative response to organisational change. (This study was based on the judgements of managers and trade union officials in a large number of firms about workers' attitudes and other responses to innovations of several kinds.) As we have previously discussed, getting the most out of flexible manufacturing systems and other forms of computer integrated manufacturing requires a substantial amount of organisational restructuring, of a type already experienced by many firms in Japan. Organisational and technological change are proving to be increasingly inseparable; and we might expect that, if the above survey questions were to be asked after more systems integration has occurred, the results may well be rather different. (We shall not venture to hypothesise whether the result will be an upgrading of organisational change or a downgrading of technological innovation.)

While there are interesting hints from these data, the firmest conclusion we can reach is that the interpretation of attitude surveys as guides to public acceptance of IT requires considerable caution. In this light, many commonplace assertions of the contributions of values and attitudes to supporting technological change are not merely facile but seriously misleading. A structuralist approach to this topic would lead us to examine the way in which cultural traditions are embedded in – indeed are reproduced by – social institutions and organisations. Here we can only suggest the directions which such an approach would take.

STRUCTURES AND PARADIGMS

A central assumption of the structuralist viewpoint is that many of our current uncertainties are a result of being at a point of transition between structural regimes. The stagnation and limits of old structures are often painfully obvious. But it is much harder to assess the viability of newer models, even as their form is becoming more discernible. A period of learning and organisational adaptation is required to capitalise on the potentials of IT; and new areas of demand are also needed, if new patterns of growth are to be established. In time new cost structures will be widely recognised, and the benefits to various actors will be more apparent.

This is decidedly *not* to say that a new technology necessarily dictates a particular pattern of organisation, but in many cases the full potential is more readily fulfilled when preceded, or accompanied, by organis- ational change. Existing structures are likely to run into problems but this does not mean that there is only *one* replacement. To talk of 'the' information society is as misleading as would be a discussion of 'the' industrial society. There may be many information societies. By way of analogy, let us consider how the organisation of entertainment has been reshaped in the light of new technologies. Traditional theatrical (and music hall) forms have not translated well on to the cinema or TV screen, although elements of both can be identified to a greater or lesser extent. But this does not mean that there is one cinema or TV form that has replaced them. Many genres have developed within these media, including melodrama, the musical, the documentary, the trailer, newscasts, and so on. National differences persist in the newer media, and there has probably been a decided segmentation of audiences with special programming for children and other groups. This is an example of cultural change, but a structuralist perspective leads us to expect a similar process with organisational change.

One area where the question of the scope for choice in organisational arrangements is particularly important concerns the formal workplace. We have also seen (Chapter 4) that one interpretation of new organisational styles – whether these are interpreted as informatisation or Japanisation – suggests that while these may result in benefits to the company and a small (or even sizable) segment of the workforce, the resulting polarisation of skills (as a range of intermediate, middle-level jobs are displaced) leads to social dualism. Perhaps this should be seen less as an interpretation of the dominant trend, and more as a depiction of one important tendency among several.[17] Whatever the case, to the extent that this pattern does develop it throws a substantial proportion of semi- and unskilled workers into a floating labour market (to be called upon or cast aside by companies as required). These workers lack security of employment, access to training, and even the facilities to organise to improve their conditions. Existing 'peripheral' sectors of the labour force – often women and minorities – are seen as being at particular risk, in part because their jobs are particularly vulnerable as members of these groups typically have low levels of training in IT-related skills.

Some forecasters see these developments as unlikely, and others as all too credible. A structuralist case would argue that the balance of outcome will be influenced by managerial and public policy choices concerning job design, labour legislation and educational efforts. And this in turn will be influenced by powers and interests of the major social actors. 'Peripheral' workers are typically not well organised: trade unions tend to represent the more stable 'core' workforce, and are only just coming to grips with the problems of involving and responding to minority groups, teleworkers, part-time workers, and so on. In many new technology industries unionism is all but non-existent. This might be interpreted as a permanent feature of new organisational styles, but we would be inclined to view it more as a conjunctural feature of (1) the semiprofessional nature of highly skilled IT work like software production; and (2) deliberate strategies of locating activities in non-industrial areas and recruiting workers with little industrial experience. In time the influence of these conditions is likely to wane, although this is not to deny that unions may experience considerable difficulties, nor that their modes of operation are liable to be changed along with those of other organisations.

From our discussion in previous chapters it can be seen that structural change is far-reaching. It affects our system of production (for example management styles, industrial relations, financial systems); and our social as well as technical infrastructures (for example training, regulations, communications). It also involves significant reshaping of ways of life (for example consumer demand and consumption; time use). Such major reorganisation may mean that it is not only companies that have fared well in the recent past which may be disadvantaged in the future, but also whole industries and countries. Much depends on the causes of past difficulties. If part of the reason that countries 'lagged' behind relates to their lack of organisational flexibility, they may continue to be tardy in their recognition of the need to create (or adopt) new structural paradigms, or in their ability to do anything about it.

Structuralist analysis typically attempts to identify key features of an emerging paradigm, most often from case studies of advanced sectors; and to outline the factors that enable, constrain and shape changes. Many of the features that are identified as likely to be part of the 'IT

paradigm' are ones we have already described as typical
of Japanese styles of organisation: just-in-time, total
quality control, strong linkages within industrial sectors
and between industries and state agencies, emphasis on
the long term. Others are related more to perceived
potentials of IT: flexible production systems (leading to
a proliferation of innovative small and medium-sized
enterprises); emphasis on retraining to meet needs for
technical skills; the design of systems to meet user needs;
and establishment of the infrastructure required to
support new IT-based goods and services. So far this
may resemble a fusion of continuist and transformist
arguments, but we would also place more stress on the
role that intergroup relations play in national differences.
Thus we would pay particular attention to distinctive
political economies – in particular the institutions and
activities of the state and the structure of economic
organisations – as conditioning the prospects for 'catching
up' and other innovation strategies.

Let us first consider political issues. There are well-
established views that macroeconomic performance takes
the form of a 'rise and decline' of nations, where older
democracies face an institutional sclerosis which restricts
their adaptability. This is seen as resulting from the
consolidation of established interest groups who are
motivated to maintain the status quo towards their
interest. More conservative commentators, in particular,
stress the way in which trade unions and corporate
bodies distort labour markets. The size of the welfare
state in OECD countries does indeed seem to be
related to the strengths of labour movements and social
democratic parties.

But other recent studies relate macroeconomic performance to political-institutional arrangements rather than
simply to the left/right bias of national governments and
bodies of elected representatives.[18] They draw attention
to other modes of interest articulation than the overt
electoral forms of representative democracy; in particular,
to corporatist structures that augment one-person-one-
vote systems with channels of communication among

major interest groups (employers, unions, and so on) and the state apparatus. Two types of 'liberal corporatism' seem to have been adopted by the most successful industrial economies; both of these forms have yielded coherent economic policies, 'concertation' in policy formation, and fairly consistently high consensus about economic fundamentals between organised capital and labour.

One model (Japan and Switzerland are perhaps the best examples) has been described as technocratic or paternalistic, with conservative-reformist policy-making. Such state bureaucracies are proactive with respect to adjustment and innovation policies but give little emphasis to social policy, Keynesian demand management and protecting declining sectors. The other model of successful corporatism (Austria and Norway are exemplars) is social democratic, reflecting the powerful role of the labour movement in these countries. This model features much more emphasis on public and social welfare, but these policies are integrated with economic initiatives rather than in stark opposition to them. In contrast to these success stories, societies with more of a war of attrition between major social classes (for example Britain), and those with only weak corporatist elements in their institutional apparatus, have faltering economies.[19]

Such an analysis tends to suggest that a transition to new structural paradigms may be inhibited by long-standing institutional factors, which prevent new policy initiatives and discourage organisational change. These factors relate to the power bases of social actors and the forms of conflict resolution available (and familiar) to them, and are reflected in the education and training experiences of managerial and technical élites (including those in public service and trade unions) and the state's 'intelligence systems' (by which we do *not* mean CIAs and Special Branches but the agencies which scan the economic and technological environment, which direct and evaluate research and industrial policy, and so on). Such institutional factors cannot be summed up at will – or easily disposed of.

New strategies may find difficulty in winning consent
and mobilising capacities. But stasis is not an option.
Political economies *are* being challenged by new patterns
of occupation and employment, of industrial leadership
and of the social concerns and movements that are
associated with these shifts. They key issues will therefore
·be how readily social changes can be accommodated
within different institutional structures, and how far and
in which way this accommodation will facilitate the
application of IT.

Our structuralist approach would go on here to draw
on interpretative studies of different policy-making
systems (rather than on the sort of large-scale comparative
analysis that provided the analysis of corporatism outlined earlier). One conclusion drawn from such studies
is that it is important to establish foresight as an integral
part of policy-making, and that the process of forecasting
which can add coherence to the planning activities of
different organisations is perhaps more important than
the establishment of specific forecasts.[20] (We return to
this point later.) Another point is that political systems
which combine high government power with relatively
closed channels of communication are liable to be less
able to cope with challenges around IT than those that
are more open (for example Sweden).[21] As IT offers
prospects for more open government it *could* be a spur
that facilitates social innovation. (Especially if there were
good examples – or 'demonstrators' – in other countries,
in local government or in social institutions, which
provided models that people wished to emulate.) If 'open
government' is associated with a high degree of inter-
agency competition, and a strong role for the judiciary,
however, it may result in veto power and costly legal
actions rather than coherent policy-making, together with
much 'behind the scenes' manoeuvring and evasion
of democratic accountability in top policy circles –
characteristics of the USA identified by some commentators.

Related to this is the importance of recognising that
IT innovation and structural change is fostering a

convergence not only of industrial processes and economic sectors but also of traditionally segmented areas of policy-making. An example of this is the distinct interweaving of industrial and cultural policy concerns posed by the new telecommunications media. In such instances a failure to bring together and concert policies may lead to contradictory or redundant efforts being made.[22]

The structuralist perspective on national differences also often highlights not only governmental institutions but also managerial style and industrial relations in the private sector. We have repeatedly referred to the debate concerning various features of 'Japanese' management styles, which appear to be particularly capable of trading on the potentials of IT. Non-Tayloristic, decentralised and high-skill profile patterns of work organisation may well be rather well-suited to IT 'styles', such as systemofacture (rather than high division of labour automation), real-time monitoring of internal processes and market environments, and distributed networks.

Many commentators have argued that cultural and psychological factors have played a leading role in the creation of Japanese management styles. Our version of structuralism, at least, would tend to draw attention to the evolution of these styles within the context of specific factor costs (for example shortages of materials and space, particular skill compositions) in post-war Japan. This latter view permits us to be more sanguine about the transfer of practices from Japan to other countries than the continuists. Indeed many 'Japanese' techniques initially originated in western management theory, and Japanese companies with plants in Europe or the USA, have apparently operated versions of them with considerable success. To the extent that cultural factors have played a central role in providing the Japanese with their current economic advantage, they may most likely be found in the highly demanding Japanese home market, the articulation of banks, manufacturing and service companies in 'zaibatsu' or the orientation of the educational system towards meeting some industrial needs

– rather than in the oft-mentioned traits of loyalty, subservience or conformity which westerners are liable to describe with a mixture of awe, admiration and abhorrence.

It may well be that there is liable to be a lengthy process of rethinking the 'commonsense' of cost-accounting in the context of new ITs, and that current (poor) linkages between financial and industrial sectors may inhibit experiments with new managerial styles and organisational structures, in much of western Europe in particular. Nevertheless efforts to learn from Japanese management are widespread, and it is likely that these will form part of an ongoing evolution towards new organisational structures in industry. Even if cultural and psychological factors should prove to be important there is no reason to assume it is an 'all or nothing' situation, or that new organisational techniques will not be developed which are more appropriate to particular conditions. One can easily envisage a situation where, for example, constraints on supplies of raw material (perhaps due to foreign exchange restrictions in a debt-ridden Third World nation) might lead to the adoption of just-in-time (or another organisation technique) *within* the factory as opposed to *the movement of raw materials into* the factory.[23]

This stress on slow but evolutionary change might sound like a continuist statement. But we expect the pace and direction of change to vary. It also seems likely that progress in the direction of these new styles will be more rapid in societies where:

● consensus-formation processes in management and government are better established
● trade unions are already organised on an enterprise basis (rather than by craft)
● systems of worker participation and consultation help promote loyalty to the enterprise and more support for plans for redeployment and retraining.

Within western Europe, Scandinavia and the FRG seem relatively well placed in these respects.

It is also worth noting that the Japanese model may

itself face particular problems of structural change. It is commonplace to hear western commentators suggesting that Japanese culture may provide less support for radical innovation than for imitation and incremental improvement. This is a position which seems largely based on wishful thinking – it lacks supporting evidence other than memories of shoddy plastic products of the 1950s. While there was certainly a large degree of imitation in those days, there was also reverse engineering and 'learning-by-doing'. Considering current and emerging consumer products, and grand schemes such as that for Integrated Network Services, sufficient evidence exists to the contrary. But more serious may be the problem of adaptation of industrial structures within Japan: changes in the organisation of lifetime employment are causing some rumblings and may weaken the legitimacy of other aspects of industrial relations. The cosy relationship between large firms and the small firm/informal sector of the economy too may be destabilised by (hidden) unemployment. Finally growing militarism, apart from further stoking the mad rush to global annihilation, may undermine R & D for civil products.

IMPLICATIONS FOR THE THIRD WORLD

Our discussion so far in this chapter has largely focused on the situation of western industrialised nations (and Japan). But, as mentioned in Chapter 4 (p. 148), one feature of the debate over national/regional capabilities to use IT as an engine for economic growth is the argument from some quarters that there is great potential for Third World countries to take advantage of the technology as a short cut to industrial development. Attempts to forecast or to generalise (or, for that matter recommend policies) between such a large number of heterogeneous nations as constitute the 'Third World' are, of course, doomed to failure.[24] Nevertheless distinct positions can be readily identified within our three schools.

The continuist perspective, as noted, is bound to be identified with most pessimistic views. Just as IT is not seen as leading to any big changes in comparative or competitive advantage between industrial nations, the same is seen as holding true for most of the Third World. In the competition between nations continuism would not expect much change in the status quo, unless it was in a widening of the gap between richest and poorest and continued progress on the part of at least some of the newly industrialising countries.

Even in those sectors in which a number of less developed countries had begun to make breakthroughs in terms of world trade (for example apparel and shoes) some commentators speculate on the return of 'runaway' industries.[25] The continuist perspective will be hesitant about endorsing such a trend – it is really something that corresponds more closely to the transformist expectation of major positional changes – but its view of IT as an incremental development of earlier high technologies still involves problems for less wealthy countries. Thus a high threshold of R & D, investment costs and infrastructure, combined with a shortage of skills are seen as restricting Third World access to the new technology.[26] Furthermore the packaging and integration trends described in Chapter 3 are expected to present additional obstacles in the adaptation of technology transferred through turnkey projects, as well as increasing the costs of reverse engineering. Only those newly industrialising countries which are big enough to muster the resources to a sufficient extent for (and politically stable enough to maintain whatever momentum may have been established in) acquisition of the appropriate technological capabilities are likely to cope with the challenge of innovation in the 'North'.

The transformist perspective is associated with more optimistic views, although expectations of revolutionary technological change can also lead to forecasts of a drastic worsening of circumstances for technologically less well-endowed countries. Some commentators justify considerable optimism by noting that IT provides the opportunity for leapfrogging over the constraints of skill shortages, poor quality, high energy costs, and so on. This is actually a twofold argument. On the one hand IT is seen as being able to enhance 'appropriate technology' as outlined in Chapter 4 – thus discussions of the 'barefoot microchip'. The implication here is that IT will enable poorer countries to forge a new route into the information age, rather than having to pass through the industrial traumas of western nations. On the other hand IT is seen as permitting poorer countries to make rapid steps in acquiring the most advanced technologies, or at least those elements of them that obviously contribute to major economic and social needs.

Following on from this, it is suggested that some Third World countries may even have an advantage over advanced industrial nations when it comes to the development of a modern telecommunications infrastructure. The high replacement costs for telecommunications equipment, for example, means there is a reluctance to discard previous generations of equipment installed in advanced industrialised nations before it is absolutely necessary. For those Third World nations starting from a less sophisticated infrastructural base complete digital exchanges and networks can be installed from the start. Of course the transformist perspective would not promote a naive expectation that all poor countries will spontaneously adopt appropriate policies; considerable diversity is likely. Nevertheless we do hear arguments from this perspective that value changes in the richer countries, associated with the shift to information society, and the greater ability of communications media to convey images of the circumstances of different parts of the world – as exemplified by Band-Aid and similar projects – will gradually transform international organisations. This would eventually lead to improved flows of skills and technological knowledge around the world, offsetting many current inequalities.

We have already in this chapter expressed our impatience with such accounts of value change (though not necessarily with the endeavours that they cite as evidence), and in Chapter 4 we reluctantly conceded the force of what we have described as the continuist approach to global inequalities. However our structuralist approach does have some points of agreement with the transformist view, and these suggest some points at which strategic choices may be able to offset the more gloomy expectations.

For example, we would agree with the point that a basis of software skills can be taught in higher education, and does not need to be acquired on the shop floor,[27] and thus that the familiar constraints on technological development that are associated with a shortage of engineering and management skills, high energy costs, and so on, may be reduced through the application of relatively simple microelectronic devices. (But we would note that many IT applications require combinations of skills that are in acutely short supply even in industrial countries.) Likewise there is much validity in the argument that the application of IT to various control and monitoring functions can regulate the use of raw materials and energy, and reduce costs that are particularly hard for poorer countries to bear. (Temperature controls on blast furnaces, for example, can reduce wastage and improve quality – in many cases achievement of these aims in Third World countries has been inefficient due to a shortage of the high skills required.)

Nor are the continuist arguments about the high threshold costs required to enter IT necessarily relevant. They tend to apply to being in the forefront of IT development, for example in chip manufacture or advanced robotics, rather than to the application of the appropriate technologies for Third World exports or production for indigenous needs. (How generalisable is the transformist-sounding argument about the shift of apparel production back to the West, for example – how many products will involve such short cycles of fashion and the like?) The transformist view that the lack of a highly evolved infrastructure in Third World countries may be less of a problem in a world of satellite communications may wrongly place attention on the development of complete networks; for a relatively small investment in developing the capacity to determine appropriate systems specifications and to assess competing suppliers' products, Third World nations (at least the better-endowed of them) could attain a more advantageous position in negotiating with multi-nationals in highly competitive markets.[28]

Yet it remains extremely unlikely that all, or even most, Third World nations will be in a position to use IT as a means of catching up with advanced industrial nations. Certain newly-industrialising countries (for example Brazil, South Korea, India, Venezuela and China), are most frequently mentioned as having the potential (financial ability, educational infrastructure, policy-making apparatus, and so on) to employ the technology successfully.[29] Poorer countries, especially those in sub-Saharan Africa, are in a much more difficult position. We can rely on neither the industrialised nor the newly-industrialising countries to seek to redress this, except in terms of stopgap solutions to intense crises. Yet in addition to the compelling moral case, in a world where nuclear and other technologies make international conflict in any region potentially threatening to the whole world (especially given the prospects for high technology terrorism), it is in all of our interests that the gloomy prognoses of continuism and structuralism are not realised.

How can there be movement towards the transformist image of the future here, if we cannot endorse transformist analyses of change? First we would suggest that it is important to complement portrayals of suffering with analyses of efforts to change its causes – including of course those that involve new technology applications. And both of these should be represented as they really are – enduring features of our shared world – rather than as sudden and surprising occurrences somewhere far away. Secondly the creation of IT applications aimed at overcoming urgent needs should not be seen as simply an opportunity to enter new markets. Technology transfer should involve the establishment of new expertise in the host countries, so that more informed choices and continuing development of the technologies (to meet evolving local requirements) can be undertaken. Thirdly those involved with the establishment of technological capabilities in the Third World – who include western educationalist and international organisations as well as the scientific and technical system in the Third World – have to emphasise ways of coupling skills in the implementation of applications (and relating these to awareness of user needs and environments) to those in the evaluation of systems and the steering forward of technical choices.

FORECASTING AND EXPERIMENTATION

Regardless of which school of thought one subscribes to, when the full range of issues around IT is considered it will be clear that both the opportunities and the problems which face us in the future are certain to be long-term, for the rich countries of the world as well as the Third World. To the extent that it has been possible, we have attempted to provide a just representation of each of the three IT schools and, while emphasising our own preferences, have pointed out that each has something of value to offer.

Perhaps the only statement we can make with certainty concerning the future with IT is that things will not stay as they are now. This does not mean that we should throw up our hands and leave the development of appropriate policies (to cope with the problems we are busily creating?) to future generations. Choices that are made today inevitably influence the future, and even inadequate attempts to identify policy issues, options and consequences (perhaps they are necessarily inadequate, given our limited experience with IT to date) are needed, for otherwise we shall simply be relying on tools made for a vanishing world. It is therefore important to design policies which attempt to take advantage of the opportunities offered by IT, and which help in the avoidance of some of the problems. Above all it is important that choices made today assist policymakers of the future by not foreclosing their options too dramatically – and that they assist us all by not foreclosing our options too narrowly as to who should be empowered to make IT policies.

The process under which choices are identified and sifted, and the final selection made among them, should be one which leads to both an enhancement in, and a spreading of, decision-making skills so as to foster debate and support the broader utilisation of information. By so doing the process can facilitate human and social development in a number of ways – at least, if these are seen in terms of our gaining better understanding of, and ability to shape, ourselves and our world.[30] We are now orienting our discussion to national contexts, but much of this argument could also be applied to international organisations, to global as well as regional and group inequalities.

It is at least arguable that increased awareness of the nature and potentials of IT can help foster:

1. the democratisation of the workplace, to enable employees to take a greater role in evaluating, choosing and modifying new technology systems and the patterns of work arranged around them (and potentially much more)
2. better social feedback more generally, so that innovations will be developed with better awareness of market requirements and users will less often acquire systems that fail to meet stated or implicit aims, while non-users will have a better chance to express their views about the 'externalities' of new systems
3. greater prospect of consensus where major technological decisions have to be made – or in the event of irreconcilable differences at least a better chance of recognising that these differences are more likely to be a matter of divergent political goals than disagreement over technical means
4. reduction of the threat of dualism, in that at least

some members of, and sympathisers with, 'peripheral' groups will be aware of the implications of technological choices and be better placed to marshall opinions in such a way as to reshape options.

There are many components to such a goal. These include educational and awareness programmes of many kinds; action from social movements as well as from authorities; roles for professionals and popularisers alike. But two activities with which we are particularly concerned, and which should be central to this process, are long-term forecasting efforts and social experiments. It is our belief that it is useful if the two are seen as complementary exercises.

Forecasting

All too rarely has long-term forecasting been recognised for the contribution it can make to policy analysis. More often than not the *forecast* is confused with the *forecasting* process. Forecasting should of course result in forecasts, but what may be at issue is less the precise details of a view of the future, than the laying bare of the factors that may be operated on to effect change in one or other direction. Speculative fiction has a valuable role to play in depicting what human responses might be to counterfactual circumstances, but forecasting also has to deal with the relation between the counterfactual future and the all-too-factual present.

We make no claims for the accuracy of any of the forecasts included in this book – our own or those drawn upon from the literature. Few, if any, long-term forecasts have ever proved to be highly accurate; indeed many would doubt their minimal reliability. Much more important is the analysis of underlying trends, and our effort to explicate factors that may bring one or other potential to realisation. In this book we have attempted to take the reader through some of the forecasting processes that we have ourselves undertaken over the last few years (with many of the edges taken off, naturally). This is a process in which we have engaged in consultation with many interested parties, many of whom are involved in their own formal or informal forecasting exercises.

Yet long-term forecasting is not well institutionalised in the UK or in other western countries. No doubt many readers will treat this book as another futurological effort, adding forecasts to the stock that is available. We would be more satisfied if, rather, we were contributing to a broader forecasting process which served as a forum within which interested parties – whether politicians, industrialists, academics or members of the workforce – were given the opportunity to exchange views on the issues they are concerned about and discuss their perceptions of the future. Such a process exists in nascent and intermittent form in the mass media, but is not generally identified as such, and thus it lacks much in the way of a 'collective memory'. This means that short- and long-term issues are confused, that fads and fashions predominate, that immediate crises preempt discussions.

Since the future is not static and new information and insights continually become available, forecasting must be an ongoing, regular activity. The aim of the forecasting process should be to increase the awareness of the goals and problems faced by different sectors of society, and the ways in which they might be achieved or affected by the forecasts. Here we are influenced by the corporatist type of forecasting exercise carried out as part of French national planning exercises and Japanese socioeconomic planning.[31] This is definitely not a matter of arguing that corporatism in general is superior to representative (let alone participatory) democracy, nor is it a plea for a greater role of technocrats in policy-making. What we are proposing is that institutionalised forecasting exercises that involve major social actors – representatives of groups such as large and small employers, regional interests, trade unions and professional associations, women's movements, ethnic groups, and so on – can enrich democratic structures and head off technocratic claims for control of thinking about IT and similar topics.[32]

It seems in the cases mentioned above that, by assessing how the actions of each group of actors will affect others, an understanding of mutual interests and the nature of positive and negative feedback effects in institutional action may be developed; and this can lead to a degree of consensus about strategic priorities, to greater commitment to solve common problems, and to the identification of ways in which to. make the most of opportunities.

Such a role for forecasting may seem highly idealised. In particular the stress upon consensus sits somewhat uneasily with the structuralist view that conflict is inherent in social institutions that will almost inevitably reflect diverse interests. Certainly forecasting cannot magically resolve all differences, and some fundamental conflicts can lead to a politicisation of forecasting activities which renders them liable to be rejected by significant actors. And, on the other hand, avoiding addressing these conflicts can result in bland and trivial exercises and results. But our stress is on forecast*ing* and consensus-*building* rather than on finalised forecasts and complete consensus. The forecasting effort can be used so as to establish areas of wide agreement as well as crucial disagreements (that may then be embodied in distinct scenarios). Obviously such forecasting will be more readily accommodated within societies that already have established consensus-building mechanisms – such as Sweden and Japan. It may be more vulnerable in other societies, but that is no reason not to try it. It may even prove exemplary for other institutional activities.

Until such time as long-term forecasting becomes a regular activity integrated into the decision-making process, policies will continue to be designed and adopted using only short-term criteria. We have argued that long-term forecasting is necessary, though for different purposes than the short-term forecasts that are a necessary part of bureaucratic activity in the modern world. The scale of change is liable to be ignored or underestimated (even the continuist vision depicts major change when its long-term projections are considered), if we only engage in short-term forecasting. Under such conditions our ability to respond to change will remain slow, with little facility to take account of either the fruitful economic and social opportunities which are created or the more threatening side-effects of new developments.

Numerous techniques of forecasting exist and no single method deserves a monopoly. Over the years we have witnessed various approaches flare up as brief fashions, to be vigorously promoted as panaceas, and then gradually recognised to be merely another more or less useful tool in the forecaster's kit. More elementary methods like extrapolation of trends and scenario-writing based on expert judgments, and more sophisticated (or at least, complicated) approaches like delphi, computer models, and catastrophe theory: all have some virtues, and more important, some major limitations. We would argue for a 'broadband' forecasting effort which draws on several methods (and is thus forced to come to terms with any divergences in results that may emerge), and that explicitly discusses different theories of social change. Such a wide approach can help avoid the danger of placing too much reliance on any single image of the future (or even on a set of images or scenarios that despite their apparent contrast are still all based in a limited view of how the world works).[33] Our own forecasts here have drawn on various methods – trend extrapolation, expert judgment, contrast of different theories. Elsewhere we have pulled together forecasts developed by different routes to establish scenarios,[34] but in this study we have been more concerned to identify possible directions of change than to construct 'histories' and 'images' of the future.

Social experiments

In addition to producing verbal (or other symbolic) images of possible futures and courses of action by forecasting, and in addition to the forecasting process being a way of bringing different perspectives, interests and sets of experience together, more concrete investigations into features of IT futures may be undertaken. There is considerable scope, in particular, for fostering experimentation with technological options and alternatives.

As we have argued elsewhere[35] social innovation is bound to occur, given the more or less rapid recognition of new technological potentials and the diffusion of systems across the economy. Social experiments, which attempt to prefiguratively construct IT systems and applications in real settings, and to establish how far they achieve the expected goals and what unexpected issues arise, are also bound to be introduced to some extent. But there is considerable scope for experiments to be articulated together and to be part of a learning process, and thus for systematic efforts to encourage the process and share the experience on the part of local and national authorities and other social actors. The questions they will need to confront are: how much experimentation on which issues; how far should experiments centring on different issues be combined; how far are efforts duplicated; to what extent is learning built into the process; how can people monitor, evaluate, and share the lessons?

The implications of experiments, in terms of what they tell us about the social relations of IT in general (or at least about the relevance of particular applications to potential user communities), can be assessed and incorporated into forecasting efforts. Social experiments can play roles other than making forecasting easier, of course:

● They can be demonstration projects, raising public and industrial awareness, stimulating debate and open policy-making.
● They can be important tools in the evaluation and dissemination of the uses and implications of information technologies. In France, for example, the experiments with Teletel in Velisy, and those now under way with broadband cabling in Biarritz, play this role.

• They can provide social and technological innovators with at the least a stimulus to thought, but also a test-bed for action.

However experiments also need to be associated with more 'grass-roots' and 'hands-on' experience in order to align new technologies to real present and emerging needs. Many social experiments have been 'top-down' affairs, where the involvement of the public is largely a marketing exercise – it is designed to bring about consumer acceptance of change, and a little fine-tuning of products to emerging demands. But citizens and social groups can also be social innovators themselves – they can identify unmet needs (and problems that may be associated with technologies), participate in the design process, set priorities for R & D, propose criteria for evaluating specific technologies or the whole experiment itself, and communicate their experiences to other actors in other places. In the light of earlier chapters, one could foresee more experiments on teleworking, alternative arrangements for transport, self-service systems and home informatics relevant to the elderly or the disabled; and demonstration projects for small firms and community groups as well as for large corporations and public authorities (for example education), as being particularly useful ones. These could provide learning experiences and the opportunity to participate in shaping the technology and the uses to which they are put.

Another area where demonstration projects and experimentation should be considered is the so-called 'home of the future'. In Chapter 5 we outlined current and likely developments towards integrated home systems – but they need not progress in the directions described. There is considerable scope for influencing the overall shape of home systems on the part of consumer electronics firms and service and information providers; and alternatives to the automated 'smart house' in the form of community networking and community information facilities might also be explored: but again we would stress that users (the general public) should not be treated as market research fodder, as passive consumers. The success of

home informatics, and the form that systems eventually
take, will be heavily influenced by the mutual shaping
of technologies and ways of life.

Furthermore, to take what may seem a more pragmatic
view, it is not inconceivable that such experimentation
could lead to products with export potential. While
competence in heartland technologies will remain important to being able to develop applications, we would
expect this latter ability to become more central to
competitiveness. If developments in home informatics to
date have one lesson, it is that increasingly products will
be sold not on the basis of their technical sophistication
but as supplying services that people really want. This
is liable to mean tailoring products to people's interests
and ways of life. Here, perhaps, Europe may retain a
comparative advantage – at least, we see aspects of
European culture and politics as being widely admired
in the contemporary world. If the ability to engage in
experimentation is restricted to a narrow segment of the
population, say systems designers, this resource may be
squandered as technically 'sweet' solutions of little human
appeal are imposed.

Within industry we are already witnessing a fair
number of demonstration projects, often with the assistance of government-provided financial support.[36] While
we would expect the private sector to increase its
involvement in demonstration projects and other forms
of experimentation as a means of facilitating its own
learning about market requirements, the public services
are well placed to play a central role in social experiments
involving IT.

Up to now, as noted in Chapters 4 and 6, the great
majority of applications of IT within the public services
have been aimed at the rationalisation of existing
functions as opposed to enhancing these services or
providing new services. To some extent this is a function
of the political context and economic pressures under
which many such services operate, together with other
special problems (to do with bureaucratic organisation,
professional interest groups, concern over security and
privacy, and so on). Public services are however among

the heaviest users of IT and as such are accumulating an enormous IT skill capability. In time, as the new technologies further diffuse throughout the public services, we would expect to find more and more creative uses of the technologies.

Also, public services are 'client-intensive': they necessarily involve considerable contact between the service providers and the people they serve. While this may inhibit some technological innovations (public acceptance is required in circumstances where other sectors may only need to win worker acceptance), it does mean that public services are well placed in terms of contact with a large section of the population. This gives them an extensive (if under-utilised) knowledge base in assessing user needs (even if these are often inadequately met). Increasingly public services around the world are placed in a position of dealing with crisis situations – of 'mopping-up' social problems – with inadequate and low quality resources. A policy which places more emphasis on social experiments involving the *augmentation* of public services could reap rewards, both in terms of their long-term ability to cope with the social changes that are reshaping society and in the promotion of awareness of the potential for individuals to engage in their own innovation. Furthermore the public services have often been an important source of technology transfer to the private sector and can be used as a means of economic stimulation through the development of new (socially useful) IT products and services.

Social experiments based on community facilities, or within public services, may also help ascertain the seriousness of the risk that IT may contribute to new forms of *dualism* in society – and to identify ways in which its application may help in the formulation of the types of action that could minimise them. The use of experiments in the assessment of such risks and the indentification of alternative strategies raises the need to align economic and social policy, since new mixes of public and private initiative are likely to be components of new structures of social organisation.

Thus public services are important actors in social

experiments with IT by virtue of their responsibilities. They are also important by virtue of their access to resources, even if they are heavily constrained by overall financial limitations. The high cost of infrastructure, the need to win public acceptance, and protection of early entrepreneurs against the high risks of entry into IT services, will often necessitate some forms of public support for experiments.[37] This has already proved to be true for telecommunication systems like teletext and viewdata, and the services they provide such as teleshopping and aids for the physically disabled. It is likely to be even more so for 'wired cities' and similar initiatives. Since these are expensive to mount, international comparisons will be even more important here if we are to gain a database to evaluate experiments. And for many countries international collaboration may be required to facilitate innovation in applications of IT as well as in the heartland technologies (chips, and so on). It will therefore be necessary to attempt to disentangle those differences that result from initial conditions (such as national culture) and those which are related to different technological and organisational initiatives.   The evaluation of experiments and experience should contribute to the intelligence function for IT policy-makers, and to more general awareness of the range of options for 'information society' – even if most initiatives to date have been somewhat limited as models of the future. While support is necessary, it seems unlikely that highly centralised interventions are appropriate, except where they provide an environment in which entrepreneurs, social activists and ordinary citizens can identify and initiate their own social innovations. However there may well be difficulties in reconciling this point with the need for international comparisons and large-scale experiments cited above; and in practice experimentation with the ways of carrying out experiments will also be essential.

CONTROLLING IT

International collaboration in developing and assessing
IT applications should not be taken to mean that all
societies will (or should) use ITs in the same way. Our
structuralist perspective leads us to focus on ways in
which different constellations of needs and interests are
liable to result in distinctive technological trajectories.
After all not all industrial societies are the same – indeed
it is one variant model (the Japanese) that has often been
seen as the likely precursor of 'information society'. But
there are many other models: Scandinavian, North
American, Southern European, and so on – not to mention Central European.

Now there are several reasons why we might be led
to expect more convergence than in the past – for
example, IT makes many services tradeable that previously
were insulated from global competition. It seems likely
that it is the lack of tradeability of many services that has
prevented a globalisation of many more features of mass
culture than we have yet witnessed, and thus preserved
some traditional national characteristics. This may be
changed by the application of IT and the emergence of
global service corporations. And the new media make it
possible to diffuse images of lifestyles and consumer
goods (in programmes as well as advertisements) across
cultures, and thus perhaps to promote convergence in
market demands, much more readily than heretofore.

But the speed of adoption of IT will still vary for
even the most universal application, and thus specific
applications will necessarily have to be adapted to specific
circumstances with different technological stocks and
skill bases as well as their own types of culture.
Furthermore IT is also a supremely malleable technology,
and given sufficient opportunities for local experimentation considerable diversity is likely to be manifest. On
the available evidence, of course, this diversity is
likely to continue to reflect differences of economic
circumstance, much as other technological differences do.
We have noted evidence for the differential organisational

implications of IT in different countries, and even in
different firms within the same country.

In the past cultural styles have been strongly influenced
by the pervasiveness of mass media, but narrowcasting
and the formation of new information communities may
lead to more differentiation around individual taste and
lifestyle in coming decades. It is likely that some national
and cultural distinctiveness will be reinfored by the
application of new technologies. In fact this may be a
deliberate ploy on the part of powerful groups – for
example to foster the tourist industry by maintaining
traditional styles or to bolster political power by a
chauvinistic manipulation of symbols of national 'superiority'. We cannot deny that such issues are liable to
arise. But there are also bound to be (1) a moulding of
IT applications by popular movements – just as video
and radio are used; and (2) a shaping of applications by
existing cultural practices and preferences (thus national
cuisine and musical tastes vary despite homogenisation).
These factors apply to subcultures as well as at national
levels. Although there may be a continuing 'levelling' of
tastes, as evidenced in the worldwide appeal of TV shows
such as *Dallas*, cultural fragmentation could also have
explosive results.

In the workplace and the media in the areas of public
services and home informatics, there is likely to be
considerable diversity within and between nations, even
if some features of the new organisational paradigms are
readily identifiable in most cases. Our point here is to
caution against the notion that future IT applications can
simply be seen as clones of current advanced applications.
Rather we have probably seen only a fraction of the
range of implementations that are available for only a
fraction of the range of applications that will be established. This means that the question of how we can
direct IT so that the more desirable potentials of
'information society' are realised is a central one.

We cannot hope to answer this question in detail –
and the answer will require considerable detail, since it
will involve welding together many currently compart-

mentalised strategies. And the whole of this book has been an effort to set out key issues that arise. But it may be helpful to consider, for the last time, what the three perspectives suggest about the answer to this question.

The continuist viewpoint proposes that IT does not really pose any new issues, that 'information society' is more of an incremental development of familiar modes of social organisation than a new-stage of development. Thus policy concerns may change, as they always do, but major upheavals in policy-making systems are unnecessary. The transformist viewpoint sees 'information society' as a completely new phenomenon to which we have to adapt if we are not to join the dinosaurs. Political institutions and policies have to 'go with the flow' of the 'third wave'. A structuralist perspective on these issues would agree that many social concerns and interests are not likely to change at heart. However 'information society' does represent a new organisation of industrial society, and thus these concerns and issues are liable to be manifest in new ways and to be joined by new problems. These will demand new policy instruments and policy-making structures, and new interventions into the process of shaping the future from all sectors of society. We have argued above for more systematic forecasting efforts and social experiments as part of these new approaches.

In the case of change in heartland technologies, the interests pushing along developments such as those described in Chapter 2 are so well entrenched that here the transformists may be right – the choice is whether or not to jump on the bandwagon. In the case of systems and applications, these heartland developments enable far more opportunity of tailoring technological change to specific goals. In addition there are social policy issues raised around technical standards, privacy and copyright law, that cannot be avoided for long by national governments and international agencies. Up to now most of the debate over these issues (other than that about technical dimensions) has been based on their use in achieving market advantage or in the degreee to which they stimulate or hinder the innovative process within the formal economy. This debate needs to be widened so as to allow an examination of, for example, the extent to which the protection of intellectual property or of narrow standards increases or restricts access to technological and information resources, and to which it may thus promote or reduce dualism.

Previous chapters have suggested that ITs can contribute to dualism – not just within the labour force and social groups within countries, but between nations as well. The worst off *could* become even more (relatively and perhaps even absolutely) worse off. Long-term developments are not, of course, solely dependent on ITs, or on any technologies for that matter: it is social change, not autonomous technological change, which will determine the shape of the future. As structuralists we do not doubt that power relationships will be manifest in determining the uses that ITs are put to – as is evident by the 'Star Wars' research programme. However if one hopes to influence the future – as opposed to merely forecasting it – then it is necessary to find ways of seizing the opportunities that the technology can also offer. For it is not enough to say that the problems are all political ones and therefore one can ignore technology. Rather technology itself is inextricably part of social and political relationships (it is not even unique in bringing natural phenomena into such relationships).

Whether – or rather how far – these technologies will be used for the benefit of humanity in general (as opposed to small or even large élites) will be determined by a number of factors. These are socially structured but not fixed characteristics of societies, such as the level of public awareness about technical issues; the access to technological resources available to different social groups; and the quality of the institutions entrusted with education, planning and other related tasks.

The world is a dangerous place and shows little sign of getting much safer. IT *could* potentially worsen the circumstances of many who live in it. All change means a trade-off: something always lost when something is gained. Often this means *someone* is a loser and someone a gainer. The new technological potentials are bound to be applied to some ends. We do not doubt that this use will often cause conflicts. Hopefully this study has helped to dispel some myths about the nature of the conflicts around IT, and contributed to wider awareness about IT itself and the broader issues associated with it. It may not be a sufficient condition, but such awareness is a necessary one for the orientation of IT to the goals of liberty, solidarity, and equality.

NOTES

1. Bessant *et al.* (1986).
2. According to systems theory, systems are ultra stable. While this does not preclude catastrophe or quantum jumps, it does mean that they accommodate changes by feedback processes; see Ashby (1956).
3. In the UK it is questionable whether privacy was the main reason behind the Data Protection Act, given that police, the Inland Revenue, and security services are exempt.
4. Soete (1981), for example, finds a high correlation between export performance of OECD countries, especially in high technology sectors like aerospace and electronics, and their technological efforts.
5. Based on the analysis by Pavitt (1979), who employed data from the 1960s and 1970s.
6. See Arnold and Guy (1986) for descriptions of national strategies in information technology.
7. British Telecom was being privatised while French telecommunications suppliers were being nationalised.
8. See, for example, the reports prepared for the Economic and Social Research Council's PANTS initiative (Public Acceptance of New Technology), especially Northcott (1985), and Hartley *et al.* (1985).
9. Who now remembers the surge of literature arguing that hippy values – 'Consciousness Three' – were here to stay? We have criticised earlier versions of 'post-industrial' value theory, in Miles (1975).
10. Hondrich (1984).

11. See, for example, studies in Roberts *et al.* (1985).
12. Yankelovich *et al.* (1983); Yuchtman-Yaar (1986).
13. Vine (1985).
14. A survey after the Challenger tragedy might have been expected to give somewhat different results.
15. Yuchtman-Yaar (1986).
16. See, for example, Northcott (1985); Daniels (1987).
17. Thus Rajan (1984) illustrates that in similar institutions, such as banks, similar IT products are in some cases used to further a polarisation of the workforce (between full-time staff on secure career trajectories, and part-time, usually women staff, who receive little training and are not expected to have much future with the firm); and in other cases are used to upgrade jobs in general.
18. Schmidt (1986).
19. Cole and Miles (1985).
20. Irvine and Martin (1984).
21. Freeman (1984).
22. McQuail (1986).
23. The concept of just-in-time implies that raw materials, goods, sub-components, and so on, arrive at the location of use at the time when they are needed – as opposed to 'way-too-early' (and therefore need to be stored) or 'just-too-late'. Too early or too late results in excess costs, poor quality, and often chaos. See Schonberger (1986) for fuller explanation.
24. Harris (1987).
25. 'Runaway industries' refers to the location of production. For a number of years firms took advantage of lower labour costs in many Third World countries and shifted production from Europe or North America to, for example, South-East Asia or South America. With the introduction of IT some commentators (see Hoffman and Rush, 1988) suggest that some of these firms may relocate part, if not all, of their production back in the advanced industrial countries.
26. From the introductory paper by Professor Ron Dore at the European Development Institutes' Association conference on New Technologies and Development, at the Institute of Development Studies, University of Sussex, May 1987.
27. From introductory remarks by Professor Chris Freeman at European Development Institutes' Association conference on New Technologies and Development, Institute of Development Studies, University of Sussex, May 1987.

28. Hobday (1985).
29. Freeman (EDIA conference, op.cit.) points out that, while few in number, these countries represent a major proportion of the world's population.
30. See the discussion of these points in Miles (1986).
31. See, for example, Irvine and Martin (1984).
32. This study in part stems from research undertaken for a body that incorporated civil service, employer and trade union views: the Information Technology Economic Development Committee of Britain's NEDO (National Economic Development Office). NEDO is generally referred to as a 'tripartite' body because of this representation of three groups. Many commentators argue that the curtailment of its role during the 1980s – most recently reflected in the closure of the IT EDC – is due to the lack of correspondence between tripartite approaches and the 'fundamentalism' of the Conservative government.
33. This is why in the preceding chapter of this book and in other publications (Bessant *et al.*, 1985) we have distinguished between discrete and systems applications of IT and between those technologies which rationalise existing activities or augment them. While it has been useful to employ such distinctions in establishing our framework, the future with IT is unlikely to be a case of either/or. (This is another argument in favour of institutional flexibility in decision-making.)
34. See, for example, Bessant *et al.* (1986); Cole and Miles (1985); Freeman· and Jahoda (1978); and Bessant and Cole (1985).
35. Miles *et al.* (1986).
36. In the UK the Department of Trade and Industry support demonstration projects on the 'office of the future'. But some Alvey demonstrators are in social services – such as the Department of Health and Social Services' expert system for welfare benefits.
37. Hartley *et al.* (1985).

Bibliography

Acero, L., Cole, S., and Rush, H., eds — (1981) *Methods for Development Planning: scenarios, models and micro-studies*, Paris, Unesco Press

Altschuler, A., Anderson, M., Jones, D., Roos, D., and Womack, J. — (1984), *The Future of the Automobile*, Cambridge, Mass., MIT Press.

Arnold, E., and Guy, K. — (1986), *Parallel Convergence*, Dorset, Frances Pinter.

Ashby, W.R. — (1956), *An introduction to Cybernetics*, London, Chapman.

Barker, J.R. — (1986), 'The physical limits of integration and size reduction in semiconductors', *Microelectronic Journal*, vol. 17, no. 1 (January/February).

Barras, R. — (1986), 'Towards a theory of innovation in services', *Research Policy*, no. 4.

Barras, R. and Swann, J. — (1985), *The Adoption and Impact of Information Technology in UK Local Government*, London, Technical Change Centre.

Bessant, J. and Cole, S. — (1985), *Stacking the Chips*, London, Frances Pinter.

Bessant, J., Guy, K., Miles, I., and Rush, H. — (1985), *IT Futures*, London, NEDO.

Bessant, J., Guy, K., Miles I., and Rush, H. (with Whitaker, M. and Turner, K.) (1986), *IT Futures Surveyed*, London, NEDO.

Bessant, J., and Haywood, W. (1985), *The Introduction of Flexible Manufacturing Systems as an Example of Computer-Integrated Manufacturing*, Occasional Paper no. 1, Brighton Business School.

Bessant, J., and Haywood, W. (1986), *Flexible Manufacturing Systems and the Small to Medium Sized Firms*, Occasional Paper no. 2. Brighton Business School.

Bhalla, A., James D., and Stevens, Y. (1984), *Blending of New and Traditional Technologies*, Dublin, Tycooly International.

British Telecommunications Engineer (1986), '565 Mbit/s optical-fibre link', vol. 5 (April).

Burns, T., and Stalker, G. (1961), *The Management of Innovation*, London, Tavistock.

Byte (1987), 'The difference in Higher Education' (February).

Child, J. (1987), 'Organisation design of advanced manufacturing technology' in Wall, T., Clegg, C., and Kemp, N., eds, *The Human Side of Advanced Manufacturing Techniques*, Chichester, John Wiley.

Christenson, F. (1987), 'Flexible specialisation in Denmark', report prepared for the FAST programme on 'Robots in new production systems: work in the factory of the future', Brussels, European Commission.

Cole, S., and Miles, I., (1985), *Worlds Apart: technology and North-South*

	relations in the global economy, Brighton, Wheatsheaf.
Daniels, W.W.	(1987), *Workplace Industrial Relations and Technical Change*, Dorset, Frances Pinter.
Feigenbaum, E.A., and McCorduck, P.	(1983), *The Fifth Generation*, New York, Addison Wesley.
Fischetti, M.A.	(1986), 'Solid state' *IEEE Spectrum*, vol. 23, no. 1 (January).
Freeman, C.,	(1981), 'Politics for technical innovation in the new economic context', in Stankievicz R., and Kristensen, P. eds, *Technology Policy and Industrial Development in Scandinavia*, Proceedings of Workshop held at the Research Policy Institute, Lund University, Sweden,
Freeman, C.	(1984), 'The computer revolution: nightmare or Utopia', Whidden Lectures, McMasters University, Canada (October).
Freeman, C., Clark, J., and Soete, L.L.G.	(1981), 'Long waves, inventions and innovations', *Futures*, vol. 13, no. 4.
Freeman, C., and Jahoda, M., eds	(1978), *World Futures: the great debate*, London, Martin Robertson
Freeman, C., and Soete, L.L.G., eds	(1987), *Technical Change and Full Employment*, London, Blackwell.
Georgiou,, L., Metcalfe, S., Gibbons, M., Ray, T., and Evans, J.	(1985), *Post-Innovative Performance*, London, Frances Pinter.

Gershuny, J.I. (1977), *After Industrial Society*, London, Macmillan.

Gershuny, J.I., and Miles, I. (1983), *The New Service Economy*, London, Frances Pinter.

Gershuny, J.I., Miles, I., Jones, S., Mullins, C., Thomas, G., and Wyatt, S. (1986), 'Preliminary analysis of the 1983–1984 Time budget survey', *Quarterly Journal of Social Affairs*, vol. 2, no. 1.

Gregory, B.L. (1986), 'Solid state: expert opinion', *IEEE Spectrum*, vol. 12, no. 1 (January).

Gurstein, M. (1985), 'Social impacts of selected artificial intelligence applications', *Futures*, vol. 17, no. 6.

Harris, N. (1987), *The End of the Third World*, Harmondsworth, Penguin.

Hartley, J., Metcalfe, S., Evans, J., Simnett, J., Georgiou, L., and Gibbons, M. (1985), *Public Acceptance of New Technologies*, University of Manchester, PREST.

Hayes, D. (1987), 'Waiting for LU6.2', *Communications*, vol. 4, no. 6 (June).

Hobday, M. (1985), 'The impact of microelectronics on developing countries: the case of Brazilian telecommunications', *Development and Change*, vol. 16.

Hoffmann, K., and Rush, H. (1988), *Microelectronics and Clothing: the impact of technical change on a global industry*, New York, Praeger (forthcoming).

Hondrich, K.O. (1984), 'Value changes in western society: the last 30 years', paper presented to Commission of European Communities Seminar, 'Technology, Capital and Labour: social and cultural aspects of economic change', Brussels.

IEEE Spectrum (1985), 'Hi-tech in the home' (May).

Illich, I. (1971). *Deschooling Society*, New York, Harper and Row.

Intelsat (1985), 'The global telecommunications cooperative', literature published by the International Telecommunications Satellite Organisation.

Irvine, J., and Martin B. (1984), *Foresight in Science*, London, Frances Pinter.

Jahoda, M. (1982), *Work, Employment and Unemployment: a social psychological perspective*, Cambridge University Press.

Jahoda, M., and Rush, H. (1981), *Employment and Unemployment*, SPRU Occasional Paper no. 12, Brighton, University of Sussex.

Johansen, R., McNeal, B., and Nyhan, M. (1981), *Telecommunications and Developmentally Disabled People*, Menlo Park, California, Institute for the Future.

Kaplinsky, R. (1984), *Automation*, London, Longman.

Kay, P. and Powell, P. eds (1984), *Future Information Technology: 1984 telecommunications*, US National Bureau of Standards.

Langrish, J., Gibbons, M., Evans, W.G., and Jevons, E. R. (1972), *Wealth from Knowledge*, London, Macmillan.

Lewyn, L.L., and Meindl, J.D. (1985), 'Physical limits of VLSI dRAMS', *IEEE Journal of Solid-State Circuits*, vol. SC-20, no 1 (February).

Lighthill, J. (1973), 'Artificial intelligence: a general survey' in *Artificial Intelligence: a paper symposium*, London, Science Research Council.

Mackintosh, I. (1986), *Sunrise Europe: the dynamics of information technology*, Oxford, Blackwell.

Martin, J., (1978), *The Wired Society*, Englewood Cliffs, NJ, Prentice-Hall..

McQuail, D. (1986), 'Policy perspectives for new media in Europe' in Ferguson, M. (ed.), *New Communications Technologies and the Public Interest*, London, Sage.

Meeks, B.N. (1987), 'The quiet revolution', *Byte* (February).

Metcalfe, S. (1986). Technological innovation and the competitive process' in Hall, P. (ed.), *Technology, Innovation and Economic Policy*, Oxford, Philip Allan Press.

Miles, I. (1975), *The Poverty of Prediction*, Farnborough, Saxon House/Lexington Books.

Miles, I. (1985), 'The new post-

	industrial state', *Futures*, vol. 17, no. 6.
Miles, I.	(1986), *Social Indicators for Human Development*, London, Frances Pinter.
Miles, I.	(1988), *Home Informatics*, London, Frances Pinter (forthcoming).
Miles, I., Rush, H., Bessant, J., and Guy, K.	(1986), 'New IT products and services,' paper prepared for the IT EDCs Long-Term Perspective Committee, NEDO.
Miles, I., and Schwarz, M.,	(1982), 'Alternative space futures: the next quarter-century', *Futures* (October).
Mortimer, J.	(1985), *Integrated Manufacture*, Kempston, Ingersoll Engineers/IFS Publications.
New., C., and Myers, A.	(1987), *Managing Manufacturing Operations in the UK 1975–1985*, London, BIM/Cranfield.
Noble, D.	(1984), *Forces of Production: a social history of industrial automation*, New York, Alfred Knopf.
Norbury, J.R.	(1986), 'Propagation and communications experiments with the Olympus Satellite, IEEE Conference 'Communications–an Industry on the Move', Birmingham (May).
Northcott, J.	(1985), *Information Technology and the Organisation*, Public Acceptance of New Technology Project, London, ESRC.

Northcott, J., Rogers, P., Knetsch, W., and de Lestapis, B. (1985), *Microelectronics in Industry: an international comparison*, London, Policy Studies Institute.

Noyce, R.N. (1977), 'Microelectronics', *Scientific American* (September).

Office of Technology Assessment (1985), *Information Technology and R & D: Critical Trends and Issues*, Washington, DC, US Congress.

O'Malley, B. (1987), 'CIM: the digital experience', in Hundy, B., ed., *Proceedings of the 5th International Conference on Automated Manufacturing*, Kempton, IFS Publications.

O'Shea, T., and Self, J. (1984), *Learning and Teaching with Computers: artificial intelligence in education*, Brighton, Harvester Press.

Pahl, R. (1984), *Divisions of Labour*, Oxford, Blackwell.

Papert, S. (1980), *Mindstorms: children, computers, and ideas*, Brighton, Harvester.

Pavitt, K. (1979), 'Technical change: prospects for manufacturing industry', paper presented at EEC workshop 'Europe in Transition: the challenge of the future', Arc et Senans, France.

Perez, C. (1985), 'Microelectronics, long waves and world development', *World Development*, vol 13, no. 3 (March).

Pfeister, J.R., Shott, J. D. and Meindl, J. D.
(1985), 'Performance limits of CMOS ULSI', *IEEE Journal of Solid-state Circuits*, vol. SC–20, no. 1 (February).

Piore, M., and Sabel, C.
(1985), *The Second Industrial Divide*, New York, Basic Books.

Poon, A.
(1988), 'Microelectronics and information technology applied to the science sector: the case of tourism in the Caribbean', submitted for DPhil thesis, Science Policy Research Unit, University of Sussex.

Prince, B., and Due-Gundersen, G.
(1983), *Semiconductor Memories*, Chichester, Wiley.

Rajan, A.
(1984), *New Technology and Employment in Insurance, Banking, and Building Societies*, Brighton, Institute of Manpower Studies.

Ranner, P.J., Horne, J.M., and Frisch, D.A.
(1986), 'Submarine optical-fibre cable systems: future trends', *British Telecommunications Engineer*, vol. 5 (July).

Roberts, B., Finnegan, R., and Gallie, D.
(1985), *New Approaches to Economic Life*, Manchester, Manchester University Press.

Robinson, R.
(1984), 'Gallium arsenide chips', *BYTE* (November).

Robinson, R.
(1987), 'How much of a RISC?', *BYTE* (April).

Rothwell, R., and Zegveld, W.
(1979), *Technical Change and Employment*, London, Frances Pinter.

Rothwell, R., and Zegveld, W.
(1985), *Re-industrialisation and Technology*, London, Longmans.

Rowland, T.   (1985), 'Satellites set to fail in favour of optics', *Electronics Times* (27 June).

Schmidt, M.   (1986), 'Political management of mixed economics', paper presented at symposium, 'Industrial societies after the stagnation of the 1970s', Villa Borsig, Berlin.

Schonberger, R.   (1986), *World Class Manufacturing*, New York, Free Press.

Soete, L.L.G.   (1981), 'A general test of technological gap trade theory', *Futures*, vol. 16, no. 3.

Trade Union Congress   (1979), *New Technology and Employment*, London, TUC.

Vine, R.D.   (1985), *The Impact of Technological Change in the Industrial Democracies: public attitudes towards information technology*, Paris, Atlantic Institute for International Affairs.

Wallich, P., and Zorpette   (1986), 'Minis and mainframes', *IEEE Spectrum*, vol 23, no. 1 (January),

Watson Brown, A.   (1987), 'The campaign for high definition television: a case study in triad power', *Euro-Asia Business Review*, vol. 6, no. 2 (April).

Weisenbaum, J.   (1983), 'The myths of artificial intelligence', *New York Review of Books* (27 October).

Whitaker, M., Miles, I., Rush, H., and Bessant, J.   (1988), *Information Technology: an annotated critical bibliography*, London, Edward Elgar (forthcoming).

Winston, H., and   (1984), *The AI Business*,
  Prendergast, eds   Cambridge, Mass., MIT Press.
Yamashita, M., and   (1985), 'The focal point of the
  Asastani, K.   future Japanese
                         telecommunications network',
                         paper presented at IEE
                         conference, 'The ISDN and its
                         impact on information
                         technology'.
Yankelovich, D. *et al.* (1983), *Work and Human
                         Values: an international report
                         on jobs in the 1980s and 1990s*,
                         New York, Aspen Institute
                         for Humanistic Studies.
Yuchtman-Yaar, E.   (1986), 'Economic culture in
                         post-industrial society:
                         orientation towards growth,
                         technology and work', paper
                         presented at symposium,
                         'Industrial societies after the
                         stagnation of the 1970s', Villa
                         Borsig, Berlin.

Index

*Printed and bound in Great Britain by
Biddles Ltd, Guildford and King's Lynn*